# *Racing Round Ireland*

## *A Miscellany*

*Compiled and Edited by*

*Fred Drew*

ORIGINAL WRITING

# The Course

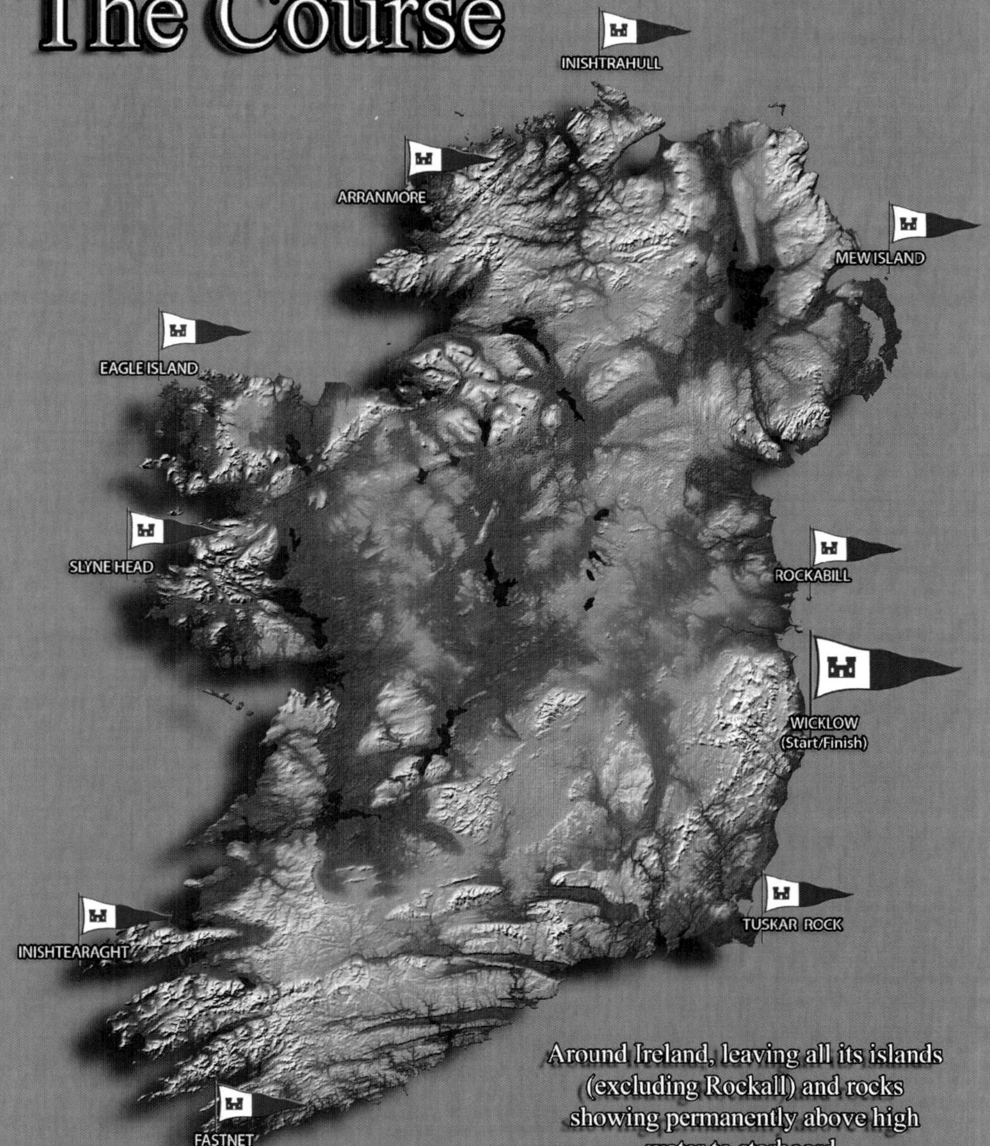

INISHTRAHULL

ARRANMORE

MEW ISLAND

EAGLE ISLAND

SLYNE HEAD

ROCKABILL

WICKLOW
(Start/Finish)

INISHTEARAGHT

TUSKAR ROCK

FASTNET

Around Ireland, leaving all its islands
(excluding Rockall) and rocks
showing permanently above high
water to starboard.

WSC Burgees indicate mandatory
reporting points.

Image courtesy of NASA Earth Observatory

978-1-907179-61-7

A cip catalogue for this book is available from the National Library.

Published by Original Writing Ltd., Dublin, 2010.

Printed in Great Britain by the MPG Books Group, Bodmin and King's Lynn.

*This Book is*

*Dedicated to the memory*

*of*

*Jim Poole and Michael Jones*

*Certainly every man that goes to sea in a little boat. . . learns terror and salvation, happy living, air, danger, exultation, glory and repose at the end; and they are not words to him, but on the contrary, realities which will ever after throughout his life give the mere words a full meaning.*

*Hilaire Belloc,*

*"The Hills and the Sea"*

# What entrants had to say . . .

Thank you for hosting a great race around Ireland. Tough sailing but memorable and far more exciting than doing another Fastnet.

*Chris Brown, Fidessa-fastwave, 2004*

May I congratulate you on a wonderful race that enjoyed unprecedented interest at every level. Aboard 02 team Spirit we had a wonderful race, enjoyed immensely by all . . . for our team the whole project was a superb experience and so rewarding in a variety of ways.

*David Nixon, Skipper, 02 team Spirit, 2004*

My first experience. Thoroughly enjoyed it. The thing that struck me the most was the warmth of everybody we met, regardless of the time of day or night. It was really refreshing in this age, the genuine warmth and friendship of everybody. This is a very unique event, obviously nurtured over the years.

*Stephen McCarthy, Nadie*

What did you do right? Almost everything except the wind. I'm sure you'll do better next time.

*Laurent Guoy, Inis Mor*

Yacht tracker was excellent. Race management was top class. Very good media coverage. Bar very good at the finish!

*Aodhan Fitgerald, Ireland's West*

Thank you, Jacky and all the team in the race office for such a well organised event. . . unfortunately the wind was not quite what we would have wanted. . . you all did a great job for the race, the club and your sponsors. Congratulations.

*Emma Moloney, Creative Play, 2006*

As always, very well organised. Some things you could improve such as a north-easterly F5 to Fastnet, then veering westerly for the rest of the way – and no calms!

*Neil Eatough, Lancastrian, 2006*

Well done on a very successful race, I hope you all feel the same. You deserve to.

*Heather and Don Kennedy, 2004*

First class organisation as ever. Thank you, everyone!

*Slingshot*

The race was a great adventure for me and I am certain for my fellow hand Donald Wilks as well. It will be a difficult act to follow and the weather made the Fastnet Race look like a walk in the park (I have done four) in comparison.

*Thunder 2, 2004*

. . a varied, exciting, challenging and elementally beautiful race.

*Richard Clubb; Darramy*

As vice commodore of our own club I fully appreciate the huge voluntary effort required from club members to pull off a successful event. We thoroughly enjoyed the race though as a double handed crew we would have liked less gales How many did they manage to fit in to four days?

We have done the race 5 times now and still are of the opinion it is "The Race"

By the way the tracking website was brilliant. Friends of ours who never stepped on a boat followed the fleet and our progress , often through the night. I was wondering why everyone looked so tired when we came home.

*Alice Kingston, Kinsale Yacht Club*

.. . . a tougher and better race than the Bermudan Race.

*Tony Hume and John Donnelly; Janey Mac*

. . .a feeling of regret that this was the end of what was a great adventure . . . a most enjoyable and entertaining trip.

*Alan Murray; Joliba*

# Racing Round Ireland

*A Miscellany*

# CONTENTS

WICKLOW SAILING CLUB                                              1

INTRODUCTION                                                     3

HOW IT ALL BEGAN                                                 8

IRELAND TO STARBOARD                                            16

ALTERNATIVE ROUND IRELAND RACE                                 22

A PRIMER FOR NON-SAILORS                                       26

A BRIEF HISTORY                                                30

ROUND IRELAND GRAND PRIX                                       33

REMEMBERING DENIS DOYLE AND MOONDUSTER                         45

LANDMARKS AND LIGHTHOUSES                                      46


THE 1994 CORK DRY GIN ROUND IRELAND YACHT RACE

1994: THE ENTRANTS                                            51

1994: THE START                                               56

WICKLOW TO FASTNET                                            58

FASTNET TO EAGLE ISLAND                                       65

EAGLE ISLAND TO MEW ISLAND                                    70

MEW ISLAND TO WICKLOW                                         72


CORK DRY GIN ROUND IRELAND 1994.

AIR CORPS 1                                                   76

ALPARA                                                        81

AQUALINA                                                      88

BLACKTIE – WICKLOW CHALLENGE                                  90

CORWYNT                                                       95

DARRAMY                                                       98

Deerstalker 100

Hobo V 104

Janey Mac 11 106

Joliba 108

Juno 114

Keep-on-Smiling 121

Marissa VIII 125

Nissan 1 132

Raasay of Melfort 135

Sty Tailte 140

St. Christopher 144

TIR na Nog 148

Tropicana 150

Ulysess 156

VSOP 158

1994 Class Results 164

BMW Round Ireland 2006 171

BMW 2008 Race 177

Appendix 1 186

Appendix 11 192

*Ireland West  (Aodhan Fitzgerald)*
*Winner of the BMW Round Ireland Race 2008.*

# Wicklow Sailing Club

Established in 1950 the club celebrates its 60th anniversary this year. From the very beginning the focus was on introducing young people to sailing. This focus on training still continues and every year the club organises ISA approved training courses for 40 to 50 juniors. Over the years the club programme has been the nursery of many fine sailors who have gone on to greater things.

The club has about 300 members and membership has remained static at around this number for some years. The major problem preventing an increase in membership of the club is the lack of moorings. Wicklow Harbour is small, fairly shallow and exposed to north-easterly winds. This means that when the wind is in that direction boats have to be taken off the moorings and seek refuge in the river. Those who don't may end up on the beach. There is also a requirement for more shore-side storage for the increasing dinghy fleet.

Wicklow Port is also a commercial port and although quiet at the present time it can be very busy and there is also the whelk fishing fleet. All of which makes for a very fine balancing act for the Harbour Master, Captain John Barlow.

Despite these constraints WSC is a busy active club with a fleet of Ruffians and other boats of that ilk. Racing competition is very keen with races held on Sunday and Wednesday during the season. The dinghy fleet is also active consisting of Wayfarers, various Lasers and 420's. Cruising is making a come-back though the restriction on the size of boats does not help.

WSC is twinned with Porth Madoc Yacht Club in beautiful Snowdonia in Wales and visits are exchanged during the season.

Over the years WSC has hosted many sailing events and national championships. In the seventies and early eighties it played host to several Folkboat Weeks. For many years it was well known for the annual Whit weekend race from Dun Laoghaire when "everything that could float made its way to Wicklow". It was also a prime mover in the inauguration of the South East Coast Regatta (Not to be confused with the Wicklow Regatta).

In 1980 the club organised the first non-stop Round Ireland yacht race-starting and finishing in Ireland (Wicklow). This year is the thirtieth anniversary of that first race and the sixteenth race in the series will take place in June. This is now a major event in the Irish sailing calendar and one of which the club is very proud. As this book is a celebration of the Round Ireland race I need not say more.

All small clubs such as ours depend entirely upon the enthusiasm of the members and their willingness to pitch in and do whatever is necessary. WSC is singularly fortunate in the wide cross section of the community it attracts and the breadth of talent within that community. It has taken sixty years and much sweat and tears to bring the club this far but all the many hundreds of members who have contributed over the years can be proud that the club continues to represent all that is best in sailing and club-life.

Like all small clubs we are experiencing difficult times. This is the first year for many years that we have been unable to find a major sponsor for the Round Ireland race but we will overcome the difficulties, helped by the loyal race competitors who are the greatest supporters of the club. Over the years we have received much positive feedback from visitors and competitors in the race. All are full of praise for the friendliness and welcome they receive from members and there is huge respect and appreciation of the clubs organisational ability as represented by the race organiser and his committee.

So why not come and join us? Social membership is open and may appeal to those who do not live locally but would like to support the club.

*A boisterous start to the race*
Photo. D. Branigan

# Introduction

This book has been a long time in gestation and one could be excused for thinking of elephants and mice.

The original plan was to write a book detailing the experiences of the competitors in the Cork Dry Gin Round Ireland race of 1994. I received considerable support from the competitors and their contributions form the core of this book, ranging all the way from brief log book entries, through knock-about comedy, to the literary (Purple shades of Herman Melville).

The initial reason for the delay in the book appearing was that I decided to expand the book to include the history of the race since its inception in 1980. However I ran into difficulties in obtaining material and also I was informed that others, better qualified than myself, were However no book appeared and I have been persistently nagged by the thought that I owed it to the competitors in the 1994 race to publish their experiences.

Another reason is that this is the 30th anniversary of the first non-stop Round Ireland race organised by WSC and it is also the 60th anniversary of the clubs foundation.

Of course a lot has happened since 1994. Another seven races have taken place and I have tried to incorporate accounts of those races where available. I have also included a section showing the results of all races since 1980 – just for the record.

Organising and running a race like the Round Ireland Race is expensive and stretches the resources of a small club like WSC to the limit. Therefore it was with gratitude that we accepted offers of sponsorship. In the early days I suspect that there was still a residual sniff of disapproval within the sailing establishment when sponsorship was mentioned; but that has long disappeared.

But the same establishment must have been somewhat chagrined when WSC announced that it was to run the first non-stop yacht race around Ireland in 1980. Some of the major clubs in Dublin and Cork had been discussing the possibility of running such a race but it was Michael Jones of WSC who had the courage to 'run with the ball'. It must have been even more of a shock when the major clubs realised that WSC could do it and intended to continue doing it.

Wm. Egan and Sons in association with Irish Boats and Yachting sponsored the first race and the second race, in 1980, was sponsored by Irish TV Rentals (John McEvoy and Ray McCulloch).

Round
Ireland
80

June 28 / July 12 1980
Sponsored by Wm Egan & Sons Ltd Cork
In association with Irish Boats & Yachting
Under the auspices of Wicklow Sailing Club

Non-stop circumnavigation of Ireland
for the Waterford Glass Premier Award
Open to boats 22 ft and over from
all countries

*Programme for the 1980 race*

Cork Dry Gin sponsored the race generously and actively from 1984 until 1998 and the development and success of the race owes a lot to the efforts of Richard Burrows and his team at Irish Distillers. It was during their tenure that the race achieved its international reputation.

I feel it appropriate at this point to include remarks made by Commodore Brendan J. Haughton in the programme for the 1988 race.

"I welcome competitors to Wicklow for the Cork Dry Gin Round Ireland '88. This is a special pleasure for me as this is my third round Ireland – as Commodore, that is.

Having been in this position in 1980 when the Round Ireland Sailing race, to give it its original title, was inaugurated by Wicklow Sailing Club, and in 1982 for the second race, I have seen it grow from tentative beginnings to the major event that it is now. I am convinced that the popularity of this course and venue will continue to grow in the future.

My sincere thanks are due to our sponsor Cork Dry gin and also to their staff. Their input and support have been of considerable help in developing the race.

I am pleased to record my immense respect and admiration for Michael Jones, the race organiser. Many yachting sages in the 1970's mulled over ideas for a Round Ireland race, mainly in the après-sail comfort of the bar; speculation and intentions which waxed glorious by night became overhung and overshadowed in the cool morning air; meanwhile Michael worked assiduously on his ideas for the Round Ireland Sailing race.

Michael presented a complete and workable plan to Wicklow Sailing Club which the Committee enthusiastically embraced. The rest is history, and each successive Round Ireland has been planned and organised by Michael with the same quiet efficiency with which he drafted and presented the original plan. Thank you Michael, and thank you R.O.R.C.

Finally on behalf of my Committee and myself, i confirm our intention to nurture and develop this race in the future with the continued assistance of our co-organisers, the R.O.R.C. for the benefit and enjoyment of sailors everywhere".

We were disappointed not to have a sponsor for the Millennium race in 2000 but Sports Ireland (Part of Failte Ireland) came on board in 2002.

BMW (Ireland) stepped in to sponsor the race in 2004 and continued to sponsor the race up until 2008 and very prestigious and generous sponsors they proved to be.

And let's not forget the continuous support the race has been given over the years by the small businesses of Wicklow town.

Before the race every boat receives a rigorous inspection by The Royal Ocean Racing Club scrutinisers, Chris and Anna Brooke, wearing their trade-mark yellow oilies and carrying fearsome looking clipboards and assisted by Simon Greenwood and Frank Jackson of WSC. Horny-handed sailors quake in their sea boots at their approach. Between them the scrutinisers leave no sail-locker unrummaged and no bilge unplumbed. It says a lot that in the entire history of the race only one entrant has failed the inspection and was left, rather forlornly, on the south quay for the duration of the race. Competitors have invested too much time and money to risk failing the inspection because of out of date flares or flimsy bolt cutters. Even so some have had to replace items of rigging following inspection and it is fortunate that Wire Ropes are adjacent.

*The race committee in session. L to R. Theo Phelan, Dennis Noonan, John Hughes, Lynn Stringer and Jacky Breathnach*

## Race Organisers.

To a huge extent the success of the race is due to the race organisers. Their work load is immense and begins months before the race with the vetting of entrants and dealing with their queries. The club has been extremely fortunate in its choice of organisers for this onerous task.

1980 – 1992 Michael Jones

1994 – 1998 Fergus O'Conchubhair

2000 – present, Denis Noonan

The present race organiser, the affable, unflappable Denis Noonan has become synonymous with the race. He would be the first to pay tribute to the enormous contribution made by his wife Evelyn and daughter Jacky Breathnach and her friend Lynn Stringer. During each race the race office is manned 24/7 by volunteers from WSC. That competitors appreciate their work is evidenced by the feedback we receive from competitors after

*Dennis Noonan*

each race. Unanimously they praise the club for the smooth organisation of the race.

A glance at the tables in the appendix will show that many of the world's greatest sailors have competed in the race; there is a galaxy of talent there. But the main support and backbone of the race comes from the 'ordinary' club sailor. There is scarcely a sailing club in Ireland which has not entered a competitor. Indeed for some clubs it has become a very personal race with fierce intra- and inter-club rivalry.

The introduction of a two-handed class proved very popular with nine entries in the 2008 race. GPS tracking was first used in 2008 and proved immensely popular. Each competitor carries a tracker which reports automatically every half-hour (via satellite) giving the boats position, course and speed. Now the race can be followed in real time from anywhere in the world and many thousands of people do so.

Finally a few words about WSC which this year celebrates its 60th birthday ('tis only a pup' some will say).

Many competitors, visiting Wicklow for the first time, are surprised that such a small club should be hosting such a major event. Sometimes we are surprised ourselves!

The success of the race is, of course, down to the competitors but it is also due to the dedicated service over the years by members too numerous to mention. We are very proud of the race and even more proud of the fact that, over the years, competitors have become old friends, very comfortable with the club and its hospitality.

## Acknowledgements

Many people have assisted me in the production of this book. Wherever possible I have tried to track down possible copyright holders. The book benefits from many contributors and without their aid the book would never have appeared.

Without the assistance and encouragement of many people this book would never have appeared. So many people have helped that it is almost impossible to mention them all. I will start with my son Adam who designed the book's cover, his wife Ciara who did the proof reading and my other son Tim who was my unpaid IT consultant. Thanks to my wife Norma whose financial prudence made the project possible. Thanks also to all the contributors who had probably given up all hope of seeing their work in print. Thanks to all those who offered the use of photographs even if I could not use them all. Special thanks go to Jacky Breathnach, Lynn Stringer, Simon Greenwood, Tim Greenwood, Simon Johnson, WSC Commodore Charlie Kavanagh, Barry O'Sullivan, John Harte, David McHugh, Richard Nairn, Kevin Desmond, and Theo Phelan.

I would also like to thank my publisher, Garrett Bonner, and designer Steven Weekes, who patiently guided me throughout the production of this book.

I have made every effort to trace the holders of copyright in text and photographs. Should there be inadvertent omissions or errors they will be corrected in future editions.

Finally. Nothing in this book is to be taken as representing the opinion or policy of the Wicklow Sailing Club.

# HOW IT ALL BEGAN

Jim Poole: *Ireland Afloat.* June 1984

Ten years ago, racing around Ireland was regarded as a crackpot idea. The 1975 Race, with only two crew allowed and with Start and Finish in Bangor and stopovers in Crosshaven and Killybegs, attracted four entries. But it established that well-found yachts had no trouble in doing the trip under normal conditions. The smallest boat, my Ruffian 23 Ruffino not only completed the race in perfect safety, but won two legs out of three, and came second overall. But the format was clearly wrong and the race Organisation needed re-thinking. Wicklow S.C., largely in the able person of Michael Jones, undertook to run a fully-crewed IOR non-stop Race in 1980. Cruisers were allowed under ECHO-type Handicaps. Brian Coad sailed RAASAY to win the latter, while my FEANOR took the IOR honours. And then came 1982. A full blown gale lashed the 17-strong fleet on the wild Atlantic seaboard, and all but a few boats ran for shelter. MOONDUSTER, STORM BIRD, FEANOR and WILD GOOSE battled through. The Round Ireland Race had arrived, as far as the public was concerned.

*Threatening skies*
photo: Norma Drew

## A small boat perspective

Larger boats always have their own special problems of Organisation, crew rostering, provisioning, etc., to a far greater extent than a one- tonner. But by and large, big boats have things easy. For them the race is shorter by a day or more, weather protection for crew is better, and the larger crew numbers make for better camaraderie and a greater sense of fun. A large boat in a force 6 is just comfortable; a small boat in similar conditions may be hard pressed. And 704 NM is a long, long race. My perspective of the Race is therefore a small boat one, written in the hope that it may help anyone interested to decide whether he and his boat and crew are up to the task. If they go, I trust it will help them to plan the race efficiently and enjoy it as much as I have enjoyed my three trips round. For others, it will give some idea of what's involved for a small boat to race around Ireland.

## A long, long offshore

The Round Ireland Race is about 100 NM longer than the Fastnet. The half Ton record stands at just under 5 days 18 hours. It could take 8 or more days if a stubborn "High" keeps winds flukey or non-existent. Participation in ISORA Races or similar is good preparation. Long coastal cruising is also to be recommended. A chat with a few Skippers who have done it will serve to clear the air. A taste for adventure will help enormously.

## A cakewalk - or a nightmare

Given idyllic June weather, the Race is a cakewalk. Glorious scenery all the way, balmy 18-hour-long days, and warm lazy nights will make it a cruise to remember. But 1982 showed that you have got to prepare for the other extreme. On Feanor, I noted in the Log "Tues. 08.30, 32 Kn Steady; 12.00, 42-44 Kn; 24.00 still 42Kn. Wed. 02.00, Max. 52 Kn recorded! 08.00, 21 Kn and falling. FORTY KNOTS PLUS HAD LASHED OUR LITTLE BOAT FOR OVER FIFTEEN HOURS. It is not likely that such a gale will be encountered again for a long time but a wise Skipper will prepare himself, his boat, and his crew for such a gale. Knowing that his preparations are well made, he can then set sail with a happy heart.

## Navigation

There is no excuse for sloppy or inadequate navigation on this race. All the nominated turning marks are major ones, and the permissible use of electronic Navigation Aids should help enormously. But don't forget that instruments require power, which can sometimes be very difficult to maintain on small boats in rough conditions. There is simply no reason for blind reliance on electronics. Do your homework every hour. Keep your log up to date. Before starting read earlier race reports. Study possible ports of Refuge in the "I.C.C. Sailing Directions". Mark on your charts the tidal streams and times of change culled from "Admiralty 40: Irish Coastal Pilot". Carry far more charts, including details of a possible anchorage, than you could ever dream of using. It's always nice to know they're there! Share Navigation duties and information with all your crew. They really need to know where they are, and why they are doing what they are doing. It's a great motivator!

## Boat safety

The race is RORC Category II this year. Check out your full safety gear. Simply nothing can be left out! Make sure everybody knows where things go, and what they are for. A favourite item for crew discussion is "SOFTWOOD PLUGS - VARIOUS". Hand them to your youngest crew member and ask for a demonstration of what they are for and how to apply them. You may be surprised (but not amused) at the response! Think about cutting away fallen rigging in a rough seaway - and go out and buy a huge pair of bolt-croppers that you can PROVE is man enough to cut rod rigging. I have seen A.C. boats carrying wire-snips that would be hard put to cut a bicycle-wheel spoke, just to fulfil the letter of the law. Don't be fooled. All your gear has to be completely seaworthy. The Atlantic, in angry mood, makes no exceptions, and accepts no excuses. Try a "man overboard" drill in sheltered waters, and have "the victim" tell the rest of your crew how horribly slippy the hull feels when trying to clamber aboard. It's a sobering thought! Seamanship saves lives; the right gear merely helps. When the cannon booms, it's a lovely feeling to know that your boat and gear are thoroughly tested. Now it's all up to you!

## Race reporting

Position reporting by radio at designated times has been suggested for the race. Its purpose is twofold. Firstly it enables Race Control to monitor fleet progress and apply safety checks. Secondly, it helps the general public to follow the race with informed interest. I have some doubts about the latter, since the public will automatically hear most about the boat leading on the water. This is hardly likely to be a small boat! But RACE CONTROL will at least have enough information to give updated lists of corrected times at major turning points. There is also the other vexed question of a position report on an individual boat being of material use to some of the opposition. All in all, though, I think it is a good thing, and should give an added measure of safety to the race, if only in the public mind.

## Crew selection

My two favourite maxims about small-boat racing offshore are:

(1) You can't hide on a 1/2 Tonner.

(2) A motivated crew is a winning crew.

Crew selecting is vital. Someone who simply is not up to the job, is scared, or seasick all the time, or just not "switched on", is a positive liability. Beware the barroom hero until he proves his worth! Some years ago off San Diego, I witnessed a spectacular broach, unquestionably caused by a scared sheet-man. Damage was impressive: but what impressed me most was the laconic comment of a truly great offshore sailor who, with me, was a silent witness of the debacle. "Yeah" he said "that's that guy's problem - he talks a great yacht". Watch out for deep-running personal incompatibilities that can make nonsense of all your crew selection. Maintain a high level of crew banter and "slagging" (including yourself) to build up rapport and mutual respect and co-operation. Keep the "Pecking Order" under constant review to reward improvement, and excellence, and effort. You'll know you're on the right lines when things get done the way you want with less and less shouting. When you can do a whole ISORA Race (and do well), while 'rigged for silent running' i.e. everyone working flat out in perfect harmony, you are probably ready for a bash at the Round Ireland. A "lash-up" crew of last-minute replacements has little chance of ever cruising in harmony, let alone racing well.

## Food

Crew must eat, and hard-working crew eat a lot. But when I hear discussions of the culinary niceties practised on some offshore boats, I smile and write them off as serious contenders. Not that I'm against good food and lots of it - my 190 lbs would prove the contrary - it's just that I believe that frequent tasty meals, eaten on the weather rail, backed up by lots of 'goodies' for instant energy, will contribute far more to small-boat speed than formal four-course blow-outs followed by a long snooze down below on a leeward bunk! I'm partial to muesli, curries with rice, beef stroganoff with spuds, Irish stew ditto, and toasted cheese sandwiches with coffee at crew changeover. Remember all food must be labelled and stowed with a view to rough weather, and to locating it by torchlight without disturbing sleeping crew. Instant meals (just add hot water) are a Godsend in rough weather. (A cold tin of Irish stew is a poor second). Creamed rice with blackcurrant jam proved a favourite for dessert on Feanor, until its staunchest proponent declared recently that he never wished to see it again! A GOODIES BAG is essential - Biscuits, Chocolate, Mars Bars, Sweets, Chewing Gum etc. Stock up for 7 days and if you're running out of food, enjoy the cruise home! You've eaten your way round too slowly to be in the race!

## Personal gear and medical kit

Allow each crew member ONE BAG ONLY, apart from his sleeping bag; otherwise the boat will be swamped. Two full suits of oilies and boots, three complete changes of clothes (each wrapped in plastic against the unthinkable but occasional fall into the bilges!) are all that is required for each crew member. Some of the Feanor crews in '82 had Thermal suits, and I'm now a convert to their efficacy in combating body damp and cold. A day's suntan can prove very painful under oilies, so bring lots of sun-tan cream and burn cream! (You'll be very popular during a gale when one of the crew, looking for something to keep out the salt water, calls out that he's "found something interesting"!) A supply of woolly caps and mittens can be most useful for night sailing. Augment your normal medical kit to ease the pain of burns, scalds, sunburns, broken fingers and the like. A doctor in your crew should be encouraged to "bring his bag". Read up about splints and sprains. Leave ALL the booze in Wicklow.

## Watching "The Watch"

Nothing underlines so clearly the difference between a 50 ft. and a 30 ft. boat in an offshore race as the attitude towards watch-keeping. On the large boats, skipper and navigator "float", and port and starboard watches are set up, with bets, wagers and repartee about "days run achieved". On a competitive 1/2 tonner, four-up and two resting below (on the outboard weather bunks) is the order of the day. If you finish any offshore race feeling rested, forget it. You simply have not being trying hard enough!

Crew weight on the rail is crucial to performance in all but the lightest airs. To have any hope of beating the big guys, the little boats must sail up to their full potential in winds from 0 to 20 KN, and must be pushed relentlessly in heavier going. So I have evolved a very flexible watch-keeping system. The only drawback is that it can sometimes demand too much for too long from even highly-motivated crew. But nothing succeeds like success, and tired crew soon recover, always in time to celebrate a good win. Frequent helming changeovers and maintaining interest through varying tasks all help to drive the boat all the time. Fully three-fifths of any long race could well be "easy-going" i.e. time to store up energy and sleep longer for the tough tasks ahead. An extra hour given to a weary crew will be repaid in full, and a crew that have mutual concern for each other's welfare is half-way to being a winning one. But don't be lulled by "easy going" into sailing badly. A mile gained in drifting conditions could make all the difference at any one of the tidal gates; the difference between first and nowhere.

## Night sailing

More long offshore races are won and lost by night sailing techniques than by any other facet of the art of sailing. How easy just to jog along on a lovely warm night knowing that soon it's going to be your turn to loll in a warm bunk below! How logical the sound of someone arguing for shorter sail, for "not pushing too much" while the skipper rests! But the foreshortened visibility at night is compensated-for by an enhanced "feel" for wave patterns and tidal effects. A really well sailed boat will be moving just as fast at night as during the day. This is where night racing experience is crucial. Good night sailing pays handsome dividends on a long offshore. You'll get lots of opportunity to practice the art on this race.

## Nets

One of the most dangerous problems is the presence of unmarked and possibly unattended drift nets. Nothing can be calculated to raise the hackles of a hardworking salmon fisherman more than the thought of yachtsmen cutting his nets, and all in pursuit of mere upper-class pleasures! Nothing could be better calculated to slow the progress of a racing yacht than getting enmeshed in a net for hours at night while the opposition sails gaily by! Unfortunately, there is no easy answer! A lookout is virtually useless at night and often just as useless by day in rough weather. The Breton Wire (strung tautly from the aft tip of the keel to the rudder) may avoid snagging the rudder on a net. I have no experience of its use. A bit of chatter on your VHF Radio can sometimes raise a helpful fisherman in advance, who will be happy to help you avoid his nets.

## Handover

The point of handing over control of the boat, especially at night, has been identified as the most dangerous interlude. On a small boat, coming up from below, and suddenly confronting a heaving wave washed cockpit in the dark can cause disorientation and confusion. I always insist that the on-coming crew sit idle for five minutes to "get their bearings" and night vision before taking over command. It also gives them plenty of time to assimilate course, weather, tides etc., so that the chain of command remains unbroken. Be totally explicit in giving sailing instructions to the new helmsman. Write it up in the log, and countenance no deviations. Leave instructions to call you should conditions alter or danger threaten. Of such joy is the life of an offshore skipper made.

## Boat speed and motivation

Apart from accurate navigation and good boat management, the attainment of maximum boat speed on all points of sailing is the most vital aspect of a successful Round Ireland Race. This begs the crucial question: "How can you keep a small boat driving at maximum speed for five days and nights, and still be prepared to do the same for another 24 or 48 hours if necessary?" In a word, the answer is MOTIVATION. If all the crew believe in the SKIPPER, in the BOAT, and in THEMSELVES then much can be achieved. Each little achievement reinforces the pattern. Every mark rounded is another success; every ploy that succeeds in cheating an adverse tide for half an hour or avoiding a hole in the breeze is a little victory that urges you on to the next part of the course. And, make no mistake about it; this is a GRAND NATIONAL among offshore races. Every "obstacle" must be tackled with resolution and cunning. Negotiating one is no guarantee of success at the remaining ones. Early successes can help, but do not guarantee an overall performance of which you can be proud. Stopping racing through fatigue, stress of weather, or gear failure is only prudent and wise; overcoming ALL obstacles is the name of the winning game.

## Enjoy it

Lastly, no matter what happens; enjoy the huge thrill of a fast cruise along some of Europe's loveliest coastline; Sluice down the Wicklow and Wexford banks on the early ebb. Battle by Tuskar and Conningbeg; Greet famous Fastnet with humility, and spare a thought for our fellow sailors who did not make it in 1979; Glory in the beauty of West Cork; Marvel at the magnificence of the Great Skelligs and the remote Blaskets; Feel the great surge of the open Atlantic as you plunge towards the North; Greet the misty Aran Islands; Salute High Island, the Stags of Bofin and mighty Achill Head; Look for the porpoise schools and maybe a lone whale; Talk of seals and mermaids as you skirt the wild coast of Mayo; Admire the stags of Broadhaven, and gaunt Black Rock, as you take the road of the lordly Salmon towards fabled Tory; Turn for lonely Inishtrahull; Sail close by Rathlin Island as the Vikings did; Fight your way down the rocky North Channel to our home waters, with their familiar beat; Come at last past

Rockabill and Kish to friendly Wicklow; tired, so tired, but full of joyous memories. And, finally, come to realise the real message of this great pilgrimage round our island home: Nobody loses - we who participate are all winners - Come On!

*Who says sailing is not a spectator sport*
photo. A. O'Sullivan

*Last minute preparations at Wicklow's east pier*

# IRELAND TO STARBOARD

Enda Padraig O'Coineen

To any nautical buff worth his salt, the circumnavigation of Ireland ranks high in the arena of achievement. Convert the challenge into a race and you have an ideal course providing a supreme test of navigational skills, seamanship and raw racing ability, the conclusion of which must at least be worth a winter's supply of G and T at the club bar.

Notwithstanding, loaded down with 12 pints of milk and 12 loaves of fresh bread for good measure, your correspondent joined the crew of "Feanor" 50 minutes before the recent non-stop Round Ireland '80 race commenced from Wicklow. It was at the kind invitation of the skipper-owner, Jim Poole, one of those rare thoroughbred breed of competitive Irish sailors and a gentle cross in origins between Cork and Dublin; Dick Burke of Galway and John O'Connor of Dublin completed our crew of four on the Ron Holland Jubilee Half-Tonner.

Minutes later the drama started. "Feanor" almost ended up on the rocks when an air-lock cut the motor while leaving harbour. Fortunately, quick anchor work and sail handling saved the day and following the last minute scramble for the line, we made it for a respectable start as organising secretary Michael Jones blasted the cannon at noon, Sunday 29 June.

*A close start to the 2000 race*

Five days, 19 hours, 19 minutes later, after heading south and turning right all the way, "Feanor" was third across the line, first boat on IOR handicap and first under 35 feet. Line honours went to "Force Tension" of South Caernarvon, Wales, in 5 days, 15 hours, 22 minutes with "Partizan" from Galway second across the line in 5, days, 17 hours, 04 minutes.

A gentle breeze from a north easterly direction blew down the Irish Sea, as we crossed the start line between a mark boat and the lighthouse on the tip of Wicklow Harbour's East Pier. The sun sparkled and a crowd gathered on the shore to watch the fleet move south with the ebb tide. Mis-judging the flow, some crossed the line too soon in their enthusiasm and had to re-cross. Brian Murphy's Hydro Half-Tonner "Gowan Fuegeot" was the first to Wicklow Head with "Partizan" starting well. However, as the wind began to fade away "Force Tension" one of the early starters, quickly made up for lost time in the light airs taking over the lead in the fleet of colourful spinnakers headed for Arklow with "Feanor" in second slot.

The forecast was for the wind to back around to a westerly direction. But instead it veered further east and it paid to keep well out into the fast south flowing stream. It was light and flukey all afternoon. Once the tide had turned we hugged the shoreline, inside the Banks which stretch right down to Rosslare, avoiding the worst of the tide. From Rosslare it was a quick dash across the tide to round the Tuskar at 22-55 hours before heading south and west for the Fastnet. Unfortunately by this time the wind, as forecast, had assumed its westerly direction making it a hard slog to weather through the first night blowing a steady force 5, gusting to 7.

Andrew Cooper Ball's unknown quantity "Snowball", a 37 foot cruising Snowgoose catamaran did not go at all in the light airs; likewise this was the case with "Garter Star", the only other multihull in the race skipper-owned by John Hall of Bray. However, when occasional gusts came on the run to Rosslare, "Snowball" caught right up with the fleet but once the wind had veered south she got left for dead meat.

Later when the wind shifted to the north-west blowing Force 7 with occasional gale gusts, it favoured the slower boats behind. Through Monday working to weather was tough going and it was not until 06.38 Tuesday morning that we rounded three miles south of the elusive Fastnet having picked up the powerful loom before the brilliant sunrise at 05.27 hours. Surprisingly there were a number of boats in sight with Dermod Ryan's "Red Velvet", a Hustler 35, one mile down to leeward.

The wind was now coming from the north varying from Force 3 to Force 4. We cut in too close to Mizen Head and were becalmed for a time, while "Red Velvet" gave it a wide berth, keeping her wind and drawing ahead two or three miles. At this stage Ivan Campbell's "Bataleur" Shamrock half-tonner of Coleraine Y.C. was going extremely well, in sight and ahead to weather of "Gowan Fuegeot" and "Partizan".

A long tack into Bantry Bay getting a good lift from the tide out past Dursey Head, the Calf, the Cow and the Bull respectively proved advantageous. Morale on board "Feanor" was good, though providing hot meals was a problem with the cooker acting up and at times everything seemed very wet. "Boat speed, Boat speed" was the catchword as we looked to Aristotle for inspiration and turned to Jim Poole for motivation. When eventually we got the cooker working, the special foil packed lightweight and nourishing airline type meals which Martin Corcoran of Swissco, Little Island, Cork, had sent up at short notice, proved an added boon and proved to be one of our "secret weapons" of the race.

By nightfall the wind died away leaving a choppy sea as the low had completely filled in, making way for a new system with southerly winds forecast. Sitting between the Skelligs and Dursey Head the lights of no less than five competing boats were visible.

## THEN MYLIE CAME OUT

Another secret weapon - one of these new fangled Mylar foresails for light airs made by McWilliams of Cork. She set like a dream and we managed to work out to sea through the night tacking through numerous wind shifts. Around 08.00 hours the following morning (Wednesday) the wind filled in from the south, up went the spinnaker and away we went north on a rhumb line straight to Blackrock off Blacksod Bay. The main bunch was behind and we had three spinnakers on the horizon astern, following "Feanor" all day.

Loop Head and the Aran Islands (though we did not see them being well out to sea) passed away to starboard representing the half-way mark. At this rate the circumnavigation looked like taking seven full days. The wind remained a steady force 5 from the south and we creamed along at well over six knots.

## FROM THE LOG

17-50 hours. Blew out floater (already torn).

20=00 hours. Haze, drizzle, reaching spinnaker set, Slyne Head 9 miles to starboard.

With no log and a weak signal from Slyne Head on the radio direction finder on account of low batteries, navigation was a concern in the haze and fog. Fortunately visibility improved for a short time - enough to pick up Blackrock with its dangerous shoals that stretch 11 miles out to sea. By this time the wind had veered around to West North West and we reached along under No. 2 Genoa.

When the navigator propounded a course of 55 for Eagle Island, leaving the Belmullet Peninsula to starboard, there was consternation and confusion on deck as it seemed we were headed straight for land but it turned out to be the bright lights of fishing boats. By dawn the spinnakers of "Red Velvet" and "Gowan Puegeot" loomed astern. The wind went back west again after rounding Eagle Island and we set our course for Tory Island. From out to sea "Partizan" came thundering up Donegal Bay as we worked hard to hold her in the freshening wind. Southerly gales were being forecast with the low centre predicted to move across Northern Ireland.

That run across the top of Ireland along the rugged Donegal coastline past Aran Island and on to Tory by dusk provided the most exhilarating sailing of the entire race. The long Atlantic swell rolled along - uninterrupted since America - powered by strong westerly winds now approaching gale force. The air was crisp and clear with visibility exceptionally good.

Bearing 60 degrees, Tory Island lay ahead with its bleak barren beauty. To starboard the Bloody Foreland stood high under a halo of cirro-stratus upper cloud. Racing neck and neck with "Partizan" this was offshore racing at its best.

"Stay clear of my ... ing nets", a salmon fisherman blared across "Partizan's" VHF radio in a sharp northern accent difficult to decipher. She altered course in time, while on "Feanor" (out of radio contact) we had to dramatically alter course and barely avoided disaster. We had to drop spinnaker and lose a hard earned two miles (or 20 minutes) in the race. Though losing all that time to "Partizan", having worked hard for it all day, was a serious matter, I could not help but find the whole business, way up there on top of Ireland, amusing. Understandably Skipper was not very pleased when all your correspondent could think of doing was to hop around the deck taking pictures.

The small fishing boat bobbed between the swells - sometimes out of view and then riding high on a crest for all to see - approached in fury to protect her nets. Undoubtedly they must have been startled by the number of racing yachts going flat-out within hours of one another; up along the coastline on an otherwise rarely visited part of the world.

"Good luck now", the skipper called - possibly from Arran Island. "And I hope you win."

For all competitors, nets proved to be a great hazard, particularly the illegal ones unattended and stretching for miles between headlands. Indeed, this was one of the principal reasons given for the early retiral of the catamaran "Snowball". The other catamaran had gear problems and ended up eventually in Foynes before retiring, where WIORA (West of Ireland Offshore Racing Association) was in full swing. "Crystal Clear", a Shamrock Half-Tonner was the third boat to retire on pulling into Galway - reportedly with crew problems.

At 12-30 hours we passed Tory on the starboard beam. The wind backed further around to SSW making it a close reach to the furthest point north, Inistrahull. The wind remained a steady 35 knots over the deck. "Partizan" revelled in the conditions and drew further ahead, much and all as we tried to hold her.

On Friday July 4th, Inistrahull was abeam at 01-50 hours, squally, rain and very overcast. Approaching Rathlin Island we encountered tides the like of which I have rarely seen before. Sailing through the dawn the scenery, with the Giant's Causeway to starboard, followed by Fair Head, was spectacular. By carrying the spinnaker longer than would normally be advised and quick sail changing we caught right up on "Partizan" before her merry crew got to work and pulled away through the early morning towards our next corner, The Maidens.

Leaving Larne and Island Magee to starboard the scenery along the Antrim coast was a joy, though the wind was drawing ahead and as we drew further south the going got tougher. We worked our damnedest to hold "Partizan" but she revelled in the 25 knot winds on her hottest point of sailing - close reaching.

Soon Belfast Lough passed away to starboard, as we stormed along drawing down past Strangford Lough by nightfall before heading straight out into the Irish Sea, making a rhumb line for the pier head at Wicklow.

Now with the wind almost on the nose, that last 12 hour slog through the night was the toughest of the race. Our wind speed indicator was knocked out but it must have at least reached Force 9 for half an hour when we dropped the main and battled on under jib alone.

Through the early morning sunrise the Sugar Loaf was a sight for tired eyes. On the final beat in we were a bit slow in shaking out a reef and allowed the tide to carry us down too far. And, to add an extra bit of drama before crossing the line, a mast runner came undone leaving us all on tenterhooks watching the bendy stick - it'll break-yes-no-yes ... Fortunately it didn't and we entered Wicklow S.C.'s hospitable bar with yet another tale worth more pints, and G and T's to last the winter.

In short, it was a good race, well run, with personality, provided challenge and achievement. Though there will always be room for improvement reasons for Feanor's success include a) Knowing how hard to push her in the blows; b) Navigation and reading the tides; c) Maintaining boat speed at all times through 24 hours a day, working specially hard in the calms.

Rhumb line: 695 miles; Est. distance 825 miles; Average speed 5.92 knots.

*(first published in "Afloat" magazine this article is interesting because it describes the events in the first ever non-stop Round Ireland race.)*

*Laurie Smith in Rothmans leads the fleet in what was to be a record circumnavigation*

*Jeep Colm Barrington at last achieved his ambition of holding the Round Ireland record. He achieved it in1998 with Jeep Cherokee. A record which stood until 2008.*

# ALTERNATIVE ROUND IRELAND RACE

David Ryan *Ireland Afloat* January 1983

*WSC's Round Ireland Race, sponsored by Irish TV Rentals, has deservedly become one of the major events on the offshore circuit. It now attracts the top boats, and inevitably the reports often feature famous household names involved. But in a fleet of this size the majority of participants will seldom, if ever, be mentioned in the race reports. So, to put the record straight, David Ryan tells the story of the "Alternative Round Ireland Race" as seen from Dermod Ryan's ten-year-old Hustler 35 Red Velvet.*

Racing is getting more and more like Formula I Motor Racing these days. This Summer's Round Ireland proves the point emphatically; it was divided into the Turbos and the non-Turbos.

Everybody knows the Turbos, Moonduster, Stormbird, Wild Goose, Shanaghee, and Feanor were reported ad nauseum in every article you read. What about the non-turbos, can you name them? Bet you can't. Well, forget all the stuff you read and heard because the non-turbos had their own Race and the winner naturally, was Dermod Ryan's Red Velvet (eat your hearts out Crystal Clear and Korsar).

These boats have different problems to face. Extra long holidays are needed. On the "Duster" all you need is a long weekend, on Red Velvet and the likes, it's at least a week with a bit of leeway from the boss just in case. Also, the Turbos don't need to carry as much grub as we do, partly because they are faster, and partly because most of their crews are "headbangers" who don't need much food anyway.

Let's concentrate on Red Velvet's Race.

In 1980, Red Velvet was second; this year, in an attempt to win, Dermod embarked on the planning with his usual meticulous care.

The crew was hand-picked (at the last minute), Harry Grimes, umpteen-times Mermaid champion (the quiet man of Sailing), Dara MacMahon, the eating machine and sometime hooker of note. Two new faces, Gerry Grimes (Harry's brother), and Sam Shields, both were incredibly keen. Myself as cook and general talker, and Dermod as skipper. A motley bunch!

Weight was cut to the maximum. Food was limited to such necessities as 1 sack spuds, 1 bag onions, 1 bag carrots, assorted other veg, 1/2 ton various tins, bags, bottles etc., etc. Enough meat to feed the Falkland's task force was stored in cold places and finally, purely for medicinal purposes of course - 1 case of Scotch and 1 case of gin. The waterline disappeared and there was hardly enough room for the crew down below. Final preparations included stuffing the broken, badly leaking stern gland with half a million J cloths.

So to the Club for a quick pre-race jar. On our way to the Club we were passed by the Turbo crews, all sober, all being shepherded back on board by their various skippers, at 10 o'clock! When the Velvet and Crystal Clear crews staggered by at an un-Godly hour, well loaded, these other crews were "zizzing" away merrily.

Saturday morning, Jazus what a hangover! Korsar, another arch rival, gave us a tow to the start as we grabbed our breakfast. Beautiful sight - all those coloured sails. The "Duster" naturally disappeared over the horizon in record time; next time we saw her it was on the following Sunday week at the Irish regatta in DunLaoire. We all had a brief period of sunshine, spinnaker work and a flying display from "Biggles" in his biplane.

You (the reader) won't really be interested in things like winds, weather and sea conditions or the best course to the Tuskar. We weren't very interested either as can be seen from the Skippers notes in the log. "Feel we should have gone inside banks" - this was written a day or two later, I think.

We rounded the Tuskar sometime during the night, most of us were indulging in Egyptian gymnastics down below. A roaring calm ensued for some hours. As Sunday progressed we spotted two yachts well astern. One may have been Challenge, the other was Partizan. We are sure because we were gradually overhauled by her during the day. (No love lost between Red Velvet and Partizan crews, after the last Round Ireland. That shower stole our entire supply of porn!) MacMahon was on the helm that evening, one minute the kite was like a giant BASS and next minute it was like ticker-tape - back to the comfort of the small spinnaker. By the way, we passed Crystal Clear somewhere around Kinsale, they were having problems with their chain plates. Naturally we were concerned and sorry for their ill luck. Oh yeah?

We rounded the Mizen in the dark, going like the proverbial clappers; we had a wake like a destroyer's, brilliant phosphorescence. Gerry expressed concern at this mad headlong rush in pitch black darkness; a hefty glass of malt eased his concern.

Then it happened. Harry Grimes came on watch at about half-five or thereabouts. In 1980, not far from where we were, he did one of his famous gybes and tried to separate my head and Dermod's from our respective bodies. So again Grimes did his thing. He has undoubtedly won the "Broach" of the Year Award. Not once mind you, he really went for broke. Suffice to say that he lost control. She lay down to leeward, then right over to weather with the spinnaker followed by the main in the water, taken back again to leeward and finally to weather again. Harry and Gerry had both been suffering from severe constipation since the start of the race, after this their difficulties were well and truly cured. We finally got the spinnaker off - not a text book performance by any means, but by God, when the hand steadied a bit, the whiskey tasted good. Common sense prevailed, we gybed the main, at about 8/9 knots, put on the no.1 and settled back to relative normality.

*"The snot-green sea" (Joyce), "Wine dark sea" (Homer),*
*"Quink blue sea" (Fred Drew)*

The weather on the west coast wasn't out of a holiday brochure. We carried on, although some of the "heavies" went for shelter.

It was not as bad as some have reported. Okay, so we pumped and bailed with buckets for hours, the electrics went on fire when we tried to charge the batteries, the spray-hood disintegrated, the main ripped, down below the boat looked like a Calcutta slum on a bad day, but things improved, they always do. The spuds and bacon were served up by the time we got to Tory.

Then we stitched the main. Hours of painstaking labour stitching a series of tears and rips. One tear was just below the last reefing point and was about 10 feet long. It looked okay, but was only suitable for winds up to about Force 2, maybe 3. The leg along the north coast was only enlivened by the inspection by one of the Irish naval boats; they didn't even report our position to base. The wind was dead on our nose- it had been since about half way up the west coast - and when we got to the top right hand corner of Ireland it was still on the snitch. Harry, by the way, had at this stage blown out the main again, so back to the hanky-sized mainsail for the rest of the race. We missed the tide at Rathlin and sat for bloody hours just off the end of the island; the only consolation was that we could relax and have a few jars followed by a typical Fingallian dish, "Tump", (i.e. spuds, carrots and onions all boiled and mashed together) and boiled bacon, parsley sauce and cabbage.

*In 2004 the 'Round Ireland' truly went international with no less than three entries from the Netherlands. Shown here is Tonnerre de Breskens (Piet Vroon). The other entrants were Zwerver (Franc van Schrank) and Second Love (Gerard Cok)*

The leg down the Irish sea was miserable, poor visibility, rain and fickle winds, still we did brighten as the time passed with the aid of a few scoops. It must have been Friday or thereabouts when we passed the South Rock LV. Gerry posed for photographs with the light-ship in the background. It was a reasonably good day; for a change the wind, what there was of it, went astern so we hoisted a kite. In such conditions sailing can be enjoyable, so we lashed into the booze with gusto, yet again quite a skinful was had by all even Sam, our star sleeper, over indulged.

Dermod got quite excited when, away ahead in the haze, he saw a spinnaker "it's Partizan, Jazus, c'mon, we are catching him". So we did because through the haze of booze we gradually caught Partizan, only it turned out to be the Kish.

*Welcome to the roughest, toughest test of stamina and endurance in the offshore racing world...*

# A PRIMER FOR NON-SAILORS

Offshore sailors are a special breed and those who compete in the 'Round Ireland' are very special indeed – so special that they keep coming back for more. Almost half of the skippers in this year's (2004) race have competed before, some as many as eight times. The race is addictive. They know they are going to suffer hardship, stress, exhaustion - and exhilaration. They keep coming back for the special adrenaline rush of the start – and because they want to win. There is a real sense of achievement in having taken part in one of the world's toughest offshore races and in having seen Ireland as few others are privileged to see it.

The rules are simple. Any boat over 30 feet in length may be entered provided the crew have sufficient experience. In fact the overall winners of the race have ranged in size from just over 30 feet to 83 feet in length. In order to have a level playing field, so to speak, boats sail under their handicap, each boats handicap being arrived at by an agreed international formula. So, theoretically, they all have an equal chance of winning, all things being equal. But of course all things are never equal and the boat that wins will have had a certain amount of luck as well as hard-driving skipper, a hard working crew and the right tactics.

Theoretically it is true that the longer the boat the faster it should be able to travel through the water and, of course, handicapping takes this into account. But there are other factors at work too. The larger the boat, the bigger the crew. A boat with a crew of 20 sets no more sails than a boat with a crew of eight (although the sails are much larger and require more 'grunt') which means that it is possible to operate a proper "watch" system where each member of the crew has more opportunity to rest and sleep. Plus the fact that such a large boat is going to complete the race in, probably, less than four days.

A smaller boat with a crew of eight may take five and a half days to complete the course and the need to push the boat continuously to the limit day and night may make it difficult even to cook meals, let alone sleep.

All boats must pass a rigorous safety inspection by official RORC inspectors. They must carry storm sails and a comprehensive list of safety equipment ranging from life rafts to bolt cutters. Any boat failing this pre-race inspection is not allowed to compete.

The fastest elapsed time for an overall winner of 3d:4h: 23m: 57s was set by 'Jeep Cherokee' in 1998 and the slowest elapsed time set by a winner was 6d: 4h: 5m: 16s by 'Imp' (a 40-footer) in the 2000 race.

(The current record holder (2008) is 'ICAP Leopard' owned and skippered by Mike Slade. The time to beat is now 2d:17h: 48m: 47s).

However this (2000) was an exceptional race because of the prevalence of light winds. In this same race the slowest boat took over 9 days to complete the course. So the time it takes to complete the course depends upon the size of boat and the weather conditions. Heavy winds tend to favour the larger boats and light winds the medium to smaller boats.

You may wonder why finishing times are given down to seconds. It may seem odd that in such a long race that takes such a long time that it should be necessary to time boats to the second. However it is vital. On several occasions what is known as the 'corrected time' i.e. the actual elapsed time adjusted by the handicap factor, between first and second boats home has been a matter of seconds. The actual winner of the race is the boat with the lowest corrected time.

This is one reason why the start of the race is such a high-tension affair, at least on the boats. Gaining those few seconds at the start is not only important itself but is good for crew morale and the temper of the skipper – and nobody wants an upset skipper! However, there is more than one race going on out there. The entrants are divided into 'Classes' so that boats with roughly similar handicaps are racing against each other. Then there is the inter-club rivalry with teams of three boats representing individual clubs competing for the team trophy – a hot one this!

The official distance of the race is 704 miles. However the real distance travelled can be much greater. Theoretically a motor-boat could circumnavigate the island of Ireland in that distance but it is virtually impossible for a sailing boat to do so.

A sailing boat is entirely dependent upon wind and tide and as it cannot sail directly into the wind it must 'tack' at a 35-40 degree angle to the wind. It is clear that distance travelled is dependent to some extent on wind direction. Then there is always the trade-off between distance trav3elled and boat speed. The boat tactician must decide if it is better to maintain the shortest course or to sail a longer course faster. In this race the first choice of this nature normally occurs after the Tuskar rock where the choice is either to hug the coast or to take a long tack out to sea and then tack for the Fastnet rock.

(All boats must have a working engine but its use is restricted to charging the boats batteries to maintain navigation lights and instruments.)

The greatest distance run in the race that I have seen logged is 890 nautical miles. However this boat did not take much longer to complete the race than other identical boats which travelled a shorter distance. It was simply sailed faster.

Over the years 561 boats have started the race and 449 have completed the course. A total of 112 boats have 'retired'. The main reason for boats having to retire is rigging failure – something breaks! More often than not it's the forestay that breaks and without a forestay the boat cannot be sailed.

The first stage of the race, from Wicklow to the Fastnet can be the most difficult. Often the boats will be sailing directly against a SW wind which means that they will be 'beating' (tacking) which can be a very uncomfortable wet form of sailing. Crews will be 'sitting-out' on the windward side of the boat, operating as movable ballast. Prolonged beating and frequent tacking is hard on crews and hard on boats. In the conditions off the SW coast, where the sea is shallow, the tides are mean and the waves are short and steep, boats and crew can take a real 'hammering' and the constant pitching of the boat puts a tremendous strain on the mast rigging.

The vast majority of boats that have retired have done so before the Fastnet Rock. Usually if a boat rounds the 'Rock' it will complete the race. After the Fastnet the boats turn north-westwards heading along the indented south west coast and, if they are lucky they will have a favourable wind. Here they head north. This stage of the race is, for most competitors, the most sublime, exhilarating – and terrifying experience. Imagine riding a high spirited horse in the 'Grand National' without any reins. This is what it is like to surf Atlantic rollers at up to 20 knots. Helming the boat in these conditions requires total concentration and is best left to someone who has done it before! Past Inishtereacht, past the Skelligs, past Slyne Head and Eagle Island, seeing the west coast of Ireland as few are privileged to see it.

Heading up the Donegal coast past Arranmore and Tory island, they see the grim Atlantic side of these islands which enables them to withstand the constant pounding of the restless ocean. Here they have to keep a careful lookout for salmon drift nets that can stretch for miles out to sea often without markers or a guard boat. Experienced sailors have developed a technique for dealing with these nets. These nets will pose a particular threat to the crews of the new two-handed class as it may be difficult to keep a constant lookout. If there is going to be a gale during the race this North West coast is normally where it happens and in the past competitors have experienced very severe conditions here.

Past lonely Inistrahull Island and the boats are now heading eastwards along the north coast, past Rathlin Island and then down the North Channel between Ireland and Scotland. Here they often experience of fierce adverse tides and a flat calm and sometimes have to anchor until the tide changes, past Mew Island and into the Irish Sea once more.

Competitors are now on the 'downhill' leg – but there is still a long way to go and quite often this leg of the race is bedevilled by light winds and some competitors head offshore towards the Isle of Man in the hope of picking up wind, others begin to measure out the water and ration the cigarettes. It can be very frustrating.

But it is all worthwhile when the Wicklow East Pier Harbour Light beckons and you glide between it and the finish mark. Down with the sails, on with the engine and suddenly you develop a raging thirst which can only be satisfied in the warm, welcoming comfort of the WSC . . . and its two years to wait until the next race.

*Fred Drew*

*Big Ears (Michael Boyd) seen here disguised as Chez Youen, won the race on handicap in 1996.*

# A BRIEF HISTORY

It is a remarkable fact, that prior to 1980, no one (according to my uncertain knowledge) had ever circumnavigated Ireland non-stop in a yacht. Since then perhaps 5,000 sailors have done so.

517 boats have crossed the starting line, 421 have finished the race, an overall success rate of 80%. However, many of the entrants have competed in the race more than once, some as many as eight times. Together they make up what is a very select group.

When we in WSC were discussing the possibility of organising a round Ireland race (in the late 70's) our first thoughts were to follow the example of Ballyholme Yacht Club and hold a 3-stage race; the idea of a non-stop race seemed somewhat bizarre. Who would enter? However, the late Michael Jones persuaded us that a non-stop race was feasible and we decided to hold the first race in 1980. Even-numbered years were chosen to avoid conflict with the Admiral's Cup as we anticipated that the race would attract similar boats. A little hubris goes a long way!

The first race in 1980 was a somewhat low- key affair – the razzmatazz would come in later years – but tribute should be paid to those pioneers.

The Round Ireland, from the very beginning, established a pattern of races within races, with, at that time, different handicapping systems in use. It also established the pattern, as the race progressed and the fleet spread out, of different weather systems being experienced by the competitors.

An extreme example of this came in the, generally, heavy weather race of 1994, although '84 had been heavy too. In 1994 the fleet was spread out over a distance of perhaps 150 miles. The large fast boats were kedged in light winds and a foul tide in the North Channel whereas the middle orders were experiencing a full gale off the NW coast, winds of 50 kts. gusting to 60 kts. being reported from Malin Head. (The leading boats had missed this).

Preparing the table which accompanies this article reminded me of just how loyal and dedicated Round Ireland sailors are to the race. Just scanning the list of entrants for the various races throws up a list of what I might call 'Hard-core' competitors who return again and again for the challenge. The table also lists the forgotten entries – the ones who finished last. There should be a trophy awarded for their sheer perseverance. There are no losers in the Round Ireland.

Take the late Brian Coad and his yacht Raasay of Melfort (a Rival 34). To Brian fell the honour of being the first overall winner of the race. Then he followed this triumph with being last boat home on four occasions. In 1982 he took over 9 days to complete the course – imagine 9 days cooped up on a 34 footer! But he persevered and never gave up – never. But then what about the appropriately named 'Damp Store', which, in the millennium race took almost 9 days and 6 hours to complete the course. This was endurance of epic proportions, especially as it would not have been too difficult to find a reason to retire – starvation perhaps.

Re-reading Winkie Nixon's entertaining account of the first race (In 'Ireland Afloat') reminded me of just how far we have come. He mentions the race committee's problem with using sponsor's names for boats – something I had forgotten about but which was to resurface in later years until finally resolved. I remember, in later years, discussions within the race committee as to whether we should allow mobile phones to be used by competitors! The theory being that those who had them had an unfair advantage as they could communicate with the shore and obtain information about the position of competitors; hard to believe now when everything is reported in real time by GPS technology.

Although the race remains the same there has been a profound change in the number and make up of entrants. The race now attracts 'state-of-the-art' yachts as well as veterans. The number of entrants has stabilised at about 40. Nowadays nobody enters or sees the race as a 'jolly'.

Predicting the winner of the race is a punter's nightmare. Literally anyone can win. It's down to luck, tactics, guile and experience. As in a horse race there is always a favourite but the wise man places an each way bet. Do you bet on the horse or the jockey? Of course weather plays a major part (something of a truism that) Light weather has tended to favour smaller boats and conversely, heavy weather the bigger boats. The race has been won by boats ranging in length from 32 foot to 82 foot.

The big question for this year is, can Eric Lisson and Cavatina win the race for a third time?' No one has won the race three times. Denis Doyle in Moonduster won the race twice and took line honours on three occasions. Colm Barrington has also won the race twice and taken line honours three times (in different boats each time).

In six of the last seven races the race has been won on handicap by boats of 40 foot or less so the statistics indicate that it is entirely possible for Eric Lisson to be the first to win the race on three occasions.

Another big question before every race is, can anyone beat Colm Barrington's 1998 record, in Jeep Cherokee, of 3d:04:23:57? Team Spirit came very close in 2004 with a time of 3d:04:48:49, just 25 minutes adrift – that was a true nail-biter.

We don't know what distance Colm Barrington sailed when he set the record but if we assume it was between 750 and 800 miles his average boat speed was between 9.8 and 10.4 kts.

A boat averaging 11 kts would similarly complete the race in between 2 days 20 hours and 3 days 1hour. Not impossible one would think, but the Round Ireland is a race full of surprises.

ICAP Leopard, possibly the most technically advanced yacht in the world and at 30m the largest boat ever to enter the race is aiming to beat the record and with a claimed ability to sail at 35 kts and a hugely experienced crew the odds must favour Mike Slade – but watch this space!

*(In fact ICAP Leopard 3 took just under 2 days and 18 hours to complete the course although I do not know the distance run).*

*Fred Drew*

# ROUND IRELAND GRAND PRIX

They were not pioneers (at least, not many of them). Nor were they the first to race non-stop round Ireland - that had been done in a race starting and finishing in Falmouth organised by the Royal Ocean Racing Club in 1978. However they were the first to race round Ireland non-stop in an event which started and finished at an Irish port, in this instance Wicklow, which WSC which inaugurated the event has continued to run, with the assistance of the R.O.R.C., on a biennial basis.

*The 2002 Race gets under way*

It was also the first time that most of them would have spent five or more days continuously at sea. The 2006 race will be the 14th in the series and after a quarter of a century it may be time to reflect on the early, now forgotten years.

13 entries started in the 1980 race and it is indicative of the attraction of the event that many were to become regular entrants over the following years. In particular, Jim Poole, who as much as anyone, helped to put the race on the map - so to speak. Jim had taken part in the 1975, two-handed,

three-stage race starting from Ballyholme Y.C. in his 23' Ruffian, Ruffino. He would be pleased to see the fleet of Ruffians in WSC. However for the 1980 race he had upgraded to a Nicholson half-tonner called Feanor which was to become a very well known boat. Sadly Jim's untimely death removed a great supporter of the race. Brian Coad won the first race on handicap in his Rival 34, Raasay of Melfort. He went on to complete a further 6 races. Brian had also taken part in the 1975 race organised by Ballyholme Y.C.

Boats such as Crystal Clear, Red Velvet, Crazy Jane and Force Tension became familiar names on what was to become virtually a Grand Prix circuit. 1980 was the first and last race in which multi-hulls were permitted to compete.

This first race was to become the template for future races although very few in WSC anticipated what a major event it would become. One person who perhaps did was the late Michael Jones, the race organiser until his death in 1993. It was due to his high standing in the sailing community and his meticulous attention to detail as well as his diplomatic skills that the race became a premier event in the sailing calendar.

## THE 'DUSTER' ENTERS, STAGE RIGHT.

For the 1982 race entries had increased to 20 and 19 boats actually started. This was the race that saw the first appearance of Denis Doyle's mighty new Moonduster. The first of about ten appearances. Denis and 'The Duster' soon became synonymous with the race. In 1982 his elapsed time of 99:45:25 not only gave him line honours, but first overall on handicap. It was also the fastest circumnavigation to-date. The, by now, usual suspects were involved in the race plus newcomers such as Kieran Jameson , Liam Shanahan, Frank Elmes, and Michael O'Leary..

A quote from 'Red Velvet' gives some idea of the flavour of the race,

". . . it was not as bad as some have reported. Okay, so we pumped and bailed with buckets for hours, the electrics went on fire when we tried to charge the batteries, the spray-hood disintegrated, the main ripped, down below the boat looked like a Calcutta slum on a bad day, but things improved, as they always do."

## MOONDUSTER SETS RECORD TIME

In 1984, in the words of Winkie Nixon, writing in 'Afloat Magazine',

"They ran out of words as they tumbled ashore from their salty boats in Wicklow's crowded little harbour.' the sail of a lifetime, fabulous' and 'the greatest' were the things they were saying. It was an experience so out of the normal way of going that one competitor summed it up for everyone: "Magic. Sheer magic"

It certainly seems an appropriate description for a race in which the record books were completely rewritten for all classes, a scorcher of a sail, which will be etched forever in the memory of all who experienced it.

This was to be the most testing heavy weather race so far and it is a tribute to the crews that only 4 out of 19 entries had to retire - mainly due to rigging failure. It was also the year that Denis Doyle in Moonduster set up what was to become the long standing circumnavigation record of 88 hours 15 minutes and 43 seconds. An amazing feat. Once again Moonduster took line honours and the overall trophy.

## DURAN DURAN AND ALL THAT RAZZMATAZZ

In 1986 razzmatazz came to Wicklow with the entry of Simon Le Bon's Maxi Drum chartered by M. O'Leary and T. Power and entered as Mazda Drum. Simon Le Bon was sailing as a crew member and the quays were packed with admiring teenagers (and not a few mums). Drum had just competed in the 'Round the World' race where she had to retire when her keel fell off. In this race she had to retire also because Simon Le Bon left the boat before the finish to meet a previous engagement. The rules state that a boat must finish the race with the same number of crew as it started with. It is thought that this rule is designed to deter cannibalism. Although Mazda Drum completed the race in 99 hours 35 minutes line honours went to Moonduster (for the third consecutive time) with an elapsed time of 116 hours 15 minutes. The race was also notable for the first all-female crew competing in the race sailing the 41' Electra and skippered by Joyce Taylor of Ballyholme Yacht Club - what goes around, comes around! Conditions did not suit the larger boats and the race was won, on handicap, by Richard Burrows in Spirit, one of the smallest boats in the race. Making his first appearance as skipper was Roy Dickson driving the soon to become famous Imp.

1988 was notable for having the largest entry to-date with 50 starters. It was also notable for the ding-dong battle in mainly light winds between Moonduster and Woodchester Challenge with Moonduster eventually taking line honours with about 50 minutes to spare from Woodchester. Again the race was won on handicap by one of the smallest boats in the fleet, Lightning, skippered by Liam Shanahan.

## ROTHMANS ESTABLISHES NEW 'ROUND IRELAND' RECORD

The Round Ireland race could be said to have reached critical mass in 1990 when 61 boats crossed the starting line. And what a line-up it was!

The prestige of the race had become so enormous that all of the world's best sailors wanted to compete (if they could get the right boat). It had almost reached the stage where the Round Ireland had become a lap of honour for those completing the Round the World races.

The 1990 event could be considered the year of the Maxi, no less than four taking part, Rothmans, (Laurie Smith); Pepe Merit, (Colm Barrington); Woodchester Challenge, (aka Atlantic Privateer, Brian Buchanan) and NCB Ireland, (Joe English).

*Presentation 1990. Richard Burrows (CDG) and Michael Jones (WSC) present Laurie Smith with the trophy for his record circumnavagation in Rothmans*

To quote Winkie Nixon yet again, "For many, crossing the starting line was an enormous relief. The many private entries had the inevitable struggle to be ready in time. For those who were sponsored there was the exhausting round of pre-race receptions. For Laurie Smith with Rothmans, there was a bit of everything. He was taking the race so seriously that the boat was optimised for the expected conditions with a new keel, and new sails were being tested less than two days before the race."

Of the 61 starters no less than 26 were forced to retire (mainly before reaching the Fastnet Rock) after running into a SW gale. Again the main reason was rigging failure, the boats taking a severe pounding in the conditions off the South coast. Even Pepe Merit who had just won her class in the Round the World race had to retire because of damage - so much for a lap of honour!

Après deluge - the calm. Although the smaller boats had to endure the gale the larger boats sailed themselves out of it only to experience frustratingly light winds for the rest of the race. Eventually, (and it must have seemed a long eventually to Laurie Smith) Rothmans took line honours with a time of 84 hours and 56 minutes thus beating Moonduster's record time - but not by much. NCB Ireland also beat Moonduster's time finishing only 1 hour and 20 minutes behind Rothmans.

## PAUSE FOR BREATH.

What had happened? Had Round Ireland fatigue set in? Had the Celtic Tiger yet to be weaned? One possible reason was the non-availability of the Round the World boats because of the timing of that race. In any event only 35 entries crossed the starting line in 1992 but between them they comprised a galaxy of Irish and British sailing talent. Returning, after his disappointment of 1990, was a determined Colm Barrington with his entry Whirlpool (aka Dump Truck) and Round the World sailor Peter Wilson was competing in Bootlegger. In the event these two big boats finished almost a day ahead of the next boat Krystal (B. Pope) which gained a very creditable third place overall. No records were broken in this race but markers were being set out.

## THE YEAR OF THE SIGMA 38's

For reasons of space this review has necessarily focussed on the overall winners of the event but it must not be forgotten that within each event there were many races, between individuals and between classes. 1994 was the year of the Sigma 38 when no less than 12 participated. This one-design competition offers the very best of challenges and it was to prove a memorable year with the emergence of Tom O'Connor, skippering a Sigma 38, Air Corps 1. He won his class and went on to greater things, although some would say that there is nothing greater than picking up silverware for a 'Round Ireland'. There was also a minor dual between Black Tie - Wicklow Challenge, a Sigma 38 with a young crew from WSC and the all woman crew of Nissan 1. No one who witnessed the end of that particular duel will ever forget it - tears were shed - I'm not ashamed to admit it.

*James S. Tyrell of Arklow has entered an Aquelina in no less than 10 Round Ireland races (1990 – 2008) and completed every one of them. Over the years the boats have changed (the current Aquelina is a J109) but the name has remained the same*

53 boats started what was to prove one of the most difficult of heavy weather races. It's a tribute to the boats and the crews that only 17 boats were forced to retire. The all woman crew of Tropicana having to retire into Arklow - along with others. Winds off the coast of Donegal reached 50 knots gusting to 60 knots. Conditions were so severe that even the mighty Moonduster had to retire hurt, with a damaged forestay.

In these conditions Corwynt, a Sigma 400, skippered by Gwilym Evans of Wales, logged 200 miles in 12 hours to finish in third place only one hour behind the eventual winner Bridgestone a J35 skippered by veteran Peter Wilson. Second place went to Richard Burroughs in Prospector with the closest finish ever, only one minute behind Bridgestone. A difference of one minute after 800 miles and almost five days of racing is quite remarkable.

## ENTER THE BIG RED ONE.

Entries seemed to have settled around the 50 plus mark with 56 starters in the 1996 event. Remarkably 55 of them completed the course - a record. The race was graced by the first contestant from the USA, the affable Jake Wood with his graceful red maxi, Sorcery. They say that down below it was fitted out with a 'Disco' and dance floor - essential requirements for a 'Round Ireland'! I know, I have the T-shirt.

*Excitement at the finish: Whirlpool takes a bow
after winning the 1992 race.*

Just reading the list of entries gives a sense of déjà vu - a roll-of-honour of 'Round Ireland' competitors. In the event, race honours went to the J35 Big Ears skippered by Michael Boyd. A pattern seemed to be emerging of this class of boat doing extremely well in the race. Second overall was Roy Dickson's Beaumont Spirit. Jake Wood took line honours with a storming time of 88 hours 15 minutes that, a few years earlier, would have been considered remarkable, giving little time for disco gyrations.

## COLM BARRINGTON DOES HIS THING.

If a prize were to be awarded for dedication and persistence it would surely be won by Colm Barrington. In 1998 it finally paid off. His entry was the Whitbread 60, Jeep Cherokee. There were only 26 entries but they were entries with a long pedigree of racing round Ireland. Jeep Chero-kee stormed home in a new record time of 76 hours 23 minutes and 57 seconds. A record that still stands (2006) for a circumnavigation within the constraints of a Round Ireland race. However, Bridgestone F1 (Ocean Marine/Mike Slade) was not far behind on elapsed time at just under 79 hours.

Worthy of mention is the WSC entry, Wicklow Racing, with Simon Greenwood as driver. They finished a respectable 13th. Proving the fickle-ness of fate, the 1996 winner, Big Ears, now renamed Chez Youen (Youen Jocob Jnr.) for this race, had to retire with a very broken stem fitting. The only other retiral was the veteran Joliba (Nigel Rollo/Jim Ryan).

## THE MILLENIUM BIG SLEEP.

Kinsale Yacht Club has always been one of the most fervent supporters of the Round Ireland race and this year (2000) was no exception in what was to prove a most tedious but also a most intriguing and testing race. What made it interesting was the almost total lack of wind for the entire race. The race started (26 boats) at 1400 hours. Those boats which opted to hug Wicklow Head got away safely. Those that didn't were obliged to kedge within sight of the start and were still there up to four hours later in sight of the start. Line honours went to the 60 footer Fenix with an elapsed time of 5 days and 12 hours. Imp, skippered by the irrepressible and indomitable George Radley Jnr., a winner at last, took 6 days and five hours closely followed by another Cork boat, Galliver, at 6 days and 8 hours. On corrected time Imp won the race but only by 6 minutes from Galliver. Even Moonduster, in what was to be Denis Doyle's final Round Ireland, took almost 6 days to complete the circuit. The trophy for courage and persistence (if we had one - and we should have one) should have gone to Damp Store (M. Davis) who took an incredible 9 days and 5 hours to complete the race.

Eric Lisson steered Cork boat Cavatina home to beat George Radley's Imp and win on handicap. Line honours were taken in 83 hours 34 min-utes by Nick Hewson in the mighty Team Tonic closely followed by Ri-chard Balding in Fenix at 90 hours and 42 minutes. 28 boats started the race, four had to retire, and one, our first entry from France, Pichenette, did not start because bad weather prevented it from reaching Wicklow in time. Looking at the results of this race and ignoring the two large boats one cannot help being struck by the uniformity of the elapsed times and, even more so, the corrected times. It's a great vindication of the handicap-ping system.

*Lobster 2004: Happy daze. The crew of Lobster celebrate their return to Wicklow.*
*Top Left, John Harte, Gary O'Sullivan.*
*Middle Row: Gary Horgan (skipper and Owner), David Boyd, Kevin Boyde*
*Bottom Row: Alan Bateman, James Long & Keith Reardon*

## THE ROUND IRELAND GOES INTERNATIONAL.

The race has always attracted the odd entry from outside the UK and Ireland, such as Austria, Germany, Switzerland, France, Malta and the USA and in 2004 there were quality entries from the Netherlands and France. One innovation introduced this year was the 'Two-handed' class in which there were five entries. Hardly an innovation really as the first race organised by Ballyholme was a two hander but with the huge difference that that was a three-stage race. Taken as a whole the fleet was probably the most powerful ever assembled for a 'Round Ireland'. It was not the largest fleet - 47 boats started the race of which 10 had to retire. Two entries, the Irish 02 Team Spirit (David Nixon) the French City Jet Solune (Jean P. Chomett) were to make a determined effort to beat Jeep Cherokee's record time. The race was one of the most closely fought so far, as befitted a quality field and, with the addition of some boisterous weather, exciting. As so often happens in the race the final stage, from Rockabill to Wicklow is the most frustrating and heart breaking. Boats have stormed round Ireland in jig time only to fall foul of light airs and an adverse tide on this final leg. This is what happened to 02 Team Spirit which seemed to disappear into a time warp after Dublin Bay. Eventually she reappeared and for a few heart-stopping minutes we thought she might break the record. But it was not to be, and her final time of 76 hours and 48 minutes was only 23 minutes outside the record. City Jet Solune finished in 79 hours 25 minutes.

*Team Tonic 2002*
*Nick Hewson drove Team Tonic hard in his attempt to break the race record. On target to do so he fell victim to the dreaded Irish Sea 'no wind syndrome'. Nevertheless he took Line Honours in the respectable time of 3 days and eleven hours.*
Photo: D. Branigan

However, as so often, the overall winner was one of the smaller boats, the brilliant Calyx Voice and Data (Eamonn Crosbie). It's hard to beat the old hands. Eric Lisson in Cavatina was having a close sniff in 3rd place. This was the first race to be sponsored by BMW Ireland and its success bodes well for the future of the race.

In an article of this length it is impossible to mention everyone who has contributed to the success of the race. The various sponsors have of course had an enormous impact on the development of the race, particularly Cork Dry Gin. And of course WSC members deserve some credit especially Denis Noonan as Race Organiser in recent years. But to my mind the real reason for the success of the event has been its appeal to the ordinary club sailor. Their support and loyalty has made the race and will continue to ensure its success in future. Thank you all.

In writing this history of the WSC Round Ireland race I have had, perforce, to rely on a somewhat suspect memory (mine), the race results in my computer files, and most of all, on the splendid reports of the race published in Afloat Magazine, mostly written by Winkie Nixon. As a competitor in the race he knows of what he writes. It is a source of disappointment to me that we do not have a proper record of the first quarter century of the race. Having said that, I accept full responsibility for any errors in the text.

*Fred Drew*

*Whirlpool (Colm Barrington) was a comfort6able winner of the 1992 race taking line honours in the process.*
Photo: D. Branigan

John Bourke    Mick McKenna    Neil Love    David Harte    John Mulcahy    Donal McClement
James O'Brien    John Lyden    Denis Doyle [skipper]    Neil Hegarty
Mark Penfold    Grattan Roberts    Brendan Fogarty

*Moonduster (Denis Doyle) Race winner in 1982 and 1984. Line honours in 1982, 1984 and 1988. Race record holder 1984 – 1990*

# REMEMBERING DENIS DOYLE AND MOONDUSTER

Is the 'Round Ireland' a one horse race? With a record of achievement like that of the late Denis Doyle and Moonduster some might think so – especially rivals. What Red Rum was to the Grand National, Moonduster was to the Round Ireland; Moonduster was overall winner of the race on two occasions, 1982 and 1984, in the latter year setting up a record Round Ireland circumnavigation time of 88 hours, 15 minutes and 43 seconds. A record which stood until 1990.

Regardless of handicap, the greatest thrill to a Round Ireland competitor is being first across the finishing line. 'Line Honours' as it is known, were taken by Moonduster on no less than three occasions, 1982, 1984 and 1988.

Moonduster was second across the finishing line in 1992, third in 1986 and 1990 and fourth in her final race in 2000 – but only 3 seconds behind Cracklin Rosie (Roy Dickson) who was third.

A study of Moonduster's race times shows their uncanny consistency. The difference between the 1986 and 1988 races is only 41 seconds and the difference between 1982 and 1992 is only 65 minutes! The difference between the 1996 and 1998 times is only 52 minutes.

Overall Moondusters average circumnavigation time for 9 races was 4 days, 13 hours and 34 seconds. To put this in perspective, in the entire history of the race only 33 boats have completed the race in less than this time. What a record! What a man! What a boat!

At every Round Ireland race, Moonduster's traditional berth alongside the North Pier remains empty in tribute to the memory of a great competitor.

## Moonduster's Racing Record

| Year | Hour:Min:Sec |
|------|-------------|
| 1982 | 99:45:25 |
| 1984 | 88:15:43 |
| 1986 | 116:15:05 |
| 1988 | 116:15:46 |
| 1990 | 131:38:19 |
| 1992 | 115:10:18 |
| 1994 | Retired |
| 1996 | 106:31:24 |
| 1998 | 107:23:04 |
| 2000 | 143:07:15 |

# LANDMARKS & LIGHTHOUSES

By Richard Nairn

The Round Ireland Yacht Race has a series of classic way points at which the competitors must report their position and time. These are all lighthouses on some of the remotest headlands and islands around the Irish coastline. The fastest sea route around Ireland measures just over 700 nautical miles (or 1,100 kilometres). But if you follow every little inlet and bay the total coastline with all its islands, measures over 4,600 miles (7,500 kilometres). This is longer than the Amazon River and even longer than the coastlines of much larger countries like France and Spain. Strung along this coastal necklace are hundreds of lighthouses, like jewels glittering in the darkness. These lights form the landmarks for the yachts and their crews as they circumnavigate the island in Ireland's premier offshore race.

*Wicklow Head Lighthouse*
Photo: D. Branigan

## Wicklow Head

Wicklow Head lies immediately to the south of the harbour where the race starts. This is the easternmost point of the Irish Republic at six degrees west. Wicklow Head has a unique history with three lighthouse towers visible from north and south. The first two of these were built in 1781 when it was decided that twin lights were needed to avoid confusion with the single lights of Howth to the north and Hook Head to the south. However, the highest point on the headland turned out to be a poor location which was often obscured and in 1818 the current lighthouse was built much lower down the cliff. In 1836, the old tower was struck by lightning and the fire which followed gutted the building. This tower has now been completely renovated by the Landmark Trust and is let as self-catering accommodation. Wicklow Head is a good place to look for Risso's dolphins as a small group feeds around here in the summer months. Looking to the south you will see the seven turbines of Ireland's first offshore windfarm which marks the northern end of the Arklow Bank. These offshore sandbanks stretch all the way to Wexford and are a significant hazard for sailors and commercial shipping.

## Tuskar Rock

Tuskar Rock lies seven miles off the south-east corner of Ireland within sight of the port of Rosslare. It is a flat rock often lashed by storms and even while the lighthouse was being built in 1812, ten men were washed off and drowned here. That same year, a ship bound for Liverpool ran aground on the rock and five people died but about a hundred survivors managed to scramble ashore. Another accident occurred in 1941 when a drifting mine hit the rock and exploded injuring two of the assistant keepers. Tuskar Rock marks the entry to Wexford harbour, a shallow estuary of shifting sandbanks. Here in the mid 19th century two large polders were reclaimed from the sea by Dutch engineers and pumped to keep them dry. In Winter, the Wexford slobs, to use the local name, hold many thousands of geese, ducks and swans from northern countries like Iceland and Greenland. Around the corner of Carnsore Point and the Irish Sea becomes the Celtic Sea with two Saltee Islands forming a gateway the south coast of Ireland. The larger island, famed for its seabird colony, is owned by the self-styled Prince Michael Neale.

## Fastnet

One of the most dramatic of Irish lighthouses is the Fastnet, which lies four and a half miles off the south coast of Cork and was often the last part of Europe seen by emigrants departing to America in the 19th century. The building of the present tower in 1900 to 1904 is captured in a wonderful series of images in the collection of the Commissioners of Irish Lights. The tower's masonry work comprised 89 courses or layers of cut granite stone made up of 2,074 blocks. The Fastnet gave its name to one of the premier ocean yacht races in Europe which started in Cowes, rounding Lands End to the Fastnet and back. The 1979 race was hit by a freak storm with many boats capsized, demasted or sunk. The West Cork coast is a great place to watch for seabirds, whales and dolphins. Big whales such as humpback and fin whales are attracted by the upwelling of cold oceanic water with abundant fish and plankton. The nearest inhabited islands to the Fastnet are Cape Clear and Sherkin Island which lie off the sailing town of Baltimore. Cape Clear is the one of the most popular birdwatching locations in Ireland as it is often the first landfall for migrants arriving from continental Europe or even from across the Atlantic Ocean. Sailing northwest from here, the Skellig and the Blaskets are among the most dramatic of Irish islands.

## Inishtearagh

Inishtearagh is the outmost of the Blasket Island group. It is a dramatic conical shape with the lighthouse built in 1870 on an extremely steep slope. The landing here was one of the most difficult of all the lighthouses and a hoist had to be used to lift the keepers from their boats. In 1900, the families of the keepers on both Skellig and Inishtearaght were re-housed on Valentia Island. Both the Skelligs and the Blaskets are internationally important seabird colonies with huge numbers of gannets, shearwaters and storm petrels. The Blaskets also have a large breeding seal colony. The largest of these islands is the Great Blasket, with its deserted village facing the mainland at Dunquin. Abandoned in the 1950s, the Blasket had among its small population, a unique group of writers including Peig Sayers, Tomas O'Criomhthain and Muiris O'Suilleabhain, who through their native Irish language, recorded the life of the islanders in the late 19th and early 20th centuries.

## Slyne Head

Slyne Head, the westernmost point of Ireland, is actually formed of a chain of small islands on the outer tip of Connemara. There were originally two lighthouses built here in 1836 although one is now disused. Navigation through these islands is very dangerous as the shallow reefs and islets are washed by strong tidal currents and overfalls. Not far away on the mainland near Clifden is the spot where the early aviators Alcock and Brown landed in 1919 having made the first flight across the Atlantic from

Newfoundland in just under 16 hours.  The Twelve Bens dominate the skyline of northern Connemara and one of the most extensive areas of blanket bog in Ireland stretches to the east.  The nearby Mannin Bay is famous for its "coral strands" which are made of the fragments of a unique submarine deposit called mearl.  Away to the north of Slyne Head a string of islands includes High Island, Inishbofin, Inishturk with Clare Island and Achill at the mouth of Clew Bay.  This is a traditional place to see the basking shark, the world's second largest fish.

## Eagle Island

Eagle Island lies to the north-west of the Mullet peninsula in Co, Mayo. The island is cliffbound and landing is almost impossible without swimming or the use of a hoist.  Two lighthouses were commissioned here in 1835 although only one is now used.  The keepers and their families who live here often had to endure periods of prolonged bad weather in winter when they were cut off from the mainland and essential supplies. In December 1894, a massive storm hit Eagle Island. Some of the dwellings were damaged beyond repair and the terrified women and children took refuge in the lighthouse tower itself. Even here, the sea broke the lantern glass and water showered down the inside of the tower.  Not far to the south are the twin islands of Inishkea, each one with a deserted village. Today the islands are used for grazing cattle and sheep which share the pastures with thousands of barnacle geese, arriving in October from their breeding grounds in Greenland.  In Autumn too these islands hold a very large colony of grey seals which come ashore to give birth to their pups. Broadhaven, to the east is the proposed landfall of the controversial pipeline from the Corrib gasfield offshore. Rounding the north-west corner of Mayo, the hills of Donegal come into view.

## Arranmore

The northern Aran Island is the largest island in Donegal with a population of about 650 people, linked to the mainland by a busy car ferry.  On the north-west point of the island, above substantial cliffs, a lighthouse was first built here in 1798 although it was rebuilt in 1865.  To facilitate landing of boats a set of steps was built down to water level where a tiny landing spot was cut into the rocks.  The western cliffs and pastures of Arranmore are used by flocks of choughs, the rarest of the crow family, which are distinguished by their red bill and legs.  To the north is Bloody Foreland, so named because of the red sunsets which light up its shores. Some eight miles north again is the remote island of Tory, which is steeped in legend and history.

## Inishtrahull

Inishtrahull is the most northernly point of Ireland (except for Rockall) lying about five miles north-east of Malin Head. The island is made of extremely hard gneiss which is one of the oldest rock types in Ireland. Inishtrahull, like so many Irish islands, was used by early Christian monks as a place of retreat and there are remains of beehive huts here. The small population which lived here abandoned the island in 1928, leaving it to the lighthouse keepers and the birds. The modern lighthouse is a massive 23m high as it occupies such an important location. In Winter barnacle geese feed here and it is often used by smaller migrant birds as a first landing place after leaving the arctic.

## Mew Island

Mew Island lighthouse is on one of the three Copeland Islands off Donaghadee. It marks the southern approach to Belfast Lough and must have been passed by many newly-built ships, including the Titanic, leaving Belfast shipyards. The original lighthouse was on the nearby John's Island but these buildings were vacated in 1884 and are now occupied by one of Ireland's two permanent bird observatories. There is a colony of Manx shearwaters nesting here and these birds migrate as far as the south Atlantic returning each year to lay their eggs in underground burrows. They only emerge under cover of darkness to avoid being eaten by large gulls. To the south of Mew Island stretches the long Ards Peninsula ending in the entrance to Strangford Lough. From here the home run begins down the Irish Sea.

## Rockabill

Rockabill lies due east of Skerries, and north of Lambay. The lighthouse was first lit in 1860 but is now better known as the location of a bird sanctuary where one of the most important colonies of terns in Ireland is located. This has been carefully protected by summer wardens and the terns are attracted to nest under cover of the dense canopy of sea mallow. Lambay has a huge seabird colony with over a thousand pairs of cormorants and in autumn a group of grey seals assembles to give birth here. From Rockabill, the yachts pass Howth Head, Dublin Bay and the Kish Light for the home run to the finish at Wicklow Harbour.


Richard Nairn is a naturalist and writer who sails in WSC. His most recent book, Ireland's Coastline: *Exploring its nature and heritage*, was published by Collins Press in 2005.

# The 1994 Cork Dry Gin Round Ireland Yacht Race

## 1994: THE ENTRANTS

Fifty three boats lined up on the starting line at 1400hrs on Saturday, 18th June, 1994. For some it was their first attempt at the gruelling 700 plus mile course, for others it was a just another circuit of Ireland!

**Alpara**, a Dufour 35, entered by Brian and Mick Carroll was one of the first time competitors. For them it was to turn out to be a seven day marathon. **Amazing Grace**, an Oyster 37 (Anthony Kingston, also of Kinsale Y.C.) had failed to complete the course in 1990. **Angel**, a Carter 34 was entered by Gerard Whiston of Poolbeg Y. and B.C., a club which has supplied many entries over the years. **Aquelina**, a Sigma 400 entered by James Tyrrell of Arklow Sailing Club had successfully completed the course twice before in 90 and 92 but this time was to find herself in a fleet of no less than eleven Sigma's competing in a race within a race for their own special trophy.

*Bridgestone Peter Wilson Sets off to win the race in 1994*

Bridgestone, (aka **Jumping Jack Flash**) a J35, (Peter Wilson, H.Y.C.), was one of the more favoured entrants and, in the event, did not disappoint. **Beaumont Spirit** (a.k.a. Scarlett, a 45', 2 tonner) entered and skippered by Roy Dickson looked very impressive in her red livery. Of special interest to the members of WSC was the Sigma 38 **Black Tie Wicklow** (a.k.a. State o' Chassis) skippered by Frank Jackson and entered by a group of young WSC members (the only crew who dressed for dinner). We knew the enormous efforts they had put into fund-raising to make their dream come true but we were also aware that they were in the most competitive group within the race.

The appropriately named **Comanche Raider** (Humphries 43), a fiercely completive boat, was entered for the third time, this time by Roy Hamilton of Carrickfergus - a combination to be respected by all competitors. Unfortunately this was not to be her year. **Constance**, a Contessa 39 (Clem Kelly), **Crown Duel**, a Dehler 36DB (Michael Fleming, Howth Y.C.) was making her third circuit and was to finish in her best time yet.

The Round Ireland race has always received enthusiastic support from Welsh competitors and this year was no exception. Gwilym Evans of the Pwllheli club was there with **Corwynt III**, a Sigma 400. Yet another Welsh entry was **Darramy**, a First 405 entered by Brian Wallace of Conwy. From Pwllheli came Anthony Jones in **Gwawr** another Sigma 38.

Travelling almost as far as around Ireland to compete came the all-conquering **Deerstalker** (S&S 34) from the Royal Harwich Y.C., fresh from her previous year's win of the Round Britain Race. One could be reasonably certain that Michael Taylor-Jones her skipper/owner had not come all that way except to pick up a 'gong' or two. Of all the entries it looked the most insignificant and least dangerous. Approaching the starting line for her third successive race was **Elusive** the Beneteau 45FS of John Sisk of the R.I.Y.C.

The smallest boats to compete in the Round Ireland are the Club Shamrock class and competing for her 5th time was **Emircedes** entered by Peter Ryan and Michael Horgan sailing under the N.Y.C. burgee. Somewhat larger than Emircedes was the entry by Bernard Freyne, a Noray 38 named **Estrellita**. **Golden Gryphon**, a Golden Shamrock was entered by well known competitor John O'Regan of the Cove Sailing Club.

The much campaigned 43 footer **Hesperia IV** was entered by the A.I.B. Sports Club but luck was not to smile upon them this year. John Bourke of the R.St.G.Y.C. was confident that his Sigma 38, **Hobo V** was going to do well. Once again the mighty **Imp**, now representing Kinsale, was present, for her 6th attempt since 1984. This time she was skippered by George Radley Jr. And was to experience a ding dong of a race with her fellow club boats VSOP and Mad Bull.

An exciting entry was the brand new J120, **Jackabout**, entered by Andrew Hall from Pwllheli. She was to give us a little excitement early on in the race. Adrian Lee, (R.St.G.Y.C) another well known Round Ireland competitor entered his Sigma 400, **Janey Mac II**. Out to give Adrian Lee some competition was Tim Little in his Sigma 400, **Keep on Smiling**, his second attempt in this boat but, like Adrian, his third attempt overall. Frank Elmes started with Marissa VI in 1984 and 86, Marissa VII in 88 and 90 and now **Marissa VIII** (92 and 94). This, his sixth race was to make it five out of six completed - a record not many can equal. The 34.5' **Joliba** was entered by James Ryan and Alan Murray of Poolbeg and they have given an entertaining account of their epic voyage. Simon Knowles (H.Y.C.) entered **Juno** an MGRS 34. Probably the most exciting entry in the race was the extraordinary Rocket 31, **Maxol Unleaded** (a.k.a. Camp Freddie), skippered by G. Peck and K. Jameson (H.Y.C.)

Yet another entry from Kinsale Y.C. was **Mad Bull**, a Swan 42 entered by Olaf Sorensen. The impressive Humphries 12M **Megalopolis** was entered by Urban Taylor of Pwllheli S.C. his fourth race in a boat of this name and destined to be his best yet. And of course the pride of the fleet was **Moonduster** (Denis Doyle, R.C.Y.C) making her seventh appearance since 1982. Twice a winner (1982 and 1984) and holder of the Round Ireland record (the only boat to complete the race in less than 100hrs. corrected time) Denis had a lot to defend. One of the two all-female crews competing, in yet another Sigma 38, was Siobhan Crowley and her crew in **Nissan I** representing Poolbeg. Representing Mayo S.C. and entered by Dr. S. Moneley was the First 30E, **Pink Panther**. Richard Burrows (H.Y.C) entered his state-of-the-art IMX 38 Prospector, no doubt hoping to repeat his triumph of 1986 when he won the race in his DB2, Spirit.

If anyone sums up the extraordinary spirit and fascination of the Round Ireland race it is Brian Coad of the Wexford Harbour S.C. competing for the sixth time in his Rival 34, **Raasay of Melfort**. Not only did he win the first ever non-stop Round Ireland race organised by WSC in 1980 but he had previously competed in the very first Round Ireland race organised by BallyHolme Y.C. in 1975 - in a Folkboat!

John Buckley (N.Y.C.) entered the smallest boat in the race, the Starlight **Samaki** and had, as they say, a good race. Entering for the first time and planning their campaign with military precision was the Air Corps. Their entry, a Sigma 38, **Air Corps I** was skippered by Capt. Tom O'Connor and sailed under the burgee of the D.M.Y.C. and very proud that club must have been of their performance.

**Arthur**, a Sigma 3800D was entered by Bray S.C. and jointly skippered by Robin Kay and Ger Dempsey. Yet another Sigma 3800D, **Rock Adventure**, (Lough Swilley.Y.C.) carried the hopes of Donegal on the shoulders of Daniel Gallagher. **Spirit of Mayo**, a Sigma 38, represented that county and was skippered by Robin Smith whilst the DB2 **Spirit of Ringsend** (once upon a time known as Spirit) was entered by the trio from Poolbeg, Michael Purcell, James Daly and Dan Crowley. The Dubois 54 **Storm Bird**, (R.I.Y.C.) no stranger to the race, was one of the largest boats in the fleet and, skippered by Ciaran Foley was expected to do well.

An English entry was the smart S&S 50 cutter rigged St. Christopher from the Flushing S.C. and skippered by owner George Fairhurst. Not to be outdone by the Air Corps the Naval Service decided to have a go and entered a Dufour 35, **Sty Tailte** (N.S.A.) under skipper Lt. Willie Roberts. In the end it probably proved that the Air Corps can sail better than the Naval Service can fly!

The Asgard Support Group entered their Sadler 32, **Tir na NOg** with Fiacc O'Broichain in command. Another entry carrying the high hopes of WSC was the Liberator 35, **Trailblazer**, owned and skippered by club member Roy Conway. The all-female crew of **Tropicana**, another IMX 38 (R.I.Y.C.), Skipper Jill Sommerville, had trained long and hard for this event and had high hopes as they set out for the start.

The classic wooden Dee 27, **Tjaldur**, (LOA 37') built by Tyrrell's in Arklow was entered by her present owner Sean Whiston of Poolbeg Y and B.C., and, as she had served as my introduction to sailing, I hoped for the best for her and her crew. From Mullingar S.C. and under the command of Pat McArdle came the highly tuned and motivated crew of **Ulysses** (a Victoria 34) determined to prove they could sail in salt water - and they did!

The Kinsale Y.C. meant business with yet another entry, John Godkin's **VSOP**, a Sovereign 400 and, from not too far away, the Royal Cork Y.C. no less, came James Donegan's Hustler 36, **White Rooster** for their fifth race around Ireland. Another entry from Howth Y.C. was the Contessa 35 **Witchcraft of Howth** entered by W.M. Nixon, E.M. Wheeler and H.A. Whelehan.

The only maxi in the fleet was **Virgin City Jet** entered jointly by Robert Dix/Power and C. Barrington and they were out for line honours. Fortunately they had two steering wheels.

*Imp.*

*This Ron Holland designed 40 footer was originally built for the American Admirals Cup team of 1977. In that year Imp was the top Admiral's Cup boat and won the Fastnet race.*

*She again represented America in the 1979 Admiral's Cup and took part in that year's tragic Fastnet race finishing in 5th place over the line.*

*Since then Imp has passed through the hands of various owners and has been owned by George Radley since the late 80's. Imp has competed in no less than eleven Round Ireland races and completed all but one. In her first race with George as skipper she was placed 4th overall. Since then she has been placed 1st. (2000), 2nd (2002) and 5th (2006).*

*If you want to know more about this famous yacht (And there is much, much more) you will soon be able to buy the book, 'The Legend of Imp', by William Barton.*

Photo: D. Branigan

# *1994: THE START*

**N**oon, Saturday 18 June, 1994 and I am not feeling too well. The head is fuzzy from the excesses of the Cork Dry Gin race party of the night before and the shenanigans in the WSC afterwards. Besides I have just attended a vinous send-off party in Phil Healy's pub for the lads (including my son Adam) of Blacktie Wicklow Challenge who are competing in the race for the first time. But now reality intrudes and I realise that the moment for which we have planned for the past eighteen months is now upon us - it cannot be put off any longer, it cannot be talked away.

The moment is the start of the Cork Dry Gin Round Ireland '94 race and I am a member of the race committee, responsible today for 'Visual Signals' (flags to you and me) and there is a knotted fist of ice in my stomach which won't go away. I meet Race Co-ordinator Fergus O'Conchobhair coming out of the race office and he looks worse than I feel - which is a relief - as he doesn't drink. "Don't worry Fergus, everything will go OK" says I and I don't even convince myself.

Suddenly I start to hallucinate. Emerging out of a crowded river comes a huge orange and yellow gennaker hiding the boat to which it is attached. What eejit is trying to show off on a day like this I wonder? However, whoever it is does it very well - only later do I find out it was Maxol Unleaded, the only boat in the race without an engine (Skippered by Kieran Jameson).

Together with the rest of the race committee we clamber aboard the RNLI 'Annie Blaker' the Wicklow station lifeboat and don our life jackets before being ferried out to the L.E. Aoife our 'committee boat' for the day.

It's not a particularly pleasant June day, cool, overcast and with a blustery SW breeze - not a good day for the spectators to be standing around. Nevertheless they are here in their thousands contributing to the festival atmosphere which has enveloped Wicklow town for the past few days.

It's also a bumpy sea and care is needed (and a scramble net) to get aboard the L.E. Aoife. We are welcomed aboard and shown the way to the flag deck. For some reason I have managed to convince myself that we will probably need to postpone the start of the race and I create a mild panic when I ask the yeoman of signals if he has an 'Answering Pendant'. He searches the flag deck lockers without success and eventually manages to locate one somewhere down below. And of course we don't need it. It's getting close to the start time now and all I have to do is to see that the four signal flags are bent onto halyards. Fortunately the L.E. Aoife has plenty of those.

Tension mounts as time for the warning signal approaches. Why, I wonder to myself, are we so wound up about the start of this race? After all, between us we have acted on race committees on dozens of occasions and for all sort of events ranging from club races to national championships and we have even rehearsed this one. Perhaps it's just the sense of occasion and the spectators and the very experienced competitors.

However, there is no problem and Fergus counts us down to the ten-minute gun and then to the five-minute gun. And then you can feel the tension. . . I check again, for the twentieth time, the individual recall flag and the general recall flag and pray that neither will be needed. Frank 'Guns' Murphy checks the cannon again (Notoriously unreliable – the cannon that is). Fergus checks his watch again. Denis Noonan, backup shotgun cradled in his arms and looking for all the world like John Wayne, looks worried as only John Wayne can look worried. I glance at Norman Long, one of our official judges for the start and think I detect just the hint of a twitch of amusement in the corner of his mouth . . . five. . .four . . . three . . .two . . . GO! Bang! I'm so concerned with the signal flags I have my back to the start and therefore I don't actually see it until I hear the laconic tones of Norman . . . "line clear - good start". Then I turn around and have a great view of 53 sterns receding in the direction of Wicklow Head.

The wardroom on the L.E. Aoife is small and snug and warm and welcoming and someone keeps filling my glass with this brownish liquid - probably cough medicine - anyway it makes me feel good and it melts that lump of ice in my stomach - until I remember that I may have to clamber down that scramble net into the RNLI 'Annie Blaker' which is coming out to rescue us from the clutches of the hospitable Naval Service and take us ashore. Rotten sense of timing.

Back on shore, and feeling no pain, the race office reminds me of nothing so much as a scene out of one of those Second World War movies when the squadron is overdue returning from its mission and the camera cuts to the clock on the Operations Room wall (tick-tock . . .) and people sit around looking worried. Suddenly a telephone rings . . . you've seen the movie.

But they didn't have computers to worry about then and Fergus and his wife Mary have a problem with the computerised race management programme - like not having one! However, like the cavalry, it's on its way. The mind wanders back to those good old days when we seemed to manage with pencil and paper and a calculator. But now the 'Media' need printouts, reams and reams of them, Rain Forests even. There's an awful lot of boring talk about handicaps and something called IMS and random circular movements, something I recall experiencing the previous night in the WSC bar.

I make my farewells and head off home for a few hours sleep - surely nothing will happen in the next few hours!

# THE FIRST LEG

## WICKLOW TO THE FASTNET ROCK

For most of the competitors gathered in Wicklow for the 1994 Cork Dry Gin Round Ireland their presence there was the culmination of months, and in some cases years, of planning, pleading with bank managers and sponsors, re-mortgaging the house, scrounging from friends and relatives, promising the wife a 'proper' holiday next year and, for the really serious ones, months of hard training through the winter months. Many of them have done the race many times and are suffering from the only recently recognised addictive condition of 'Round Ireland Syndrome'. For others it is their first time and they are easily recognised by the 'what am I doing here?' expression on their faces.

Possibly there is no other race like the Round Ireland which involves people with such a wide spectrum of sailing experience - from Laurel-browed, garlanded heroes of the 'Round the World' to humble horny handed club sailors. Possibly no other race where everyone enters actually believing that they have a chance of winning. After all the race has been won by boats from a little over thirty feet in length up to world girdling Maxi's. The days have long gone when crews would embark on the round Ireland as a 'jolly' or an extended 'cruise in company'. Now it's serious but it's serious fun.

This is an offshore race - not an ocean race - unusual, possibly unique with regard to tidal effects and their influence on tactics - this is above all a tactical race - not just about crew stamina, morale and boat speed. And, lest we forget, it is also about luck.

It's also a race of sufficient duration, for the majority of competitors, such that they will experience at least one gale and for sure they will also have at least one day without any wind at all. It's also an exhausting race for the majority of competitors on small boats with crews of between six and eight, the difficulty of maintaining a watch system, the difficulty of keeping dry, preparing a hot meal, getting real sleep. No two days are the same, it's impossible to establish a ship's routine and, just as you are finding your sea legs the race is over.

There were fifty three yachts with a combined crew of almost five hundred sailors jousting for the best position on the starting line. If it had been possible to bottle their combined outpouring of adrenaline and feed it to the Irish soccer team not only would Ireland have won the World Cup but the rugby Grand Slam as well!

The pier end of the line appeared to be favoured as with the wind from the SW clean air could only be got there. The Maxi, **Virgin City Jet**, was primly letting the smaller fry jostle for position knowing that when the starting gun went she would slice through the smaller fry like a hot knife through butter and so she did. But what was this? Sporting that huge gennaker the relatively tiny **Maxol Unleaded**, starting with the speed, as someone so aptly put it, "of a rat up a drain-pipe," was snapping at her heels - but not for long. Other boats tried to fly shy spinnakers but they soon disappeared as did the crew of **Black Tie Wicklow** as they rushed down below to change from dinner jackets to wet gear.

Off to 'the Head' and a cruel lumpy sea and what was, for some, to turn into a nightmare beat of up to three days to the Fastnet. The flooding tide and a 20+ Kt on the nose SW breeze meant that after rounding Wicklow Head most skippers opted for a close inshore course which would take them inside the Arklow Banks. Disaster struck almost immediately. Just past the Head and about 2 nm NW of the Wolf Rock the Club Shamrock, **Emercides**, jointly skippered by Peter Ryan and Michael Horgan radioed in they were retiring with a broken spreader. At least that was not life threatening but, almost immediately afterwards came the report that there had been a gas explosion on Bernard Freyne's **Estrellita** just 7 miles after the start. The explosion started a fire but cool heads soon brought this under control and the Race Office received a message that they would be able to make it into Arklow unassisted. Of all the things that can happen at sea a gas explosion must be the most feared but in this case the damage was not too extensive and no one was injured except skipper Bernard Freyne, who suffered burnt hands and hair, fortunately not serious.

Meanwhile the remainder of the fleet were involved in a hard tacking match. **VSOP**, after a shaky start, was exchanging tacks with her fellow Kinsale yachts **Imp** and **Mad Bull** in what proved to be the beginning of an epic struggle.

In the months leading up to the race the crews of **Air Corps 1, Nissan 1** and **Black Tie Wicklow** had often found themselves together at the same promotional/fund raising events and a friendly rivalry had developed between them by the time the race started. All had entered Sigma 38's. The men on Black Tie Wicklow were to chase the girls on Nissan 1 to a nail-chewing finish. **Deerstalker** had made a good start and immediately began to prove that her reputation as a superb windward sailing boat was well deserved as she gradually wore down and passed **Amazing Grace, Nissan 1, Wicklow Black Tie** and **Witchcraft of Howth**, another boat doing particularly well. **Juno** was going well until problems resulting from a headsail change caused her to lose considerable ground.

**Mayday! Mayday! Mayday!** The dreaded call was heard by most of the competitors at about 2130 hrs. Andrew Hall's J120 **Jackabout** was in trouble. In fact she was in danger of sinking. Her keel bolts had worked loose and a crack had developed in her hull. **Aquelina** and **Corwynt**, the nearest yachts, responded immediately and headed for Jackabout to stand by until the **Rosslare Lifeboat** arrived. Eventually Jackabout reached Arklow and safety but the real gravity of the situation only became apparent when she was lifted out of the water and the keel fell off!

Many competitors who listened to this drama unfold over their VHF's were later to praise Andrew Hall for his calm, professional handling of this potentially very dangerous incident.

Meanwhile another 'race within a race' was developing between **Raasay of Melfort, Alpara, Sty Tailte and Ulysses** who were to see a lot of each other over the next few days.

Retirals continued during the night and the following morning. **Maxol Unleaded** with a stretched forestay headed for Arklow where frantic efforts to find a replacement failed. **Trailblazer** from Wicklow retired into Dunmore East with headsail problems. **A.I.B. Sailing** reported breaking her mast and also retired into Dunmore as did **Tropicana** when her skipper Jill Sommerville decided it was too dangerous to continue with a badly flexing mast - a sad end to what had been months of planning, organisation, training and dreams. At 0601hrs on the Sunday morning the race office was informed that **Comanche Raider**, some 25nm SW of Tuskar had retired and was returning to Wicklow where she arrived back safely that evening. And then the unthinkable, **Moonduster** reported losing her forestay and almost her mast just 20nm south of the Tuskar. She managed to make it safely to Crosshaven. **Tjaldur** with a very ill skipper, Sean Whiston, retired into Cork to have him rushed to hospital where he soon made a complete recovery. With **Pink Panther** also retiring this made a total of eleven boats out of the race in the first twenty four hours. A lot, you might think but conditions had been very difficult and boats had received a ferocious pounding and in the circumstances rigging failures, particularly in highly tuned boats, were only to be expected. An analysis of the quality of the boats retiring would suggest that no amount of boat preparation could have prevented the rigging failures.

(Only 208 different boats have been entered in the Round Ireland race since it's commencement in 1980, although, because many boats have entered the race more than once, the total number of starters has been 296. Of these 296 starters 79 (26.6%) have failed to complete the course. In only one year, 1986, were there no retirals at all but this was a year of light winds for the race. Almost 50% of retirals have taken place before Dunmore East and over 90% before the Fastnet Rock. So this year was, eventually, to be above average with 17 retirals out of 53 starters (32%)).

While all this was going on **Virgin City Jet**, leading the fleet and about one hour ahead of **Stormbird**, was experiencing a litany of problems. A broken runner, torn mainsail, loss of the top mainsail batten, a broken rigging strut and the mainsail boltrope pulled out of the mast track. Any one of these happenings would perhaps have put a smaller boat out of the race but Virgin's crew managed to carry out the necessary running repairs and continue with the race.

By now the surviving competitors had made the turn at Tuskar and were making the decision whether to continue to hug the shore or head to sea. The wind was forecast to back to the south but in the event it only made a token effort to do so and those who went out to sea on the basis of the forecast came unstuck.

Now some 24 hours or more into the race some sort of routine was being established on most of the boats although conditions made it extremely difficult for the smaller boats and some crews were not to get their first hot meal or a change into dry clothing for another day or two.

Almost exactly 24 hours after the first **Mayday** call came another, this time from the angling boat **Sharkhunter**. After some confusion its position was established at $51^O$ 50.3N $07^O$ 53.2W. **Aquelina** whilst on route to assist relayed the stricken boats position to **Ballycotton lifeboat** which was already on route and **Hobo V** stood by in sight of Sharkhunter until the lifeboat arrived. Other competitors who abandoned the race temporarily to assist were **AirCorps 1**, **Nissan 1** and **Black Tie Wicklow**. Sharkhunter was escorted safely into Ballycotton by the lifeboat.

Despite her problems Virgin City Jet was still race leader at the Fastnet (all times are elapsed times) which she rounded at 1850 hrs. On the Sunday, Stormbird rounded just over an hour later at 1952 and then Megalopolis who was having a storm of a race was round at 2251. Bridgestone rounded at 0030 on Monday 20th. And then within a nine minute spread came Prospector (0130), Beaumont Spirit (0135) and Keep on Smiling (0139). Janey Mac II rounded in solitary splendour at 0250 and then an hour later came the Kinsale Killers still fighting their private battle but as a team taking on the rest. Only 17 minutes separated the three boats, Imp was first to round, at 0354 followed by VSOP. (0408) and Mad Bull (0411). Corwynt, who had lost time standing by Jackabout, rounded at 0517 to be followed by a positive traffic jam as eight boats rounded the Fastnet in thirty five minutes, Crown Duel (0710), Marissa VIII (0712), Amazing Grace (0715), Gwawr (0723), Juno (0730), Deerstalker (0737), Spirit of Mayo (0740), and Witchcraft of Howth (0745). Then came the Sigma's, Aquelina, who had done very well considering the time lost standing by Jackabout and Sharkhunter, (0809), Hobo V (who with Nissan 1, Black Tie Wicklow and Aquelina had also lost time going to the assistance of the fishing boat off Ballycotton), (0825), Air Corps 1 (0830), Rock Adventurer (0834), Nissan 1 (0945), Black Tie (0950). Arthur was well behind and rounded at 1105. Sandwiched in between the Sigma's came White Rooster (0922).

Joliba rounded at 1150, Darramy at 1310 and Spirit of Ringsend at 1320.John Buckley's Samaki rounded at 1437, St. Christopher, whose crew were enjoying their cruise, at 1502 and then the four tail-enders intent on their own particular race. Alpara at 1938, Sty Tailte at 2026, veteran Raasay of Melfort four minutes later at 2030 and finally, Ulysses at 2109.

But what had happened to Tir na nOg? They almost made it to the Fastnet, within ten miles in fact, but, in skipper Fiacc O'Broichain's own words, "sixty-eight hours of solid beating and two sea-sick crew (out of six) wore us down." An adverse weather forecast convinced them it would be foolish to continue and they retired into Kinsale.

This has been the fate of many a crew. The tendency is to think that the race starts at the Fastnet and getting there through those so familiar waters is a doddle. But this is not cruising - this is racing and not everyone is prepared for or experienced enough to put up with the demands made on body and spirit required to drive a boat to the maximum day after day (and night after night). It is difficult enough for an experienced racing crew but to expect an inexperienced crew who, again in O'Broichain's own words, "the first time the full crew were on the vessel at the same time was 1100 on the morning of the race!" to do so is somewhat naive. The entry rules lay down stringent requirements regarding experience of skipper and crew but it would be impossible for the race committee to vet every single crew member for suitability and in practice they have to accept the crew lists given. However, Bill Snaith (of Figaro fame) would have had little sympathy with this point of view:-

*"In the matter of race committee certification: A crew must have demonstrable experience. If a ship is lost and everyone drowns, the papers will be filled with public wailing's. The committee will be properly sad, of course, but, worse, it might endanger the sport. The drowning must, therefore, be on your own head. The committee cannot [allow itself] be placed in a position of blame as being lax and frivolous in certifying a boat ready to race."*

*Bill Snaith, "On the Wind's Way"*

But I digress . . .

On corrected time **Bridgestone** was in the lead (CT: 1:12:05:13) with **Megalopolis** second (CT: 1:12:45:33), **Prospector** third (CT: 1:13:46:19), **Stormbird** fourth (CT: 1:13:52:15) and surprise, surprise, in fifth place was **Deerstalker** with a CT of 1:13:54:46. Way down the field behind **Witchcraft of Howth** in thirteenth position on corrected time was **Virgin City Jet** (1:16:46:13).

If the Tuskar Rock is the first turning point on the course the Fastnet Rock is the psychological turning point. Even though it is slightly less than one third of the total distance of the race there is a tendency to think it is the half-way point. Most crews who get this far will eventually complete the race. For many it will be their first sight of the famous rock and all will gaze with awe at this marvellous feat of engineering and maybe reflect as they look at it from a calm sea level that on several occasions Atlantic waves have swept over the top of it and smashed the glass in the lamp house . . . that is awesome. Some, who were there then, will say a prayer for their friends lost in the Fastnet race of 1979. For many this will be their first experience of the Atlantic, their first feel of a different motion which animates the boat. Many will experience a little *frisson* of fear as they contemplate the next two days sailing up the west coast, an unfamiliar, iron bound, lee shore on the very fringe of a mighty ocean.

The first Fastnet light was illuminated on 1st January 1854, on top of a 91ft cast iron tower. This was Halpin's light. The present masonry tower was erected between 1896 and 1903 and when the last granite block was placed in 1903 it was placed by the foreman, master mason James Kavanagh of Wicklow town who had personally put in place every one of the 2,074 blocks used in the towers construction. James was to die before the new light was displayed. The official name of the tower is the William Douglas Tower after its designer but locally it is still known to some as Kavanagh's Tower. By an incredible coincidence when the light was automated in 1989 among the final party taken off the rock was one James Kavanagh [stone-mason], of Wicklow town, grand nephew of the James Kavanagh who had supervised the building of the tower. ( I got these facts from a book every Irish sailor should have on the bookshelf, preferably on the boat, 'Bright Light, White Water' the story of Irish lighthouses and their people by Bill Long).

## Position and Time at Fastnet.

| Yacht | Entered By | Date/ Time | Elapsed dd:hh:mm | Corrected dd:hh:mm:ss |
|---|---|---|---|---|
| Virgin City Jet | Dix/Power/Barrington | 19/1850 | 1:04:50 | 1:12:05:13 |
| Stormbird | Ciaran Foley | 19/1952 | 1:05:52 | 1:12:45:33 |
| Megalopolis | Urban Taylor | 19/2251 | 1:08:51 | 1:13:52:15 |
| Bridgestone | Peter Wilson | 20/0030 | 1:10:30 | 1:13:52:15 |
| Prospector | Richard Burroughs | 20/0130 | 1:11:30 | 1:13:54:46 |
| Beamont Spirit | Roy Dickson | 20/0135 | 1:11:35 | 1:13:58:02 |
| Keep On Smiling | Tom Little | 20/0139 | 1:11:39 | 1:14:37:12 |
| Janey Mac II | A Lee | 20/0250 | 1:12:50 | 1:15:11:26 |
| Imp | George Bradley Jnr. | 20/0354 | 1:13:54 | 1:15:15:09 |
| V.S.O.P. | John Godkin | 20/0408 | 1:14:08 | 1:15:16:38 |
| Mad Bull | Olaf Sorensen | 20/0411 | 1:14:11 | 1:16:08:11 |
| Corwynt | Gwilym Evans | 20/0517 | 1:15:17 | 1:16:29:51 |
| Duel | Michael Fleming | 20/0710 | 1:17:10 | 1:16:46:13 |
| Marissa VIII | Frank Elmes | 20/0712 | 1:17:12 | 1:16:52:13 |
| Amazing Grace | Anthony Kingston | 20/0715 | 1:17:15 | 1:17:35:49 |
| Gwawr | Anthony Jones | 20/0723 | 1:17:23 | 1:17:40:47 |
| Deerstalker | Michael Taylor-Jones | 20/0737 | 1:17:37 | 1:17:51:59 |
| Spirit of Mayo | Robin Smith | 20/0740 | 1:17:40 | 1:17:57:46 |
| Witchcraft of Howth | Nixon/Wheeler/Whelehan | 20/0745 | 1:17:45 | 1:18:07:30 |
| Aquelina | James Tyrrell | 20/0809 | 1:18:09 | 1:18:32:34 |
| Hobo V | John Bourke | 20/0825 | 1:18:25 | 1:18:53:00 |
| Air Corps I | Tom O'Connor | 20/0830 | 1:18:30 | 1:18:58:03 |
| Rock Adventurer | Daniel Gallagher | 20/0834 | 1:18:34 | 1:19:02:06 |
| White Rooster | James Donegan | 20/0922 | 1:19:22 | 1:19:05:00 |
| Nissan I | Siobhan Crowley | 20/0945 | 1:19:45 | 1:20:08:38 |
| Black Tie | Frank Jackson | 20/0950 | 1:19:50 | 1:20:13:33 |
| Arthur | Robin Kay/ G. Dempsey | 20/1105 | 1:21:05 | 1:20:18:56 |
| Joliba | James Ryan & A. Murray | 20/1150 | 1:21:50 | 1:20:45:48 |
| Darramy | Brian Wallace | 20/1310 | 1:23:10 | 1:21:34:45 |
| Spirit of Ringsend | Purcell/Daly/Crowley | 20/1320 | 1:23:20 | 1:23:34:43 |
| Samaki | John Buckley | 21/1437 | 2:00:37 | 1:23:41:08 |
| St. Christopher | C.G. Fairhurst | 21/1502 | 2:01:02 | 2:00:25:19 |
| Alpara | B & M Carroll | 21/1938 | 2:05:58 | 2:01:38:58 |
| Sty Tailte | Lt. William Roberts | 21/2026 | 2:06:26 | 2:02:04:34 |
| Raasay of Melfort | Brian Coad | 21/2030 | 2:06:30 | 2:02:18:30 |
| Ulysses | Par McArdle | 21/2109 | 2:07:09 | 2:02:30:51 |

# *Fastnet to Eagle Island*

(Approximately 201 nm rhumb line)

Now the magic begins. The Cork Dry Gin Round Ireland race is not, as someone described it, 'the Fastnet race with scenery,' but scenery in which the Fastnet merely plays an incidental part - after all the boats have to turn somewhere! Later in this book some of the competitors will describe their experiences on this leg of the race and I will leave it to their words to describe the sheer magic and beauty of the experience of sailing up the Atlantic coast of Ireland. This leg takes the competitors out past the Bull Rock and the mysterious Skelligs. Depending upon position competitors were to experience everything from a flat calm mid summer's day to a 50Kt+ gale, from continuous rain and or fog to comforting sunshine. The leading boats probably never had as much wind as they would have liked and the middle of the fleet probably had more than they needed. But that's the Round Ireland.

By the time the last boat had rounded the Fastnet Rock there was a fifty hour spread between it and **Virgin City Jet** the first boat around. Effectively this means that not only do we have different races within the race between the boats but those races may be subject to widely different weather patterns. Boats rounding on Sunday 19th still had a $230^0$ - 15 Kt. breeze which, as the day progressed backed to $210^0$ where it stayed for the next twenty four hours. However it piped up to 20 kts+ and gave the leading boats an exhilarating ride to Inishtereacht, the next reporting point. Inishtereacht, on the rhumb line, is approximately 60nm from the Fastnet and the leading boat on the water, **Virgin City Jet** covered this distance in less than six hours at an average speed in excess of 11 kts. **Stormbird** and **Beaumont Spirit** each averaged almost 9 kts. **Megalopolis**, still on a 'flyer', averaged almost 9.5 kts, **Bridgestone** 8.8 kts. **Prospector** seems to have experienced problems as their estimated average speed was less than 7.5 kts. The tail-enders suffered hard times from a freshening breeze and the Atlantic swell. From Fastnet to Inishtereacht **Ulysses** made an estimated 3.8 kts. **Alpara** and **Raasay of Melfort** 3.5 kts. And **Sty Tailte** a mind and bumb numbing 1.5 kts. After surviving these conditions they were then to be frustrated by light winds on the nose, rain and fog.

**Virgin City Jet** was first to romp past Inishtereacht on Monday 20th June at 0030, followed by **Stormbird** (0244), **Beaumont Spirit** (0545), **Meg-**

alopolis (0655), **Bridgestone** (0833) and **Prospector** at 0945. Keeping well in touch was **Keep on Smiling** (1020).

Next came the intrepid trio from Kinsale with only 29 minutes separating **Mad Bull** (1140) from **Imp** (1209) with **VSOP.** sandwiched between them at 1147. The middle of the fleet was still very compact with no less than nine boats passing Inishtereacht between 1500 and 1600 on Monday afternoon. At this point **Deerstalker** (1550) was only just holding off the challenge on the water from **Witchcraft of Howth** (1555).

Early on Tuesday morning **Samaki** and **Spirit of Ringsend** reported in and then there was to be a long gap until Tuesday 22nd at 1300 when **Ulysses** reported in followed by **Alpara** at 1300 and **Raasay of Melfort** at 1315 - still only fifteen minutes between the three of them on the water. The crew of **Sty Tailte** had been through a character forming experience (see their story) and it was not until 1145 on the Wednesday that they reached Inishtereacht.

With approximately 250 nm of the race completed at this stage the positions on corrected time were first, **Bridgestone** (CT: 1:20:30:26), second **Deerstalker** (1:21:23:53), a really astonishing performance, third, **Megalopolis** (CT: 1:21:47:09) fourth **Beaumont Spirit** (CT: 1:22:28:04), fifth **Prospector** (CT: 1:22:33:00) and sixth **Stormbird** (CT: 1:22:34:40).

Still trailing **Witchcraft of Howth** was **Virgin City Jet** in 14th position (CT: 2:00:46:59). Leading the Sigma 400's was **Keep on Smiling** (CT: 1:23:12:54) and the leading Sigma 38 was Spirit of Mayo (CT: 2:01:59:38).

On the morning of Monday 20th June the coastal station at Belmullet was recording winds of between 20 and 30 kts from 190 to 200. However, later that day the winds were to veer and moderate to less than 10 kts. Therefore the leading boats experienced a considerable lift from the wind. **Megalopolis**, for instance, eating up 148 nm in a 12 hour spinnaker run, an average speed of 12.6 kts. This must have been hairy stuff. Some of the Sigma's reported reaching speeds of 16 to 18 kts.

# Positions and Times at Inishtearacht

| Yacht | Entered By | Date/ | Elapsed | Corrected |
|-------|-----------|-------|---------|-----------|
| | | Time | dd:hh:mm | dd:hh:mm:ss |
| Virgin City Jet | Dix/Power/Barrington | 20/0030 | 1:10:30 | 2:00:46:59 |
| Stormbird | Ciaran Foley | 20/0244 | 1:12:44 | 1:22:34:40 |
| Beamont Spirit | Roy Dickson | 20/0545 | 1:15:45 | 1:22:33:00 |
| Megalopolis | Urban Taylor | 20/0655 | 1:16:55 | 1:21:47:09 |
| Bridgestone | Peter Wilson | 20/0833 | 1:18:33 | 1:20:30:26 |
| Prospector | Richard Burroughs | 20/0945 | 1:19:45 | 1:22:33:00 |
| Keep On Smiling | Tom Little | 20/1020 | 1:20:20 | 1:23:12:54 |
| Janey Mac II | A Lee | 20/1027 | 1:20:27 | 1:23:17:41 |
| Mad Bull | Olaf Sorensen | 20/1140 | 1:21:40 | 1:22:56:43 |
| V.S.O.P. | John Godkin | 20/1147 | 1:21:47 | 1:23:09:25 |
| Imp | George Bradley Jnr. | 20/1209 | 1:22:09 | 1:23:01:37 |
| Corwynt | Gwilym Evans | 20/1224 | 1:22:24 | 2:01:13:49 |
| Duel | Michael Fleming | 20/1457 | 2:00:57 | 2:01:46:56 |
| Juno | Simon Knowles | 20/1515 | 2:01:15 | 2:01:09:05 |
| Amazing Grace | Anthony Kingston | 20/1520 | 2:01:20 | 2:00:00:05 |
| Spirit of Mayo | Robin Smith | 20/1527 | 2:01:27 | 2:01:59:38 |
| Gwawr | Anthony Jones | 20/1530 | 2:01:30 | 2:02:11:35 |
| Marissa VIII | Frank Elmes | 20/1544 | 2:01:44 | 2:01:20:08 |
| Aquelina | James Tyrrell | 20/1545 | 2:01:45 | 2:04:50:04 |
| Deerstalker | Michael Taylor-Jones | 20/1550 | 2:01:50 | 1:21:23:53 |
| Witchcraft of Howth | Nixon/Wheeler/Whelehan | 20/1555 | 2:01:55 | 2:00:25:09 |
| Rock Adventurer | Daniel Gallagher | 20/1700 | 2:03:00 | 2:03:33:40 |
| Nissan I | Siobhan Crowley | 20/1716 | 2:03:16 | 2:03:49:50 |
| Black Tie | Frank Jackson | 20/1815 | 2:04:15 | 2:04:49:29 |
| Darramy | Brian Wallace | 20/2142 | 2:07:42 | 2:08:18:46 |
| Arthur | Robin Kay/ G. Dempsey | 20/2200 | 2:08:00 | 2:08:36:58 |
| Joliba | James Ryan & A. Murray | 20/2210 | 2:08:10 | 2:04:47:48 |
| St. Christopher | C.G. Fairhurst | 20/2315 | 2:09:15 | 2:10:44:19 |
| Samaki | John Buckley | 21/0000 | 2:10:00 | 2:04:39:50 |
| Spirit of Ringsend | Purcell/Daly/Crowley | 21/0130 | 2:11:30 | 2:12:52:07 |
| Ulysses | Par McArdle | 22/1300 | 2:23:00 | 2:16:28:05 |
| Alpara | B & M Carroll | 22/1309 | 2:23:09 | 2:17:27:29 |
| Raasay of Melfort | Brian Coad | 22/1315 | 2:23:15 | 2:14:12:05 |
| Sty Tailte | Lt. William Roberts | 23/1145 | 3:21:45 | 3:15:00:00 |

Virgin City Jet was to pick up a lot of time on this leg. Although I have no information other than the race office records, it is fair to assume that they experienced a run all the way from Inishtereacht to Eagle Island, a distance of c. 141 nm, a distance they covered in eleven and a half hours which computes to an average speed of about 12.2 kts. Not exactly southern ocean stuff but impressive enough.

She rounded Eagle Island on Monday, 20th June at 1200 followed by **Stormbird** at 1430, **Beaumont Spirit** (what a race they were having!) at 1730, **Megalopolis** at 1743 and then quite a gap before Bridgestone rounded at 2211 and Prospector at 2307.

The first to round on Tuesday was **Janey Mac II**, sailing a canny race, at 0322 then **Corwynt** at 0544.

Kinsale's finest had changed positions again. Now only fourteen minutes separated the three boats. It was **VSOP.'s** turn to lead the pack, rounding at 0609 then **Mad Bull** at 0619 and **Imp** at 0623.

Meanwhile **Black Tie Wicklow** was steadily losing ground to their arch rivals the girls of Nissan 1.

At the Fastnet they had been five minutes behind, at Inishtereacht fifty nine minutes and now at Eagle Island they trailed Nissan 1 by three and a half hours when they rounded at 2100.

But what was this? **Witchcraft of Howth** reached Eagle Island at 1452 some three minutes ahead of **Deerstalker** (1455). Deerstalker had not found the lighter winds to her liking and had floundered about and lost time.

A ten hour time spread had developed in the Sigma 38 fleet. **Gwawr** rounded at 1255, **Spirit of Mayo** at 1334, **Hobo V** at 1523, **Air Corps 1** at 1525, **Rock Adventurer** at 1700, Nissan 1 at 1750 then **Black Tie Wicklow** at 2100 followed by **Arthur** at 2330. The final boat to round on Tuesday was **Darramy** at 2345.

**Spirit of Ringsend** rounded on Wednesday at 0130 followed by **Samaki** at 0224. Then was a gap until **Alpara** at 0920, **Raasay of Melfort** at 1225 and **Ulysses** at 0420.

The race office received no report from either **Keep on Smiling** or Sty Tailte at this point but all was well with both boats. In fact Keep on Smiling, a Sigma 400, had a memorable run of 200 miles in 24 hrs - an average speed of 8.33 kts.

Now after 388 nm of racing the corrected time leader board was showing some changes. A magnificent leader was **Megalopolis** (2:09:52:15), second, **Bridgestone** (2:10:46:04), third, **Beaumont Spirit** (2:12:12:13), fourth, **Prospector** (2:12:46:20), fifth, **Stormbird** (2:13:29:53) and moving up from fourteenth to sixth place was **Virgin City Jet** (2:17:02:38).

**Deerstalker** had dropped to eleventh place (2:18:25:38) and **Witchcraft of Howth** was in fourteenth place (2:22:40:50).

On corrected time the Kinsale trio were almost as close as on elapsed time with **Imp** in the lead (2:17:36:24), **VSOP** (2:18:04:28) and **Mad Bull** (2:18:07:03).

## Position and times at Eagle Island

| Yacht | Entered By | Date/ Time | Elapsed dd:hh:mm | Corrected dd:hh:mm:ss |
|---|---|---|---|---|
| Virgin City Jet | Dix/Power/Barrington | 20/1200 | 1:22:00 | 2:17:02:38 |
| Stormbird | Ciaran Foley | 20/1430 | 2:00:30 | 2:13:29:53 |
| Beamont Spirit | Roy Dickson | 20/1730 | 2:03:30 | 2:12:12:13 |
| Megalopolis | Urban Taylor | 20/1743 | 2:03:43 | 2:09:52:15 |
| Bridgestone | Peter Wilson | 20/2211 | 2:08:11 | 2:10:46:04 |
| Prospector | Richard Burroughs | 20/2307 | 2:09:07 | 2:12:46:20 |
| Janey Mac II | A Lee | 21/0322 | 2:13:22 | 2:17:17:39 |
| Corwynt | Gwilym Evans | 21/0544 | 2:15:44 | 2:19:37:16 |
| V.S.O.P. | John Godkin | 21/0609 | 2:16:09 | 2:18:04:28 |
| Mad Bull | Olaf Sorensen | 21/0619 | 2:16:19 | 2:18:07:03 |
| Imp | George Bradley Jnr. | 21/0623 | 2:16:23 | 2:17:36:24 |
| Aquelina | James Tyrrell | 21/1224 | 2:22:24 | 3:02:45:53 |
| Duel | Michael Fleming | 21/1225 | 2:22:25 | 2:23:36:50 |
| Gwawr | Anthony Jones | 21/1255 | 2:22:55 | 2:23:54:34 |
| Juno | Simon Knowles | 21/1325 | 2:23:25 | 2:23:16:26 |
| Spirit of Mayo | Robin Smith | 21/1334 | 2:23:34 | 3:00:21:14 |
| Marissa VIII | Frank Elmes | 21/1345 | 2:23:45 | 2:23:10:34 |
| Amazing Grace | Anthony Kingston | 21/1350 | 2:23:50 | 2:21:53:38 |
| Witchcraft of Howth | Nixon/Wheeler/Whelehan | 21/1452 | 3:00:52 | 2:22:40:50 |
| Deerstalker | Michael Taylor-Jones | 21/1455 | 3:00:55 | 2:18:25:38 |
| Hobo V | John Bourke | 21/1523 | 3:01:23 | 3:02:11:26 |
| Air Corps I | Tom O'Connor | 21/1525 | 3:01:25 | 3:02:13:27 |
| Rock Adventurer | Daniel Gallagher | 21/1700 | 3:03:00 | 3:03:49:30 |
| Nissan I | Siobhan Crowley | 21/1750 | 3:03:50 | 3:04:40:03 |
| White Rooster | James Donegan | 21/2044 | 3:06:44 | 3:05:14:15 |
| Black Tie | Frank Jackson | 21/2100 | 3:07:00 | 3:07:52:08 |
| Joliba | James Ryan & A. Murray | 21/2310 | 3:09:10 | 3:04:17:48 |
| St. Christopher | C.G. Fairhurst | 21/2313 | 3:09:13 | 3:11:19:42 |
| Arthur | Robin Kay/ G. Dempsey | 21/2330 | 3:09:30 | 3:10:23:47 |
| Darramy | Brian Wallace | 21/2345 | 3:09:45 | 3:10:38:57 |
| Spirit of Ringsend | Purcell/Daly/Crowley | 22/0130 | 3:11:30 | 3:13:25:14 |
| Samaki | John Buckley | 22/0224 | 3:12:24 | 3:04:38:07 |
| Alpara | B & M Carroll | 22/0920 | 3:19:20 | 3:12:01:36 |
| Raasay of Melfort | Brian Coad | 22/1225 | 3:22:25 | 3:10:25:33 |
| Ulysses | Par McArdle | 24/0420 | 4:14:20 | 3:15:28:14 |

# Eagle Island to Mew Island

**N**ow was to begin what was, for almost all the competitors, the most exciting, fearful, magical, exhilarating sail of their lives. Most of the boats in the middle of the fleet were to experience a 'hooley'. The wind gradually veered into the west and increased to gale force. Malin Head reported 10 minute winds of 40 kts. + and some boats were to record over the deck wind speed in excess of 50 kts. Some competitors opted to head out to sea and ride it out. Others set all the sail they dared and had the sail of a lifetime. Unfortunately this meant they arrived at the North Channel just as the tide turned against them. Tides had not entered very much into calculations sailing up the west coast but here on the north coast they were to make all the difference, for some boats, between winning and losing the race. It was here that Megalopolis, then leading the race, lost it, much to the chagrin of skipper Urban Taylor. They had sailed a brilliant race and now were the victims of their own success. Hitting the tidal gate at the North Channel they could only watch as boats which had been six hours behind them, still carrying a favourable tide caught up with them. Urban believes that an offshore race which has tidal gates is no good: "some boats are lucky and some are not". Precisely! But tides are a component of the race and the skipper/navigator has got to use them just as he would use the wind but whereas predicting the wind is difficult, predicting the tides is not and in a situation such as the notorious North Channel it is a wise skipper who bases his plans on the tide and not the wind.

# Position and times at Mew Island

| Yacht | Entered By | Date/ Time | Elapsed dd:hh:mm | Corrected dd:hh:mm:ss |
|---|---|---|---|---|
| Virgin City Jet | Dix/Power/Barrington | 21/1500 | 3:01:00 | 4:07:13:19 |
| Stormbird | Ciaran Foley | 22/0107 | 3:11:07 | 4:09:23:31 |
| Beamont Spirit | Roy Dickson | 22/0200 | 3:12:00 | 4:02:11:46 |
| Megalopolis | Urban Taylor | 22/0223 | 3:12:23 | 3:22:25:30 |
| Bridgestone | Peter Wilson | 22/0555 | 3:15:55 | 3:19:57:39 |
| Prospector | Richard Burroughs | 22/0715 | 3:17:15 | 3:22:57:43 |
| Janey Mac II | A Lee | 22/0739 | 3:17:39 | 3:23:23:15 |
| Keep on Smiling | Tim Little | 22/0805 | 3:18:05 | 3:23:56:20 |
| Corwynt | Gwilym Evans | 22/0817 | 3:18:17 | 3:23:47:26 |
| V.S.O.P. | John Godkin | 22/0854 | 3:18:54 | 3:21:37:37 |
| Mad Bull | Olaf Sorensen | 22/0947 | 3:19:47 | 3:22:21:12 |
| Imp | George Bradley Jnr. | 22/0949 | 3:19:49 | 3:21:33:40 |
| Duel | Michael Fleming | 22/1350 | 3:23:50 | 4:01:27:45 |
| Aquelina | James Tyrrell | 22/1416 | 4:00:16 | 4:06:14:07 |
| Amazing Grace | Anthony Kingston | 22/1619 | 4:02:19 | 3:23:39:44 |
| Air Corps I | Tom O'Connor | 22/1640 | 4:02:40 | 4:03:45:07 |
| Gwawr | Anthony Jones | 22/1643 | 4:02:43 | 4:04:05:55 |
| Spirit of Mayo | Robin Smith | 22/1710 | 4:03:10 | 4:04:15:27 |
| Marissa VIII | Frank Elmes | 22/1753 | 4:03:53 | 4:03:05:03 |
| Witchcraft of Howth | Nixon/Wheeler/Whelehan | 22/1827 | 4:04:27 | 4:01:26:11 |
| Deerstalker | Michael Taylor-Jones | 22/1858 | 4:04:58 | 3:19:58:50 |
| Rock Adventurer | Daniel Gallagher | 22/2157 | 4:07:57 | 4:09:05:36 |
| Alpara | B & M Carroll | 23/0031 | 4:10:31 | 4:01:59:43 |
| Nissan I | Siobhan Crowley | 23/0315 | 4:13:15 | 4:14:27:06 |
| St. Christopher | C.G. Fairhurst | 23/0400 | 4:14:00 | 4:16:51:36 |
| Black Tie | Frank Jackson | 23/0712 | 4:17:12 | 4:18:26:43 |
| White Rooster | James Donegan | 23/0843 | 4:18:43 | 4:16:32:13 |
| Arthur | Robin Kay/ G. Dempsey | 23/0843 | 4:18:43 | 4:19:58:43 |
| Darramy | Brian Wallace | 23/1117 | 4:21:17 | 4:22:34:24 |
| Joliba | James Ryan & A. Murray | 23/1300 | 4:23:00 | 4:15:51:36 |
| Samaki | John Buckley | 23/1310 | 4:23:10 | 4:12:12:12 |
| Spirit of Ringsend | Purcell/Daly/Crowley | 24/0850 | 5:18:50 | 5:22:01:35 |
| Sty Tailte | Lt. Willie Roberts | 24/2222 | 6:08:22 | 5:21:23:47 |
| Ulysses | Par McArdle | 24/2335 | 6:09:35 | 5:19:27:13 |
| Raasay of Melfort | Brian Coad | 25/0026 | 6:10:26 | 5:14:49:13 |

# Mew Island to Wicklow

Thursday morning at 04:00 and Theo Phelan (who would normally be competing in the race himself but is shore-bound this year) and myself are standing the night watch in the race office. It's just about dawn and there is a grey haze hugging the water and limiting our visibility. I walk to the light at the end of the East Pier (the shore end of the finishing line) hoping that with the aid of my binoculars I will get a better view. We know from the crew of VSOP, which had finished at 0140, that Imp and Mad Bull are close behind them. But how close? For the previous four and a half days these three boats had rarely been out of sight of one another dipping and diving and alternatively stealing the lead from one another. Now it was all over. Well almost.

Suddenly through the patchy haze I spot a boat just off Six Mile Point just where I would expect it to be. But just one boat and because of the distance and the visibility I cannot identify it. By now I have called Theo to join me. (Its amazing how one panics on these occasions. I know full well that a boat in that position and with barely a whisper of a breeze could not possibly reach the finishing line in less than an hour yet I had to have the cannon and the timer ready NOW!). I routinely scan the north to east quadrant of the horizon and then spot another boat out there but this one is almost due east of the finishing line but about the same distance as the boat approaching from the north. I know that these must be Imp and Mad Bull. But one or both could be visiting yachts. It wouldn't be the first time that a visitor got a bang of a welcome.

Theo and I start to bet on which boat will finish first. There is barely any wind and what there is is coming from 70-800 and virtually no tide as it was low water at Wicklow at about 0400. One boat was on a run and the other on a reach. While we watched them, Theo and I had plenty of time to philosophise about the meaning of life and the price of pints - and hedge our bets.

It was Imp, we could now clearly identify her distinctive colour scheme, and she crossed the line at 0455 to receive our feeble cheers. Just over thirty minutes later (0526) Mad Bull - for it was she (?) - finished.

What a race these three, VSOP, Imp and Mad Bull, had run. On corrected time VSOP. was the clear leader (4:14:54:47) which gave her 6th place overall in the race. Imp had a corrected time of 4:17:02:27 which placed her 9th overall and Mad Bull had a corrected time of 4:18:33:44 to finish 11th overall. A magnificent team effort and they well deserved the Team Trophy which they won.

As no other boat was expected until much later in the morning Theo and I turned to our more important duty which was opening up the special small bar we have for these occasions. It's a little known fact that competitors in the Cork Dry Gin Round Ireland race develop a raging thirst not at all connected with the water shortages which some of them experience during the race. A thirst which can only be slaked by copious pints of black or amber liquid. Before we did this humanitarian service however we did another and woke up the chap from Kinsale who had taken to sleeping every night in one of our shower cubicles. Such devotion to his absent friends!

And you know what? I have completely forgotten who won the bet!

Late on Thursday night we received the news that Black Tie Wicklow and Nissan 1 were making their final approach to the finishing line. Nissan 1was still in the lead although Black Tie had managed to whittle down the four hour lead held by Nissan 1 at Mew Island. WSC was packed with the crews of the boats which had finished earlier in the day (and week) and the many supporters of the crews of the two boats. Naturally the WSC members, having to be impartial and neutral in these matters, were to a man, woman and child, rooting for Black Tie Wicklow, although common sense informed them that the result was a foregone conclusion and that the girls of Nissan 1 could not be caught in the time remaining.

By 0030 on the Friday morning more than two hundred spectators/supporters were crammed on the end of the East Pier watching Nissan 1 approach the line. It was almost flat calm and the tide was just starting to ebb. Closer and closer Nissan 1 came to the line, to the deafening cheers of the crowd. But something was wrong. She was being carried to seaward of the mark on the outer limit of the finishing line. Desperate efforts on board by the crew, now clearly visible to the spectators on the pier, were to no avail and Nissan 1 drifted slowly past on the wrong side of the mark. With no wind and the tide against them they acted with remarkable presence of mind and speed and dropped an anchor which brought them to a stop just about a cable length beyond the mark. You could almost feel the wave of sympathy sweep through the crowd. On board Nissan 1 some of the crew wept.

And now, just visible up towards Six Mile Point were the masthead navigation lights of Black Tie Wicklow. First green then red, then green then red. . . Gary Haughton on the helm was using all his considerable skill and local knowledge of the tide to push Black Tie Wicklow in towards the shore. Between Six Mile Point and the finish they put in over twenty tacks. Agonisingly, slowly, on each tack they gained a few metres. To their supporters on the pier it was painful to watch those alternating navigation lights but slowly it became clear that they would make it. And they did. But they only shaded it by a few feet - to an enormous cheer from the crowd.

My parental pride at their achievement (my son Adam was in the crew.) and my pride as a member of WSC that our very first entry (crewed, with one exception, by WSC members) had made it, was severely tempered by sadness as I looked out at the forlorn crew of Nissan 1. But they had not given up. Even as the echoes of the cheers for Black Tie Wicklow could still be heard they were raising the anchor to take advantage of a slight breeze and by some skilful sailing they managed to cross the finishing line at 0144 some twenty seven minutes after Black Tie Wicklow.

Back to the club and a party until dawn! Perhaps it was this party which upset Jonathan Bradshaw (Marissa VIII - see his contribution) so much. It appears not to have occurred to him that not everyone can 'do' the Round Ireland. That's for the chosen few. Not to recognise the genuine outpouring of emotion at the safe return of loved ones and friends from those who had worried and waited for the best part of a week is crass. It's not the sort of attitude we want to encourage in sailing. I, personally, would love to do the Round Ireland but I know I am not a good enough sailor. I can live comfortably with that and I am content to make my contribution in other ways as do so many other people. Perhaps people did scurry off to the bars after the starting gun. That seems very appropriate and natural to me. Not everyone finds staring at an empty sea interesting or therapeutic, especially for a week.

But now it was the finishing gun that people were celebrating in a glorious mish-mash of hand-shaking, back-slapping sailors, weeping mums, and dads with lumps in their throats. When the girls of Nissan 1 walked in the roar of welcome fully equalled that which greeted Ireland's goal against Italy just a week previously. The talk - so much to tell - the jokes, the tall stories, the light staring out of tired eyes. This **was** the Round Ireland. The glory of it all was overwhelming and I never felt so proud in my life as to be part of it all.

But the race was not over. There were still ten competitors out who had not retired, many of them veterans of the round Ireland race. White Rooster, Joliba, Arthur, St. Christopher and Darramy finished within the next seven hours then Alpara, Raasay and Spirit of Ringsend leaving just Ulysses and Sty Tailte to slog it out. Ulysses finished with the boat's doctor Willie Fearon nursing a broken scapula and Sty Tailte after an interminable drift down the Irish Sea crossed the line in a squall.

Undoubtedly the performance of the race was by Peter Wilson, veteran round the world skipper who brought home Bridgestone, a J35, to become outright winner. His time of 3 days and just over 16 hours was remarkable by any standards and it just shows that size (just over 35 feet) isn't everything but ruthless determination is.

# Position and times at Wicklow (Finish)

| Place | Yacht | Entered By | Type | CHS TCF | Elapsed Time | Corrected Time |
|---|---|---|---|---|---|---|
| | | | | **Cork Dry Gin Round Ireland 1994 - Overall Results** | | |
| 1 | Bridgestone | Peter Wilson | J 35 | 1.046 | 3:16:30:33 | 4:11:21:36 |
| 2 | Prospector | Richard Burroughs | IMX 38 | 1.064 | 3:23:46:57 | 4:13:13:30 |
| 3 | Corwynt | Gwilym Evans | Sigma 400 | 1.061 | 4:01:45:45 | 4:13:59:31 |
| 4 | Janey Mac II | A Lee | Sigma 400 | 1.064 | 4:02:35:15 | 4:14:18:10 |
| 5 | Megalopolis | Urban Taylor | Humphreys 12m | 1.119 | 4:06:38:19 | 4:14:19:10 |
| 6 | V.S.O.P. | John Godkin | Sovereign 400 | 1.030 | 4:06:39:18 | 4:14:54:47 |
| 7 | Keep On Smiling | Tom Little | Sigma 400 | 1.065 | 4:07:40:05 | 4:14:58:10 |
| 8 | Deerstalker | Michael Taylor-Jones | S & S 34 | 0.911 | 4:07:40:05 | 4:15:06:42 |
| 9 | Imp | George Radley Jnr. | Sloop | 1.019 | 4:08:11:48 | 4:17:02:27 |
| 10 | Beamont Spirit | Roy Dickson | 2 tonner | 1.169 | 4:11:40:57 | 4:18:17:04 |
| 11 | Mad Bull | Olaf Sorensen | Swan 42 | 1.028 | 4:14:55:59 | 4:18:33:44 |
| 12 | Amazing Grace | Anthony Kingston | Oyster 37 | 0.973 | 4:15:26:31 | 4:20:33:27 |
| 13 | Witchcraft of Howth | Nixon/Wheeler/Whelehan | Contessa 35 | 0.970 | 4:18:50:30 | 4:21:10:37 |
| 14 | Marissa VIII | Frank Elmes | sloop | 0.992 | 4:22:17:57 | 4:23:53:57 |
| 15 | Air Corps I | Tom O'Connor | Sigma 38 | 1.011 | 4:22:39:36 | 4:23:57:55 |
| 16 | Hobo V | John Bourke | Sigma 38 | 1.011 | 4:22:47:29 | 5:00:05:53 |
| 17 | Duel | Michael Fleming | Dehler 36 | 1.017 | 4:22:59:03 | 5:00:18:37 |
| 18 | Gwawr | Anthony Jones | Sigma 38 | 1.014 | 4:23:47:31 | 5:00:39:00 |
| 19 | Stormbird | Ciaran Foley | Dubois 54 | 1.268 | 5:00:45:17 | 5:01:27:08 |
| 20 | Aquelina | James Tyrrell | Sigma 400 | 1.062 | 5:00:48:03 | 5:01:57:43 |
| 21 | Spirit of Mayo | Robin Smith | Sigma 38 | 1.011 | 5:00:51:58 | 5:02:04:59 |
| 22 | Virgin City Jet | Dix/Power/Barrington | 73 Maxi | 1.414 | 5:01:58:00 | 5:05:09:07 |
| 23 | Rock Adventurer | Daniel Gallagher | Sigma 38 | 1.011 | 5:09:34:06 | 5:10:59:37 |
| 24 | Samaki | John Buckley | Starlight | 0.910 | 5:11:17:30 | 5:11:47:35 |
| 25 | Black Tie | Frank Jackson | Sigma 38 | 1.011 | 5:11:44:36 | 5:12:44:09 |
| 26 | Nissan I | Siobhan Crowley | Sigma 38 | 1.011 | 5:14:39:56 | 5:13:11:33 |
| 27 | White Rooster | James Donegan | Hustler 36 | 0.981 | 5:18:14:53 | 5:15:37:17 |
| 28 | Joliba | James Ryan & A. Murray | Nicholson 345 | 0.940 | 5:18:22:21 | 5:16:50:07 |
| 29 | St. Christopher | C.G. Fairhurst | Cutter 15.2 m | 1.026 | 5:23:07:17 | 5:18:10:01 |
| 30 | Arthur | Robin Kay/ G. Dempsey | Sigma 38 | 1.011 | 6:00:49:39 | 5:19:53:41 |
| 31 | Darramy | Brian Wallace | First 405 | 1.011 | 6:01:34:10 | 6:00:41:45 |
| 32 | Alpara | B & M Carroll | Dufour 35 | 0.920 | 6:17:44:13 | 6:19:09:40 |
| 33 | Raasay of Melfort | Brian Coad | Rival 38 | 0.873 | 7:09:20:57 | 6:21:04:56 |
| 34 | Spirit of Ringsend | Purcell/Daly/Crowley | DB2 | 1.023 | 7:14:35:51 | 6:21:27:25 |
| 35 | Ulysses | Par McArdle | Victoria 34 | 0.908 | 7:21:05:52 | 6:21:47:55 |
| 36 | Sty Tailte | Lt. William Roberts | Dufour 35 | 0.928 | 7:22:17:10 | 7:08:35:08 |

# CORK DRY GIN ROUND IRELAND 1994

## *The competitors tell their stories...*

### *Air Corps 1*

"Jaysus. There'll be a lot of dancing in Dublin tonight." This was a comment made by a member of my watch as we listened on the radio to the after match celebrations that followed Ireland's famous victory over Italy in the World Cup.

Picture the scene. It is the first night of the Cork Dry Gin Round Ireland Yacht Race and four of us have just come off watch. Outside a gusty Force 6/7 south-westerly blows as we pass the Tuskar Rock off Wexford in a very lumpy sea. Everyone is soaked wet and things are in a bit of a heap down below due to the rough seas. Half the crew are sea-sick. However this does not deter the conversation of the off-watch crew and there follows a fascinating and in-depth discussion of what kind of people, places and positions would be involved in the above mentioned entertainment. This discussion carried us through until our next watch - four hours later. This "cumann" of the Air Corps Theosophical Society convened often over the five days of the race and discussed matters such as medieval architecture in Galway, the decline of the breeding numbers of the Corncrake in Ireland, the Wonderbra (a form of sail, you'll understand) and its uses in Ireland today and other such uplifting matters.

But to get back to the action. The race started beside the L.E. Aoife anchored off Wicklow at 1400 on 18 June. This was the start of the race but the end of six months hard preparation and fund-raising by the team. The cold wet hours spent in the Irish Sea over the winter and spring were now distant memories but would nonetheless stand to us over the coming few days.

The final preparations were carried out the week before the race when we collected our Sigma 38 from Sail Ireland Charters in Kinsale and delivered it back to Wicklow. The days of organised chaos flew by as we assembled food, safety equipment, charts etc., lifted the boat out for a scrub down and carried out a thorough check of rigging and sails. In between all this we had to fit in some training and familiarisation as none of us had sailed on this particular type of boat before.

The boat had quite a sophisticated instrumentation system on board and many hours were spent perusing manuals trying to figure out how to get the best out of this. To add to this we fitted a mobile cellular phone and a Global Positioning system (GPS) chart plotter. This latter piece of equipment was kindly donated to us for the duration of the race by Racal Ireland. This system gives pinpoint position information obtained from satellite, and this is integrated with a small screen on which one can zoom in or out of all the Admiralty charts for Ireland, contained on one small computer disk. Captain Ned Kelly fitted the above items for us. Indeed, when it became known that he was such an electric's wizard, his services were very much in demand around Wicklow.

And so, from a position of mild confusion a state of order spread over the boat and all was now ready for the start. Well almost. Cork Dry Gin sponsors the race and it is customary to have a reception in Wicklow the night beforehand. This reception includes a free bar for three hours. Not a very good idea when planning to sail into rough weather the next day. So the crew were honour bound to moderation and I can safely say that most people found those three hours more difficult than the five days ahead.

## Day One

The race started amidst a carnival atmosphere in Wicklow. This did not last long after the start as the wind rose and we settled down to the serious matter of racing. It was close tacking as the fleet of fifty four boats set off down the Irish Sea.

The wind and the seas continued to rise and by daybreak more than ten boats, including some of the highly fancied challengers, had retired due to gear failure. We rounded the Conningbeg Lightship off the Saltee Islands and into the teeth of a strong south-westerly and headed for the Fastnet Rock. Our tactics on this stretch were to stay close inshore on our way across to the south coast. In Ballycotton Bay we, along with four other yachts, responded to a "Mayday" call from a sinking fishing boat. Bally-cotton Lifeboat was quickly on the scene and dealt with the matter.

## Day Two

Our tactics paid off and by 0930 we were rounding the famous rock, heading for Mizen Head. At this stage we were lying third in the Sigma 38 fleet just behind Hobo V, another Sigma 38 that we were to see a lot of over the next few days. Hot on our heels came the rest of the Sigma fleet. Having rounded the Fastnet the wind was now on the beam to the boat which meant we were reaching, a faster and more comfortable point of sailing. This gave us a chance to tidy up down below, but as the rain continued for another 24 hours it was not until we got to Donegal Bay that we got a chance to dry anything. We had a crew of nine, which was divided into two watches of four, with a floating man. The watch's duration were four hours on, four hours off during the evening/night and six hours on, six hours off during the day. Basically the job of each watch was to keep the boat going as fast as possible without endangering the lives of the crew or, more importantly, damaging the boat (crew always being expendable). With this in mind we attempted to fly the spinnaker in very heavy conditions off the Blasket Islands. After three hairy attempts at setting this sail we decided discretion was the better part of valour, granted victory to the spinnaker and packed it away. (There were to be many thrills and spills with this self same spinnaker over the next few days). In hindsight it was just as well we didn't fly it as the winds soon gusted over forty knots, which would have been very interesting with the "spinny", to say the least. So as the evening and mists rolled in we lost sight of the other boats in the gloom. Based on the forecasts we decided to head out into the Atlantic in the hope of finding more favourable conditions. Visibility was less than 300 mts. And for the next twelve hours we did not see another boat. During this time paranoia can set in where you convince yourself that you may have made a wrong move and the rest of the fleet are slipping past you. Only time would tell if this was the case.

## Day Three

*The crew of Air Force 1 receive encouragement from a colleague.*

The rain stopped at last and the sun came out but the wind died so we found ourselves stopped dead for four hours. Very frustrating. As the mist cleared we spotted a boat just inside us and through the binoculars we confirmed it to our old friends Hobo V. So as we passed Eagle Island off Mayo (a compulsory reporting point on the marine radio) we were neck and neck with Hobo, two hours behind a boat called the 'Spirit of Mayo.' This was quite a gap in sailing terms.

The Dauphin SAR helicopter came across us while on exercise in Donegal Bay. What a coincidence! Of course no outside assistance is allowed in the race but it was nice to see some familiar faces to remind us where we came from, and where we were going to! Once again the wind continued to rise and night fall found us bearing down on Tory Island. Now sailing around Donegal at this time of year brings its own particular problem. It's called the Salmon fisherman and it's not so much the man himself (they're helpful enough when you can understand what they're saying) that is the problem but the miles of nets he sets out.

It is difficult enough to see these nets in daylight but at night, in a rising gale, doing 10 kts under spinnaker in a 4 metre swell, trying to decipher the directions of a fast talking Tory islander - need I say anymore? The up-shot of it all was that we "broached" whilst attempting to avoid one such net. Now, one meaning of the word broach is a lovely ornate piece of jewel-lery worn by a lady in evening wear etc. In sailing terms in the conditions listed above it has slightly more serious connotations: your whole world turns over on its side as the boat is pulled over to 70 or 80 from the verti-cal, the helmsman is powerless to do anything about it, the rest of the crew hang on for dear life and the air is filled with the sound of flogging sails and the roaring of colourful expletives. In short, all hell breaks loose.

Having survived the broach with nothing worse than frayed nerves we packed away the spinnaker and carried as much sail as we dared in what was now a full blown gale. We pushed the boat quite hard for the rest of the night and started to close on the class leaders.

## Day Four

Wind gusting over 40 kts. surfing down 20 ft. waves on a 5 tonne surf-board, getting the boat up over 14 kts. In the crisp morning air - there's only one thing comparable, and that had already been well covered by the Theosophical Society. We were now screaming across the north coast in exhilarating sailing conditions. All the crew were up on deck as nobody wanted to miss the 'sail of the century'. My theory is that they felt a lot safer up there rather than lying down below listening to the whoops and roars as the boat surfed spectacularly downwind.

But something was wrong. We were now leading our class. This wasn't in the script. Sure didn't we just get the boat the week before the race? We didn't have a new set of sails, for God's sakes. All the experts back in the bars in Wicklow said we'd be lucky to get around. Surely they couldn't be wrong, could they? When I say we were leading our class, it was only just. Off our port quarter lay the spectre of Hobo V, whose presence we just could not shake off. It was to be nip and tuck between the two of us all the way to Wicklow.

In an effort to break clear we once again set up to fly our old friend the heavy spinnaker. In hindsight the conditions were probably a tad fresh for it. The exuberance of youth prevailed and up went the kite. A spectacular broach followed with the usual results. This particular sail was just des-tined not to fly for us. It came down with a healthy tear along the length of it which meant, thankfully, we were never to see it again for the rest of the race. Crew injuries were nothing worse than severe rope-burn, a dislocated little finger and a collective dented pride. Evening saw us past Belfast Lough and back into the Irish Sea. The wind had started to drop and by evening we were completely becalmed. This was to last for six long hours.

## Day Five

Dawn thankfully brought some wind for the stretch back to Wicklow. A leak in our water tanks meant that we were down to our last few litres. This was used for copious cups of coffee interspersed with cigarettes (only one person smoked at the start, but by the end five of the crew were back on the fags, his fags - thanks Ronan). The Theosophical Society had now been transformed into a born-again prayer group as we exhorted assistance from every possible God in our bid to win.

And so it was neck and neck down the Irish Sea. In the end we won our class by the shortest of short heads - a mere three minutes. Pretty close when you consider that we had been racing nonstop for nearly five days.

The event had been a tremendous success for our first entry. It is an excellent test of teamwork, endurance, navigational skills and of sailing tactical awareness. We won because we had a good crew, a good boat and our fair share of good luck. On tying up in Wicklow we bought a few large bottles of lemonade, made some cucumber sandwiches and whiled the night away singing auld sea shanties and telling stories. And one or two of us even had a "dance"!

Crew:

Tom O'Connor, Kevin Nunan, David Carolan, Derek Madden, Ciaran Parker, Mike Baker, Ronan Verling, John Kilmartin, Jimmy Quinn.

Finishing Position: 15th Overall (4:23:57:55)

1st Sigma Class

# *Alpara*

**Sat. 18 June:**

1300         Last checks carried out. All sails properly stored and bags numbered, water bags filled. Went through our roles for one of the longest races we would ever do.

1400         Crossed starting line with 51 other yachts. We started with No.1 headsail and full main. Weather overcast, winds south westerly.

1630         Wind southerly, 30 knots. Put second reef in main. Dropped No.1 and hoisted No.3. Tacked at heading of $260^0$, stayed on this tack for eight hours. Seas became choppy which made it uncomfortable below deck. Report came over radio of A.I.B. snapping mast.

2400         1st. watch on deck, seas began to worsen, winds gusting over 30 knots.

**Sunday, 19 June.**

0300.         2nd. Watch on deck. Course set for Tuskar Rock, compass heading 300. Seas began to worsen and it was difficult to hold course.

0600         Between 0300 and 0600 we had been blown off course and lost some distance. We still had to pass Tuskar Rock but were glad daylight was here after the night we had experienced. Other yachts which had the same problem as we were now in close contact with others.

0900         1st. watch stayed on to give 2nd. Watch extra rest as they had been in the worst of it during the night. Began to make good ground as seas became calmer and winds dropped to 20 knots.

1200         Rounding Coninbeg Light Ship. Set bearing for Old Head 247. Sailed at 180, tacked as we thought best.

1500         Could now see yachts in distance, did not know who as not much was coming over the radio. Helicopter film crew began circling us. We were all stars for a few minutes and spirits were high after they left.

1800        Removed reefs from main and hoisted No.2 genoa, boat speed steady seven knots with wind gusting to 25 knots.

2400        Hoisted No.1 genoa. Winds light, seas calm. 1st watch back on deck (0100). Trouble with fishing nets off Ballycotton. Progress slow. Made contact with Golden Griffin - she was heading for Crosshaven with an injured crewman. We found that eleven yachts retired or were forced to pull in due to weather conditions on the first night.

## Monday, 20 June

0500        2nd crew on watch. Passed mouth of Cork harbour. Yacht Raasay in sight. Had trouble with nets near Sovereigns, changed tack for 10 miles. Back on course for Old Head. Winds rose to 25 knots. Hoisted No.2 genoa and put reef in main. Passing Old Head hoisted No.3 Genoa as winds were gusting. Doing steady six knots. Could see five yachts behind us. Tailte (our main rival) made radio contact - she was behind, to our good fortune. Set course for Galley Head.

1000        1st. watch on. Small problems with fishing boat. Took reef out, speed 5 - 7 knots. Passed Galley Head, set course for Fastnet 259. Wind south westerly. All crews on deck to maximise speed.

1530        Passed Stags with Raasay and Tailte behind. Not much distance between us and Raasay. Passing Baltimore winds blew up to 30 knots. Second reef put in main. Caught in tidal race - seas became violent. Lot of water coming over the deck. Raasay dropped her genoa and lost ground to us. Passing Fastnet we radioed our position to Bantry Bay. Passed a French yacht going the other way. We all must have thought the same "are they mad?"

2000        Set course for Mizen Head. High winds and heavy rolling seas. Winds were blowing force 6-7. Sailing our fastest yet - almost 9 knots. Yacht receiving a real pasting coming off waves. Radio check found Raasay pulled into Cape Clear.

2100        2nd. watch on deck. Helmsman badly sick so helmsman from 1st. watch stayed on. Very heavy seas. Passed Mizen Head and set course for Bull Rock.

2400        1st. watch on. Problems with finding Bull Rock on account of heavy mist and near miss on rocks. Everyone on deck in case of unforeseen danger. Almost lost life-raft overboard. Passed Bull Rock about 0130, set course for Great Skellig. Watch crews were in disarray with such bad weather.

## Tuesday, 21 June.

0330        Coming up on Great Skellig yacht Tailte radioed us as she was on our port side. Passed each other at rock, set course for Inistearaght at 050. Winds changed to southerly. Hoisted spinnaker, wind again changed to north easterly as we reached Inistearght light house at 1030. Set course for Black Rock. Weather, raining, with light winds.

1300        Back on deck winds dropped, seas calm, even so forecast was bad. Rolling seas and south westerly gales. It was a good time to clean up and get our gear dried. Had our first cooked meal and, of course, dessert and Fosters!

1700        School of Dolphins off our bow. Nav. lights checked and sails folded and bagged. Winds non-existent, boat speed down to one knot. Radio report told us Raasay snapped Genoa halyard. Tailte well behind.

1900        Wind picked up. North West - westerly. Doing steady 5 knots. Mick and Dermot on watch. Bottle of Gin opened. Went well with Pat Barret's stories. Crew in good spirits.

2000        2nd. Watch on. Seas calm, boat speed steady seven knots. Sky's darkening, bringing up seas, winds gusting to forty knots. Put second reef in main.

2400        1st. watch on. No change in weather. Sea's rolling heavily, main spilled out.

## Wednesday, 22 June

0400        Passing by Inishmore. Winds gusting 30-45 knots. Hoisted storm jib. Seas very heavy. Watches were set for three hours as going was very heavy. Owen assisted from 1st. watch.

0700        Only two on watch, Mick and Pat. Large rolling seas. On course for Black Rock.

1000        Weather worsened. Hatch door on and locked in position. Mick and Pat taking turns at the wheel. Yacht being engulfed by waves at times. Passed Black Rock and set course for Eagle Island. Winds dropped to 20 knots and seas becalmed to slow rollers. Weather clear and sunny. Made contact with Belmullet radio west of Eagle Island lighthouse. Found out that Virgin finished at 0600 today. South westerly-westerly gales had been forecast for afternoon.

1300        2nd. Watch on. Winds 10-20 knots, clear and sunny. Boat speed, steady 6 knots. Hoping to reach Tory Island by 0100 at compass course of 61, covering 78 n.m.

1700        Night sailing would again be done by 1st. watch. 43 n.m. to Tory Island. No radio contact with Tailte, no yachts in sight. Hoisted spinnaker as winds had changed.

2200        Passing Aran Island Lighthouse, can see Tory Island in distance, should round it by 0030. Yacht offshore but cannot decide who it is as no contact has been made with Tailte. Wrong GPS heading for Tory Island bringing us onto Inishbeg.

2400        1st. watch on. Encountered nets on our course for Tory Island. Had to drop spinnaker and hoisted No.1 genoa. Fishermen guided us to end of nets, taking us away from Tory Island. We again hoisted our light spinnaker.

## Thursday, 23 June

0230        Went to jibe spinnaker, lost wind and it wrapped around the foil. Everyone was on deck as rocks were in close distance. Could not unravel spinnaker, the only way of getting it down was for some-one to go up the mast and slide down the foil bringing sail with him. Brian Gray went up with two safety lines (just in case) attached to him. Three of the crew held torches as he made his way down the foil. He was successful but we had lost almost two hours on time.

0400        Passed Tory Island and set course for Inishtrahul, com-pass heading 87, distance 35 n.m. Dropped light spinnaker, hoisted heavy, held for about two hours, dropped and hoisted No.1 genoa getting 5-6 knots. Whilst 1st. watch sleep we fried up what wasn't bad - it was heaven - all the other watch got was the smell! Passed a number of fishing boats, did not have to alter course as their work was done. Made contact with Malin Head Radio. Found that Decibell passed only seven hours before us. 10n.m. to go.

0700        1st. watch on. Passed Inishtrahul at 0930. Changed course for Rathlin Island, compass course 101, distance 20 n.m. Sea flat, winds light. Could see Decibell in distance

1100        2nd. Watch on. No change in weather. Rathlin Island in sight, should pass it in 3-4 hours.

1400        Winds lightened. Trouble with fishing boats. Not much progress made.

1700        Wind picked up. Two reefs in main. Held No.1 until winds reached 30 knots and then changed to No.3. Doing steady 6 knots. Rounded Rathlin about 0730. Set course for East Maiden.

2100        Winds lightened. Removed reefs and hoisted No.1. Winds strengthened later and made good progress with tide in our favour.

2400        1st. watch on. Winds lightened. Strong currents on out-going tide made progress slow. Passed East Maiden at 0200 and set course for Irish Sea at 203 off South Rock.

## Friday, 24 June

0300  Off Belfast Lough. Light winds dropped and began drifting with tide. It was hairy at times with so many vessels going in and out of Belfast. Made 1n.m. in three hours.

0600  Began to make progress at last. Our E.T.A. at Wicklow could be lunch time on Saturday.

0900  Strong winds. 2nd. reef in main, changed from No.1 to No.2. Weather cloudy with 20 knot winds. Doing steady 8 knots with the help of the tide.

1200  Winds lightened. Hoisted No.1. Later flew heavy spin-naker. Winds began to gust to 30 knots. Dropped spinnaker and hoisted No.2, later No.1. Everyone sitting out on rail to maximise speed. Heavy rain and thunder in mid-afternoon with winds lighten-ing. E.T.A. back by six hours!

1730  No wind for four hours. Repairs carried out on main sheet block. Royal Navy paid us a visit and wished us luck.

2000  With no wind morale was low so the cooks on board served up a four course dinner. Went down very well, opened a few cans of Fosters. After learning forecast, 3-4 knots of wind and heavy fog began to move as 2nd. watch came on. Wind held for one hour, with heavy fog - we began drifting again.

2400  No change in wind. Still losing ground in heavy fog.

## Saturday, 25 June

0300        Wind picked up for two hours, made about 6n.m. Could hear ships in distance but could see nothing in fog.

0600        Wind rose to 20 knots. Hoisted spinnaker. Spinnaker blew out as 2nd. watch came on. E.T.A. at Wicklow should be about 2100.

1200        No.1 hoisted. Doing well, speed 6 knots. Hopes are high of getting in early.

1500        Last of Gin opened, wished each other well and began making plans for our finishing party.

1730        Reached Outfall Buoy off Wicklow Harbour. Could see finishing line. Spirits were high. But we couldn't cross finishing line for another 6 hours as winds dropped and we were caught on the north-going tide. After five sail-changes and once having to anchor we crossed the line at 2330 on Saturday 25th. June. It was the toughest battle against wind and sea we would ever do - but we succeeded where others failed.

Sunday 26 June

2300        Everyone sick!


Crew:    1st. Watch                    2nd. Watch
         M. Carroll (Helm)            B. Carrol (Helm)
         P. Barret (Nav.)             V. MaGibbon (Nav.)
         D. Cobham (Sail trimmer)     B. Gray (Foredeck sail)
         O. McCarthy (foredeck)       M.Tobin (Sail trimmer)

Race Position: 32nd. Overall (6:19:09:40)

# Aqualina

by Brian Dempsey

## Day One.

Start at 1400 under main and No.1 genoa. Wind SW 3. At 2158 received PAN PAN developing to MAYDAY from yacht Jackabout in position 52' 17.3'N 06' 07'W. Stood by with Corwynt until 2258 when MAYDAY was stood down and Jackabout making her own way to Arklow under escort of a local fishing boat. Wind during the day was S to SW 3 becoming 5 to 6 gusting 7.

## Day Two.

1230 1.5' SE Helvick Head with 1st reef in main and No.3 jib with SW 5-6 winds. At 1718 received MAYDAY from fishing vessel Sharkhunter in position 51' 49.7'N 07'52'W which was sinking. Relayed position to Mine Head radio and to any yachts in the vicinity. Mayday position updated by crew of Shark Hunter shortly after to 51'50.326N 07'53.249W. Stood by with Nissan 1, Black-tie, Hobo and Aircorp 1. 1755 restart race after clearance given to proceed from Ballycotton lifeboat. Wind during this day SW 5 to 6 decreasing in evening to SW 3 to 4.

## Day 3

By 1315 position was 1.5' SW of Skellig Michael proceeding under full main with No.2 jib. Wind starting from SW 4 increasing 5 to 6 and gusting 7 until late evening when it had veered and decreased to NW 2 to 3 by 2130.

## Day 4

Morning started with a WSW 3 breeze under full main and spinnaker making Eagle Island report-in station by 1224. Wind becoming W 2 to 3 veering WNW 3 to 4 by evening and backing W by S later. Met man was giving a blow so safety checks carried out and rig checked.

## Day 5

Starts with wind W 5 to 6 increasing to 7 and 8. Tramping along under full main and spinnaker. Reducing to first reef by 0513. By 1415 reported position of due east of Mew Island Light under No. 1 reef in main and No. 4 jib. Wind W8. By 2300 wind had enough and decided to call it a day. We waited patiently for the day. 16' E by S of Clogher Head.

## Day 6

Starts with no wind but filling in from the SW to 1100. Crossed finish line at 1212.55 just ahead of Crown Duel. Tied up and in WSC by 1300 to report our completion of Round Ireland Race having got lost at the bar for 30 minutes. This time was not logged in the log book for reasons unknown to those who have not participated in crossing the start line.

The first 48 hours from the start line to north of Skellig Michael proved to be the hard slog of the race, quite like the '92 race. However the run to Aranmore off Co. Donegal was relaxing - even Factor 12 stuff. The run along the north and north east coast was exhilarating stuff especially along the north coast under spinnaker achieving boat speeds of up to 16.6 knots. We came to an abrupt stop east of Clogher Head drifting and ghosting southwards. The breeze gradually filled in off Dublin Bay to carry us across the finish line.

*Aquelina 1994. Crew: (Back, left to right) Ken Hudson, Max Hill, Derry O'Sullivan, Paul Fallon, Fiacra Mullen. (Front, left to right) Sheila Green, Geoff Dean, Brian Dempsey, Matt O'Connor and Tom O'Reilly*

# Blacktie – Wicklow Challenge

By Charlie Kavanagh

Our story began in late summer '93 when Gary Haughton announced that the owners of "State o' Chassis" (a Sigma 38) would favourably consider loaning the boat to members of the regular crew and interested members of WSC - all we had to do was purchase a new set of sails for the boat. By now we had the hard core of a probable crew and a boat but no money. Before Ireland qualified for the '94 World Cup we had the good fortune to have Declan and Linda Lucas as part of our crew and even though work now prevented Declan from competing in the race Linda stayed with us as our PRO. We immediately set ourselves deadlines for raising funds, starting with a New Years Ball in the sailing club, selling T-shirts, raffle tickets, St. Patrick's Day parade, Newspaper features, sponsorship from local firms and constant approaches, mainly through Linda, to nationally known businesses with a package deal as our main sponsor. We were finally introduced to Niall O'Farrell of Blacktie Dress Hire and thanks to some very protracted negotiations on our behalf by Linda a deal was eventually hammered out and we could at last concentrate on sailing instead of money. Our final budget for everything came to just over IP10,000 and the effort was well worth it as we were now ready for the start on 18 June. We certainly cut a fine dash as we made our way to the start line in our black tuxedos and our skipper, Frank Jackson in his (Fred Drew's) top hat and tails. [It is an urban myth that, as part of the deal, the crew had to dress for dinner every evening. Ed.] Our starting helm, Gary, decided to go for an inside start and his judgement proved correct as we approached Wicklow Head in the first third of the fleet with all the big boats.

It was a dull overcast cold June day as we punched into the last few hours of the flood and a fresh south/south-westerly wind. Even though Wicklow is our home port I doubt if many of our crew had seen the beaches of Wicklow from such close quarters from sea before, as we literally beach-hopped in company with most of the other Sigma 38's down the coast. The big surprise was to see the graceful lines of Michael T-Jones' S&S 34, "Deerstalker" sliding through the fleet of bigger boats as if to say "catch me if you can", and he went on to prove you don't have to have a new, state of the art, flying machine to win honours in offshore racing.

As the day progressed we had wind against tide and conditions were deteriorating down along the Wexford coast. Some of our less experienced offshore sailors were now beginning to call Huey and were glad the watch system was now in place to get in out of the misery. We adopted a 4 hour/2 man system with a change every two hours leaving the skipper free to be available when required.

Our VHF started to come to life about 2000 with the first retiral - yacht "Estralita" put into Arklow after a gas explosion on board. Hot on their heels came the cool voice of the skipper of the new J120 "Jackabout" who put out a MAYDAY after discovering that his boat was filling with water after his keel came loose. He explained his predicament in very clear terms and kept the rescue services and fellow competitors "Aquelina" and "Corwynt" who were standing close by, fully informed on his boats condition and his intentions - an excellent lesson in how to conduct oneself in an emergency. They safely made it back to Arklow where the keel finally decided to part company with the boat on being lifted out.

All the Irish crews now had matters on another field to distract them from the serious business of yacht racing - Ireland v Italy in the World Cup in New York. I'm sure the few gulls brave enough to be out on a miserable Summers' night like it were wondering what all the shouting was about when Ray Houghton hit the back of the Italian net 3000 miles away. Ole, Ole, Ole was rivalling the wind in the rigging and any boats still in earshot of each other were celebrating a famous victory, making believe that they were back in their local soaking up the special atmosphere only to be found in an Irish pub on such occasions.

Midnight finally saw us off Tuskar Rock and the VHF was alive again - first we heard AIB "Hesperia IV" was dismasted and then the saddest news for all Round Ireland fans, the illustrious Denis Doyle in "Moonduster", the grand old lady of the race, had retired. By midday Sunday a total of 12 boats out of 53 starters had retired, sure testimony to the difficult conditions thrown up by the south Irish Sea. On board, our crew were slowly getting their sea-legs and fortunately bade

*Frank Jackson, skipper of Blacktie-Wicklow Challenge, wears the only top hat known to have circumnavigated Ireland*

adieu to the heebies for the rest of the race. We were disappointed to hear our fellow club boat, "Trailblazer" was one of the retirals, but a chat on the mobile phone ascertained all was well. We were only in sight of a few boats now and a helicopter came out to film us off Ram Head which gave us something to cheer about.

During the afternoon, another MAYDAY came over the VHF and after some confusion over the position we discovered we were in its vicinity. A fishing boat with five persons on board was taking water and was requesting assistance. We downed sails and motored in the direction of a vessel we could see fitting the description of the casualty. However, before reached this vessel a message came over saying that "Hobo V" another Sigma 38, was alongside and disembarking the crew from the casualty "Sharkhunter" and was awaiting the lifeboat from Ballycotton to arrive. We were now released from the rescue by rescue control in Shannon and we resumed racing. As a result of all this activity we now found ourselves in close proximity to Siobhan Crowley's all-female crewed Sigma 38 "Nissan 1", who were to become enemy No. 1 right down to the finish line

With an ebb tide setting west the tactic was to stay offshore and follow the favourable stream, however the desire to show the girls how to sail resulted in us following them inshore thereby passing up the probable advantage to match race. We were neck and neck into the hours of darkness towards midnight or so, until we lost sight of them in the early hours of the morning. Daybreak found us about four miles south of the Stags, with a boat about three or four miles ahead between us and the Fastnet Rock, which we hoped wasn't the enemy, and another race was on. With Adam Drew now helming and a fresh SSW4/5 making a fetch a daunting task to which he rose admirably, slowly but surely we hauled in our rival ahead, and had our worst fears confirmed when "Nissan 1" checked in at Fastnet Rock five minutes ahead of us. The Fastnet Rock was a magnificent sight in the fresh bright morning sunshine and a few more sailors achieved another notch in their sailing logs.

Now finally able to free off the wind we had an enjoyable days sail up the Kerry coast, averaging speeds of 10/11 knots at last and, from the boats calling in at Inishtearaght, we were still in reasonable shape in our fleet, being quite close to a number of Sigma's. As we made our way up the west coast the wind fell away and we found ourselves becalmed for the best part of the next day about 25 miles off Inishturk Island with only a few Dolphins to break the monotony. When finally we got moving again we made our approach to Eagle Island off the north Mayo coast and discovered we had lost a lot of ground in our fleet, with some boats now seven hours ahead. In the midst of our gloom Tim Greenwood renewed some culinary memories with the crew of "White Rooster", on which he had done the previous Round Ireland, and who were just ahead.

As evening became night and we approached the Donegal coast the wind started to freshen to SWS 7/8 and we were down to two reefs and a poled-out No.2 making speeds of 12/13 knots in steadily building seas. Now was the time for the real hero of our crew to stand up - Mad Dog Dwayne Lysaght - our only import on board, and the value of his selection now became evident as he took the helm for a solid eight hours in very testing conditions, almost reminiscent of the Southern Ocean footage from the Whitbread race.

With some of the crew preferring the comfort of their bunks, he thrilled in getting up to 16 knots under NO.2 jib alone off the back of the huge Atlantic rollers taking us up past Tory Island next morning. His reward was the last shortcake biscuit and a good sleep through similar conditions for the next 10 hours or so. "Nissan 1" had called in about 2 hours ahead of us at Inishtrahull so we had a major task ahead of us now to beat them. All along Adam, our gismo expert, was shooting video footage with a view to launching his TV career, but alas most of his talent ended up in Declan Lucas' rubbish bin with 49 hours of other hopeful's efforts (Declan Lucas was the RTE editor responsible for putting together the RTE film of the race).

As the evening drew in the wind abated somewhat and we were finally back in the Irish Sea approaches. We crossed Belfast Lough under spinnaker and prayed that we would hold enough breeze to cheat the tide. Next morning gave us the inspiration we were hoping for - "Nissan 1" was still only two hours ahead and as this was hopefully our last day our skipper Frank rallied the troops for one last effort. Instead of following the girls this time and giving them an incentive to stay ahead we set off into the Irish Sea towards the Isle of Man and away from the coastal course they were taking. For the next 18 hours the whole crew remained on deck - eating, reading, sleeping etc., on the rail, and we maintained radio silence all day, just using the mobile when necessary.

Nightfall saw us approaching Wicklow and the wind was starting to desert us. Work came back from the Club that the girls had not finished - but they were in the bay!! We now renewed our efforts to find every whisper of breeze as the tide ghosted us down towards our destination - but no sign of the foe in front of us. Suddenly, a large flash of lighting lit up the whole of Wicklow Bay, and there, sitting at anchor on the wrong side of the line, were the girls. Our magician, Gary Haughton, was on the helm, calling for bodies to distribute weight in his last fling for some miracle to get us to the line on the right side for some compensation after five and a half days at sea and 890 miles later. By putting the boat across tide he managed to get some drive from the apparent wind and slowly but surely snook us down through the finish line at 02.30 to a tumultuous roar from about 200 family and friends gathered on the East Pier to welcome us home.

Even though we felt sorry for the manner in which the girls were pipped good fun was had by all in the WSC and next morning still had some crews partying after a gruelling but hugely enjoyable 'Round Ireland'.

# Corwynt 111

by Huw Tudor

Preparations for Corwynt III to participate in the race were made by the owner, Gwilym Evans, with the usual meticulous care and attention to detail. If things don't quite go as well as they should on Corwynt it can never be said that any blame is attached to the preparation of the yacht or her equipment.

We made an early decision to race with a crew of nine but our plans were thwarted by injuries to two blokes at the last moment. The response to enquiries resulted in a complement of eleven at the start line. It proved the old adage, that there is never a shortage of crew for winning yachts! The skipper for the race was Richard Tudor, well known in Irish Sea waters and renowned for his successful circumnavigation of the world as skipper of British Steel II in the Chay Blyth toughest yacht race ever - British

*This is what the Round Ireland is all about. Ask Gwilym Evans.*

Steel Challenge.

The Cork Dry Gin Round Ireland race was not without drama and excitement for Corwynt from the start gun to the finish at 17 minutes 27 seconds after midnight on 23rd June, an elapsed time of 106 hours, 17 minutes and 24 seconds. This time included deviating to accompany Jackabout. At 2138 hours on Saturday night Corwynt responded immediately to a MAYDAY transmitted by Jackabout, a J120. We had been alerted that there were problems and that she was taking in water but had not appreciated the seriousness of the situation until the distress call. We were not the nearest yacht to Jackabout but we were tacking to windward at over 7 knots with a good 2 knots tide under us, speed made good 9+ knots. At precisely $52^0$ 17' N; $6^0$ 07.9'W; 5.5n.m. from Tuskar we jibed to escort Jackabout on a course northwards in a heavy following sea against a tide of 2 knots. A true wind speed of 22 knots and direction $235^0$ was recorded on our log. A listening watch was maintained on Channel 16. Quite soon we were accompanied by Aquelina, another Sigma 400 which had also ceased racing to stand-by Jackabout. Both Corwynt and Aquelina stood by until Rosslare lifeboat instructed us, at about 2300 hours, that we could stand-down. At 2303 hours Corwynt resumed racing from position $52^0$ 23.6N;$06^0$ 10.9W. It had taken us 1 hour 25 minutes to accompany Jackabout northwards. By the time we reached the same latitude at which we had ceased racing at $52^0$ 17'N it was 2353 hours, the wind had veered and the ebbing tide was weaker. When we arrived at Tuskar at 0029 hours on the following day we were beating against a foul tide at a boat speed of 7.7 knots in a true wind of 23 knots.

The yacht behaved superbly on the hard beat to Fastnet but modifications to the Dorades, carried out by our local boatyard, because of slight leaking, resulted in a greater volume of water down-below than we had ever experienced. It resulted in swamping, not only of five loaves of bread but also a hand-held VHF!

The culinary expertise on Corwynt III cannot, we feel, possibly be matched by any other yacht. We operated, under Richards's advice, two watches. It was arranged that Brian, our regular Corwynt Chef, and Keith, one of the urgent crew replacements and winner of the 'Best Chef Trophy' on the British Steel Challenge, were on opposite watches. The result: superb cuisine, including two hot meals every day no matter what conditions. Apart from the galley, care was taken that the two watches did not vie with each other. There is no gain in telling the oncoming watch at 0200 hours that a certain gain to windward or miles made good have been achieved and challenging the next watch to better it. Our watch system disintegrated totally after rounding the Bull at 0845 on the 20th. The reach and then the run up the west coast were so exhilarating that everyone was on deck to experience it. There was a time we whooped with joy to see 12 knots on the 40:40 display - no more. We had 15 knots for long…long…spells as Richard manoeuvred Corwynt to ride those big Atlantic rollers. But the high point was when 18.2 knots flashed with Gwilym on the helm. We kept the spinnaker trimmed with hands on helm, guy, sheet, kicker and main from The Bull to Eagle Island and had two hot meals a day.

The experience of a heavy displacement yacht on a sleigh ride is impossible for a simple navigator to describe. We were creating, for the most part, our own private route in the waves and surging forward at 15 knots with white foam above the height of the guard rails on each side without a drop falling on deck. We give compliments to Rob Humphreys, who designed the yacht, his brother Wil, our mainsheet trimmer and Richard our helmsman. There was never any suggestion of a broach, even in those big seas.

One of our last minute crew replacements, known as Huw McEars (McEars, because, in his own words . . . "I have a big nose, big hands and big feet, size 14 feet, and small everything else"), who had only done a little Cardigan Bay sailing previously. His classic remark to Gwilym was echoed by us all . . . "This is the best day of my life . . ."

We all hope that the Cork Dry Gin Round Ireland race will continue to be supported for the excitement and genuine competition that it gives. The exploits of Corwynt alone could fill a book. The superb experience of the North Channel and the excruciating final hours in no wind at all into Wicklow deserve chapters on their own.

Sailing is not for the faint-hearted or the grousers. Nevertheless on Corwynt we can justifiably claim if ONLY we had not lost those valuable hours and that favourable tide we MIGHT BE the overall winner.

Finishing Position:    3rd. Overall
                       3rd. CHS Class 1
                       1st. ISORA
                       1st. Sigma 400/Combined

Crew: Gwilym F. Evans, Richard G. Tudor, Gwyndaf Hughes, Brian Jones, John Rickards, Keith Mundell, Tino Highland, Huw Tudor, Huw Williams, James Evans, William Humphries

# Darramy

by Richard Chubb

We enjoyed both WSC and Wicklow town, culminating, of course in the eve-of-race reception victualled generously by "Cork Dry Gin". It was here that we suffered our first casualty when one crew member whilst bunk-bound in a premature escape from a sea of gin, was struck by a falling line of decorative "Dry Gin" cardboard coasters (fortunately not of the "dirty British" variety), sustaining a minor forehead abrasion. Predictably, the sympathy forthcoming was minimal in view, not only of the trivial nature of the injury and the anaesthetised state of the patient at the time, but also because of the unforgivably early retreat from the first - and potentially hardest - leg of the race.

The friendly interest in the race displayed by the public climaxed, for us, in the exceptional attention which our craft - Darramy - and crew attracted on race day. Some have suggested that the press and T.V. cameras were focusing upon our neighbouring boat (the all-female crew sponsored by "Tropicana") but we knew better that it was the colourful basket of geraniums suspended from the end of our boom, the exotic 'though quiet parrot clawed to our skipper's hat and, above all, the natural photogenicity of our crew which made us the target of the Irish Paparazzi.

We were in danger of developing injury paranoia when a second accident overtook us as we cast off the quay. Who would have thought that after hours of practice the previous evening a crew member should be unlucky enough to lacerate his hand whilst releasing, through the porthole, a farewell rocket balloon? We had been told that this race held in store hazards most varied but this was becoming ridiculous!

I suppose we were not alone in being unable to come off the wind until rounding the Fastnet and the first third of our race was marked by a shifting crew scramble for the least uncomfortable bunk, the complexity of which would have left Short and Kasparov wallowing off Kinsale. The crew who though he had it cracked with a relatively dry bunk for the anticipated largely Port-tack circumnavigation, belatedly realised that he was berthed atop the food supplies and many an otherwise weary watch was enlivened  by watching him progressively approaching the bilges as we consumed (faster, no doubt, as a result) our rations.

It was after two days of this beating that our aforementioned balloon-launching crew member presented his battle-scarred hand with an accompanying sick note (courtesy of our medical man aboard) to our skipper at the start of his watch. The skipper's somewhat unsympathetic response would have been a credit to any N.H.S. minister of the Thatcherite era. It was around this time, also, that our rather unsteady cook took it upon himself to redecorate the walls of both galley and saloon. It was imaginative, if perhaps unoriginal of him to choose a decor of goulash and mixed vegetables but then to pebble-dash the whole with boiled rice displayed a true genius for improvisation.

Meanwhile, the magnificent cruising grounds of the South-West and the stunning hills of Connemara provided all that we needed in the way of visual stimulation; occasionally leaving us regretful that it was not a cruising rally since it seemed sad to pass such beauty without closer exploration. However, these were the only regrets and they were briefly held. It was our consensus that such a circumnavigation course provided not merely the variable sailing conditions and navigational challenges one would expect, but also introduced the interest of a rolling "land-view" which is so obviously absent in many other races.

The forecast gale took a long time in coming and when it did it coincided with our decision to prepare spinnaker around midnight off Donegal when the true wind-speed was around twenty knots. Fortunately, the arrival speed of the gale rather surpassed that of our foredeck team, coming - as it did - before the actual hoist and we soon found ourselves heavily reefed with storm jib and running excitedly before forty to fifty knots and waves the size of which had reached twenty foot in the telling even before the end of the race! We have no startling tales of heroism or, fortunately, disaster to relate during the hours of passage of the severe gale (remember, we had experienced our share of injuries before the starting gun!) but, for most if not all of us, the running, surfing and near-broaching represented the greatest of thrills.

Hours after the gale subsided, we experienced the contrasting but, nonetheless, memorable thrill of a spinnaker, ghosting, moonlit sail of silent majesty in sight of Co. Down, Rathlin and Mull of Kintyre. Hours later again, of course, we were drifting astern, windless in a foul tide in the Irish Sea but such frustration was insufficient to mar the pleasure and privilege of completing a varied, exciting, challenging and elementally beautiful race. Also, I do believe we won the rocket-balloon competition.

Finishing Position:    31st. Overall
                       15th. CHS Class 2
                       1st. Rocket-Balloon Competition

Crew: Bond, Brankin, Clubb, Stanley, Graham, Davies.

# Deerstalker

by Michael Taylor-Jones

Immediately prior to the Round Ireland race Deerstalker was located in Scheveningen having just completed a North Sea race. We left Scheveningen on 29 May and arrived in Wicklow on 13 June, a passage of 700 miles including a stiff beat down the English Channel from Eastbourne to Penzance - where the delivery crew gave up on 6 June because of fatigue and lack of time. We motored from Penzance to Wicklow in flat calm between 11 and 13 June. We anchored in Brittas Bay for the night of 12 June. Our fuel was nearly gone and we had a foul tide. Beautiful morning of deserted golden beach with the Wicklow mountains in the background and drifted into Wicklow on the morning tide. What a splendid way to arrive!

13-18 June. We repaired electrical/charging problems on engine, replaced the engine starter battery and much appreciated the help we received from Paddy Goodbody of Wicklow Marine.

16 June. Lifted out for a scrub, filled and rubbed down dents and had a polished bottom with 800 grade wet and dry. Opposition commenting on our efforts in the bar of Wicklow S.C.; Winkie Nixon says "you may get to the rock (Fastnet) OK, but those S&S's can't run for peanuts!" Answered by a polite smile.

17 June. Crew arrive, morale good, menus planned and food shopping list drawn up. Fresh meat and veg. for the first three days then pasta, curries etc., from tins. An off-

*Deerstalker  A shark disguised as a minnow*

shore sailor sails on his stomach. Scrutineered by Anna Brooke, who had sailed on the boat with its previous owner (Joe Isaac, East Coast RORC measurer). She knew what to look for but fortunately we had filled all the gaps in Joe's safety equipment.

18 June. Good start in clear air and centre of line. Shy spinnaker reach to Wicklow Head. Soon sat on by overtaking Sigma 38's etc., and floundered briefly under the wind shadow of the Head. Then beating down the coast. Full main and No.2, foul tide, close tacking inshore. Overtook Amazing Grace, Nissan 1, Wicklow Black Tie (black looks - we had been told to follow him as local expert), and after a struggle, Winkie Nixon in Witchcraft of Howth.

That evening, as the tide turned we are only 7-8 miles south, but count 20 yachts astern, some hull down (4-5 miles). Lamb chops, green beans and potatoes with gravy and all washed down with red wine. As wind builds change to No.3 with one reef in main. See Maxol return to Arklow, then Tropicana and two unidentified yachts coming back. Much banging and crashing with wind against 3-4kt. tide. Stand on south, away from coast.

19 June. Dawn - 20 miles offshore, tack onto port and increase sail in smoother sea. Afternoon - close tacking towards Cork to cheat tide. Identify Witchcraft astern and Juno, Gwawr and Arthur close ahead. For a short period overtake Juno and Gwawr but lose them again as wind drops to 3/4.

20 June - 0737 round Fastnet. Juno ahead, Gwawr, Spirit of Mayo and Witchcraft astern. Difficulty with radio contact. Gwawr kindly passed on our rounding time.

1130 approx. Witchcraft closing, buzzed by helicopter - broach reaching with No.2 and 1 reef. Hoisted spinnaker but helicopter cameraman did not return. Witchcraft under white sails slides away backwards.

1550 - sea building, forced to drop spinnaker rounding Inishteracht. Wind SSW 6.

21 June

0245 - Fine night, 2 yachts in sight, wind W 3/4

0650 - Witchcraft abeam

1305 - Nice sunny day, drying bedding, slow progress

1455 - Rounded Eagle Island

2030 - Wind W5, changed to heavy spinnaker

## 22 June

0030 - Wind backing, changed to big spinnaker, dead run.

0100 - Wind increasing, changed to heavy spinnaker. Jim damaged finger catching it between halyard and winch. Changed again to boomed-out No.2 and gybed.

0510 - Gybed to clear Inishtrahull, wind gusting to 35 knots over deck, surfing at 10 knots, lots of salmon nets and one or two fishing boats gesticulating! The nets roll away under our keel, no problems, certainly no way of avoiding them. Wind WSW8+.

0645 - Heard Gwawr, then Juno, round Tor Rock.

0725 - Rounded Tor Rock, Witchcraft alongside, bear up across her stern, then gybe.

1135 - Rounded Rathlin Island, Wind WNW7. Superb views of coast in brilliant sunshine. Jim fully recovered and wanting to steer.

1630 - Run 182M in 24 hours, (previous best 165 on route to Cadiz in 1990). It shouldn't be possible for a heavy displacement yacht of 24 ft. waterline length to average 7.6 knots. Can't run for peanuts be damned!

1756 - Rounded Mew Island.

2310 - Wind variable 2. Much frustration.

## 23 June

0045 - Brief spurt at 5 1/2 knots - then totally becalmed.

0500 - Some wind again; 4.2M in three hours, the quick boats will have finished by now.

0750 - Wind ENE2, sailing 6 1/2 knots under spinnaker.

1130 - Off Dublin Bay, wind S4, dead beat to finish, no yachts in sight.

1559 - Finished, sails down, motor into Wicklow, tie up astern of Witchcraft. Nixon forced to eat his metaphorical peanuts. Crew vote it the best race ever. Heard we had won Class 3. To win overall we needed more head winds and not to be becalmed on the last night.

25 June

Denis Noonan appears with all our spare gear, taken off before the race. Skipper now alone on board and is invited to lunch. Discover mutual interest in model making and steam engines.

Deerstalker is a Sparkman and Stephens 34 built in 1974 by a neighbour of mine, Joe Isaacs, the RORC East Coast measurer for many years. I bought her in 1988 and since then we have done two Fastnets (1st. in class in 1991), the Brent Walker Cadiz race in 1990 and we were overall winner of the 1992 Round Britain and Ireland race.

Since competing in the Round Ireland this year Deerstalker has competed in the Cowes - Cherbourg race on 16 September winning Class 3 and overall. Spinnaker all the way once more averaging 7.6 knots, probably the maximum for an S&S 34.

Crew:

Will Taylor-Jones, Richard Dean, James Gibbon, Fiona Conway-Hughes, David Conway-Hughes.

Finishing Position:    8th. Overall
                       1st. Classic Class
                       1st. Class 3

# Hobo V

by John Bourke

Following the Fastnet Race in 1993 I decided to race with a crew of eight instead of the permitted nine on my Sigma 38.

We went for a pier-end start and hit it more or less exactly, to the great pleasure of our supporters nearby on the pier. Our first tussle of many with our sister ships was with 'Rock Adventure' as we tacked down the shore against the tide. Approaching Arklow we appeared to lead the Sigma 38's but then I tacked out to sea with the changing tide. As it happened, this was not a good tactic and a bit more coast-hopping would have been better. We seemed to lose heavily that evening and into Sunday morning despite good boat speed.

Saturday evening was also the time of the great match, Ireland v Italy. I settled down at the chart table and turned up the volume. There was little reaction from the soccer-mad crew below, as they drew further into their sleeping bags in the rising seas. Anyway I enjoyed it thoroughly, and they did manage a cheer despite all, when we won.

At 1725 on Sunday, beating towards Ballycotton, we heard a Mayday call from Sharkhunter. After some confusion, she gave a position almost on ours and set off a flare which we saw. I took down the sails and announced on the VHF that I was motoring down to her. Sharkhunter motored very fast towards us but stopped as we came alongside. Apparently she was leaking and the skipper had rightly taken no chances with the several anglers standing on board with rods held upright. We motored round her briefly until Ballycotton Lifeboat arrived and then hoisted sail and went back to our starting position and off we went again. Our watches told us that the entire episode took only 20 minutes: it seemed much longer.

Having tacked up the coast I took a long leg out at the Cork buoy, hoping for the wind to back. It did, and let me up almost to the Fastnet Rock on port tack, just ahead of 'Air Corps', with whom we were to match race for virtually the rest of the course.

The wind freshened as we cracked off up the west coast. I flew a spinnaker for a while but the wind at 35 knots and a big quartering sea, kept tipping the stern into another broach, and we went to two sail reaching with some relief. At 1554 on Monday we passed 'Great Yoze' going fast, but as we went into Tuesday lighter variable winds and drizzle took over.

At 1523 we passed Eagle Island just behind 'Air Corps' and had a lovely neck and neck to Tory Island, just regaining the advantage. At Tory the wind freshened again into a really dirty night. I set the heavy spinnaker and wrapped it quite horribly, losing two halyards and bending the top of the seastay. Having sorted that out we poled out our No.2 and with one reef, proceeded comfortably at virtually top speed.

At 0640 on Wednesday we passed Inistrahull with the dark menacing shape of Malin Head behind it in the morning sun. The forecast said Malin Head 29 knots gusting 50 knots. It felt like it!

At Rathlin I stayed out a bit, remembering the strong winds and tide there when I was navigator on Moonduster in '82. That time the big boat was swept by big seas several times. This time, I need not have been so cautious.

We arrived at Fair Head by 1100 with 'Air Corps', and now, 'Gwawr', right there inside us. At the Highlandman Beacon off the Maidens we reached down just ahead of them, but by Mew Island we were just behind, in a good but lightening wind. Later, in Dundalk Bay, it went very light and became a beat. We ghosted slightly ahead and carried on into a nice beat to the finish at 1307 on Thursday, just inside the five days. Gwawr was just ahead but gave us time. Air Corps was twelve minutes behind us but had more redress from the 'Sharkhunter' affair and beat us into second place in the Sigma 38 class by 8 minutes.

Our consolation was to win the IOR division overall. The second consolation was to have enjoyed the best boat for boat racing on a long race that I can ever remember.

Finishing Position:     16th. Overall
                               1st. IOR Class 8

Crew:
John Bourke, Skipper
Gerry Mulvin, Watch leader
Caroline Mulvin
Michael Steveley
Declan Tyrrell
Brodie Sweeney
John O'Reilly
David Hammond

## Janey Mac 11

by Adrian Lee

For me the start was the launch of Janey Mac II in the Havant on February 11th. After that the work began.

Wicklow was a great experience. Saturday night was rough, most of us seasick and fed up listening to rescue after rescue. Feeling that most of my crew needed a rest we tacked into Dungarvan Bay for flatter sea. I made the breakfast and we were running fast. At Cork a helicopter joined us - maybe we are in front! Spirits do lift. We had no idea where we were placed at any stage in the race. We felt we should not call Wicklow hot line as it may be against the rules.

We had a good passage to the Fastnet which we rounded at 2.40 am Monday. Then onto the Skelligs At about 1100 we hoisted the Spinnaker and surfed at over 14 knots with "Keep on Smiling" beside us for a few hours. This sailing was the most hairy stuff I have ever done after the whole crew being up for over 6 hours and having worn out 4 spinnaker grinders. I took the kite down as we approached overfalls north of Skellig. At the time we had 30 knots of wind and a large Atlantic sea following. This was a difficult decision and rather unpopular. As skipper I knew we could not have lasted the next 400 miles and this was not a fast race around the cans in the Solent or Dublin Bay. We had been beating for two days and the spinnaker going down was sad, but as I said to the crew "We'll get it up again". We did, from Eagle to Mew. We goose winged the No2 and sped up to Black Rock. We did 210 miles in 24 hours, saw Dolphins and listened to Richard Burrows call in to the press office. I spoke with my father "Reggie Lee" several times pleading with him not to tell us anything we should not know (this was for me the most difficult challenge - he knew we were doing well, but could not tell us.) I felt cruel when I asked him not to call us again.

We had mostly a spinnaker run to Rathlin where we hugged the coast to fight the tide. My brother Philip burned his hands as he lowered a spinnaker. Whiskey helped the shock. We beat down to Wicklow playing songs and looked cool in our gear and sunglasses as we finished in Wicklow at 21:40 Wednesday. When we arrived in Wicklow what a shock! Only four boats ahead of us - we had done so well! We had not had water on the boat for the last one and a half days and instead before a drink we had a pint of water! We had got third overall! And that on IMS. Then it was downhill. Corwynt Sigma 400 was given two and a half hours redress for a rescue of Jackabout. Bridgestone had not given her IMS entry correctly so when corrected beat us.

Footnotes: I had three of my crew from the USA, Henry Find, Tony Hume and John Donnelly. I had billed the race as better than the Bermudan Race. They all agreed it was a tougher and better race - and will be back.

*Adrian Lee.*

*Ruth Lee, daughter of Janey Mac skipper Adrian Lee plays a few 'shantie's to encourage the crew.*

# Joliba

by Alan Murray

## Saturday 18th June

Our aim was to run down the start line on starboard - close hauled – and get the best position at the pin end, near the harbour mouth. This plan was formulated through a gin soaked haze induced by the Cork Dry Gin Reception the night before. Only lunatics and sponsored yachts go for a "best start" with 52 other boats bearing down on the line at the beginning of a race that could take a week to complete! In the end we shot across the line in approximately 6th position and the crew vowed to buy me a bottle of that fine gin before every race in the future.

*Joliba at the start of the 1994 race*

After Wicklow head we were trying to decide how soon we could tack inshore to go tide dodging when we were beaten to it by the canny Mr. Nixon on "Witchcraft". We tacked immediately after him and worked what we called the 5 meter line - when the depth sounder reads 5m - tack out to sea. Thus began the long slow slog down the East coast.

Of course the Decca died off Wicklow head and did not rise again until we were almost at the Tuskar. Don - "Did we just hit the Blackwater Bank?" Me - "No-way, that's out there" - "Then why did we just slow from 6 kts to 3 kts and go back up again?" - "Bad Batteries. Start the engine and charge them" Navigators always know exactly where they are!! That night Fiacra was taken aback by the number of retirals and the litany of problems experienced by those boats, he was also quite alarmed when the red flare from "Jackabout" went up. I must congratulate the skipper of "Jackabout" on the calm and collected way that he handled his yacht in that crisis and the professional tone of his radio transmissions - lessons for all of us there! We did not suffer any gear failures - though seasickness had claimed one or two victims and the spirit on the boat was jocular - a typical "Royal Poolbeg on Tour".

### Sunday 19th June

Sunday morning saw us beating south from the Tuskar. My plan was to go south while anticipating a Southerly wind shift and to tack before the wind backed. This hopefully would enable us to reach the Fastnet on one tack on a lifting hand (more gin soaked hazes). I also felt that the steeper and shorter seas inshore would not suit the boat, so we sailed south until we were way off the chart! Liam, his first ever attempt to chart a position, - "I must be doing something wrong, I have us off the lip of the chart table between the clasp and the tea-stain!" Finally we tacked and on rejoining the human race, by creeping back onto the chart, we found ourselves pointing at Kinsale. True to form the Irish weather forecasters had got it right and we started to get lifted. All this talk about lifting caused our Decca to take it to heart and it re-evaluated our position and told us we were half way up a mountain in Cork! I made all the necessary adjustments to correct the problem only to find that the position search function - green light and all - had us descending the North face of the same mountain. Suspicions arose and our stocks of Cork Dry Gin were checked but to no avail, the Decca had gone mad all on its own. Our land based sailing lasted for two hours when, all of a sudden, we were immediately transferred back to sea - without by your leave or explanation. Now I know what the transporter does on the USS Enterprise - It doesn't send you anywhere, it merely reprograms the instruments and you hallucinate the rest yourself!

### Monday 20th June

By now we were all wet and tired (not emotional unfortunately) and the Sock Monster had followed me here too. One by one my socks went missing and the reading material - donated by two of our friends on the quay wall just before the start - could not be found either. They had warned us - "You are not to open this bag until you are at sea" - fine job if you could find it!

The Fastnet glistened and smiling faces warmed in the morning sunshine, while Mr. Eastman made another few dollars from our pathetic attempts to capture the awe inspiring rock on film. The one tack on a lifting hand had worked and we rounded the rock and eased sheets for the first time in two days - Hurray.

We spotted a couple of larger yachts behind us - had the going to sea gamble worked? - I think so. We knew we were not real contenders in the CHS race but we had set our sights on doing well in the Classics Division. I knew that "Deerstalker" would hammer us to windward in those conditions to the Fastnet so we were playing catch-up all the time - with the wind dying. One of the more pleasurable moments at sea is when a school of porpoises play in the bow-wave of your yacht. We were privileged to be afforded such a display by these amazing creatures in the bright sunshine of that afternoon. In the evening we reported in to Inishtearacht and received a call from that magnificent yacht "St. Christopher" who were eager for a chat. That lasted about ten minutes until their batteries started to go down but we agreed to make contact the next day.

**Tuesday 21st June**

Galway Bay, Galway Bay, Galway Bay on the most beautiful day of the year. Sunshine - No Wind - No Clouds - No Clothes, or rather - the deck looked more like Kelso Laundry with everything and I mean everything, hung out to dry on every available spot. We now had our first proper meal since leaving and it began to dawn on us that perhaps we had brought too much food.

Suddenly Liam found the bag of books and passed them round. Our mouths fell open. We were given the whole top shelf of a sleazy bookstore. A nice How-dy-do for six men and one woman at sea for a week! We needed a calming so we opened another bottle of that fine Cork Dry Gin and lamented our lot. One of the sleeping crew woke up to find six of the books in his bunk and two on his chest - slagging time!!

"St. Christopher" called us to wish us a happy mid-summers day and we nearly had grown men leaving Joliba to swim over to them after the descriptions of the girls in bikinis on board. We had populated the area west of Slyne Head for about twelve hours, when a zephyr of wind enabled us to set the spinnaker and take off for Black Rock and Eagle Island. We were in high spirits and looked forward to an easy sail to Tory. Little did we know that Neptune had other plans! I called "St. Christopher" and wished them a happy midsummer night's dream!

Wednesday 22nd June

We skirted Black Rock under kite and made our way to Eagle with the wind building all the time. "St. Christopher" passed within twenty yards of us at about one in the morning and we all came up on deck and sang Olé Olé Olé to them. There seemed to be multitude on board and they gave us the Mexican wave in reply. In the words of their radio operator "It's nice to know there's someone else out here".

Our spinnaker has always had a mind of its own and when it wants some time out it jumps free from the pole and broaches us. We could even hear it screaming "GET ME DOWN" - or was that my imagination? As the night became dawn we were running under a double reefed Main and a No. 2 Jib. The Main was boomed out with a slightly slack preventer (if we broached there was enough slack on the preventer to allow the boom to rise with the water) and the Jib was trimmed for close reaching - even though we were almost dead running. The purpose of this was to give us way and steerage in a broach - e.g. when the yacht lay beam on to both sea and wind, the Jib filled and by straightening the rudder we could maintain our momentum and return to our original course almost immediately. These precautions were necessary due to the fact that our anemometer was reading 40 kts+ at times and the following sea was quite daunting. Clodagh knew the words of the Paul Brady song "The homes of Donegal" and we rewrote the last two lines of each stanza to wit: ". . . . *And your seas are like your mountains in the Hills of Donegal".*

The most nerve tingling times were not the numerous round-ups but the surfing and such was the excitement that there was stiff competition to get a turn on the helm. Once, while steering I asked the cockpit crew to watch and tell me if we were going to be pooped - "Why is that dangerous?"- "No it's just that I have a hole in my right boot and I want to lift it clear of the water".

While off watch, during this madness, a couple of us tried to play a game called "Pass the Pigs". This game is similar to dice except you throw two small plastic pigs and score points according to how they land. In the broaches there was plenty of makin'-bacon (game terminology) and pig hunts. Definitely not the usual occupations of an offshore racing crew! Once more we were wet through. Nigel came on watch wearing his last set of dry clothes. He said that he had kept these for arrival in Wicklow but now he had to wear them. I soon saw to it that on a sideways surf - the yacht surfed on its side with the starboard half of the boat underwater - the water ran up Nigel's left leg, across his chest and down his right leg - so much for his Sunday best! The same surf sent gallons of sea-water down through one of the forward facing air vents and drenched the owner in his bunk. No-one would own up to being on the helm at the time.

We had started across Donegal Bay just as the gale began and as we rounded Inishtrahull the wind and sea abated - what a nice present Neptune had concocted for us! Rathlin Island beckoned and we rounded just before the notorious tidal gate closed. That night saw us drifting towards the Antrim coast in light airs against the tide.

**Thursday 23rd June**

The slow beat to Mew Island held our interest until the "DON'T DRINK THE WATER" syndrome struck. One crew down - up and down and up and down would probably describe it better - and all water now had to be boiled.

Our vacuum sealed meat rations had fared well up to this point but now they looked very suspicious - they quickly became fish food. Break out the tins - Yuk!

The day wore on and the wind stayed about 10 kts on the nose. I gave the crew a course and retired. Soon afterwards I could hear them discussing a short cut and one of them came below to ask if we could go through the gap through which the trawlers had come. After rising from my bed and taking it on me that the on watch crew were not aware that the South Rock Lightship was a mark on the course. Thankfully they had kept to the original course and we cleared the mark and began our run for home. That night provided us with one of the most spectacular lightning storms we are ever likely to see. With 15ft of anchor chain tied to the mast and trailing over the side we picked our way towards the Lambay Roundabout with stabs of electricity slashing the surface of the sea all around us. We hoped that Zeus was punishing Neptune for all he did to us in Donegal Bay and that he wouldn't hit us by accident!

**Friday 24th June**

The Kish Lighthouse holds a special place in the hearts of our crew - we spent three and a half hours studying it from all angles on Friday morning. With no wind some of the crew got so frustrated - to have come this far only to be stopped outside our own front door - that they took to their bunks and buried their heads (at least one in a good book!).

As the wind picked up we started on the final leg to the finish. There was an air of anti-climax and a general feeling of regret that this was the end of what was a great adventure. We had "Gelled" together as a team and there was never a word spoken in anger. We had fun, the craic was 91 and we all loved it. The camaraderie with the other yachts and the banter and slagging on our own made for a most enjoyable and entertaining trip. Our youngest member of the crew, Fiacra, brought the boat home over the finish line and the bang from the gun signalled the ending of a crusade and the opening of the champagne. As for our position in the race - our target to do well in the Classics Division worked out with a 2nd place and we also achieved a 2nd place in Class 6 IMS. Not bad - considering.

WSC welcomed us with open bars and lots of mugs of beer and we finally met with the crew from "St. Christopher" who didn't have those pints on the bar waiting for us as promised!

**Crew:**
James Ryan, Alan Murray, Liam P. O'Cleirigh, Fiachra O'Cleirigh, Nigel Rollo, Clodagh Cullen, Dan Breen

*Konica Minolta Zana*

# *Juno*

by C. Buckley

*Juno. Conditions are never too adverse to miss a photo opportunity*

Juno was entered from Howth Yacht Club in the 1994 Cork Dry Gin Round Ireland Race having been kindly loaned to us by Andrew Knowles (a man of immense faith). Eight friends assembled from near and far with the objective to win while never letting humour or having a good time out of their sights. Jim Newport travelled from Los Angeles, John Flynn from the United Kingdom and John Mordaunt joined us from outer space! The majority of the crew had previously raced in the Round Ireland and/or Fastnet, whilst all had extensive sailing experience. Three of the crew were fully certified I.S.A. Yachtmasters (Offshore). Rumours among our competitors were abound that JUNO was merely entered so that we could avail of the free drink prior to Race day and the chance to introduce ourselves to the two competing female crewed boats whenever possible. This was not entirely true as we were confident that our boat could perform despite the limited aggregate intelligence of the crew on board. So on the morning of the 18th June 1994 after many months of deliberation, practice and preparation an accountant, a dentist, a banker, a film maker, a couple of computer buffs, a double glazing salesman and a test pilot for Armitage Shanks cast off from Wicklow harbour leaving behind a nervous smiling Andy Knowles for perhaps a few of the most eventful few days we could have hoped for.

## DAY ONE

Start 14.00 hrs. at Wicklow. JUNO started midway on the start line; spirits were high on board not to speak of alcohol levels of one or two members of the crew from the previous night! After the first number of miles we were leading all Sigma 38 footers with only three Class II yachts ahead of us. Increasing winds up to an apparent of 28 knots forced us to reduce our Genoa No.1 to a No. 3. During the change, halyard problems left us sailing bare head losing an estimated 20 minutes on the competition. Wind on the nose down the Irish Sea. As we approached the Tuskar Rock it was nightfall (Ireland V Italy). Our problem headsail change rendered our bowman Neil Power prostrate below. A previously incorrigible football fan slept through the entire Ireland V Italy match, dreaming of hundreds of sheep.....well, we'd better not go into that! The remaining crew were on deck alert and a little apprehensive as a Pan Pan, followed shortly afterwards by a MAYDAY was sent out by "Jackabout". The Lifeboat from Rosslare crossed our bow shortly after we heard the MAYDAY en route to the stricken Yacht which had been taking water through some of her Keel bolts. Time of incident was approximately 21.30 hrs. Not many volunteers to grab a few hours below bar our overworked bowman who was contentedly sleeping like a baby elephant. After Tuskar JUNO tacked out to sea as the wind was forecast to go southerly in the early morning. This did not materialise and so we tacked back inshore at daybreak to the joint leading pack of Class II yachts, south of Dungarvan. Morale at this point in the race was decreasing among the crew of JUNO and the Darina Allen of the yacht was not in the mood to venture below no more than any of the other "ah....I just haven't quite got me sealegs yet" brigade to prepare food. To cap it all, the up to then fully reliable compact wonder of Japanese engineering decided to act up and the sewer king Shane O'Flaherty took to the dark dank depths of the bilges to try and sort the engine out. Battery power was low and despite Shane's every effort we were all trying to stave off the idea of retiring knowing that without power a jaunt up the west coast would be foolish to say the least. Shane, up to the time of our engine problems, was the dark horse of the crew. A quiet good living chap with little boating experience save the occasional ferry trip to England to escape the authorities, he emerged as a true leader. His stomach of iron and uncanny knowledge of diesel engine mechanics astonished the entire crew to a man. While JUNO battled against the elements, the sewer king had his head stuck in the diesel only to emerge a few hours later with an expression of elation on his face that, to be frank, left the crew somewhat disturbed.

## DAY TWO

Having remedied our engine problem morale rose considerably in the knowledge that we were back in the race so to speak. JUNO got into a brisk tacking duel with MARISSA VIII and CROWN DUEL off Cork harbour at approximately 19:00 hrs. which brought blood back to the veins and raised spirits even more. At 22:00 hrs. our halyard problems resurrected themselves and true to form one of the people more susceptible to vertigo was up the mast and sorting out the problem in the form of Simon Knowles. He refutes totally the notion that he scaled those dizzy heights to escape the constant drone of John Mordaunt heaving over the leeward side. Anyway John found his sea legs and Simon having regained his colour was rewarded with a banana for his heroic endeavours. At this stage of the race we were off the old head of Kinsale with a south-westerly wind force 5-6 in strength. Our resident seamstress, Jim Newport, worked an absolute miracle on a ripped No. 1 Genoa and all agreed that he had a lost vocation in dressmaking. We had 33.5 nautical miles before we would reach the Fastnet Rock. I suppose you are wondering what we survived on with all the energy we were burning up. Well the cooking quality was basic but sufficient given the facilities available on board. None of the crew starved nor did anyone suffer from food poisoning. Colm 'Darina' Buckley coped reasonably well, being more used to cooking facilities available in Le Frere Jacque a la Coq Hardi. He adapted to the two ring gas stove producing such culinary masterpieces as bundy a la chicken, with croutons, surpassed only by his speciality Reefed Stew which he marinated carefully in the bilges ! We operated a two watch system, four crew members on each, which afforded us 3-4 hours sleep every other 4 hours. This system worked very well, however, I must mention that there was a vast difference between the two watches in terms of racing ability and consequent results! It soon became apparent that there was in fact a racing watch and a cruising watch. I noted in the log for JUNO that the skipper recorded that competition "is increasing between the two watches", which is a polite description of the unfolding events. I mentioned already that we had some exhilarating racing between CROWN DUEL and MARISSA VIII, culminating in our catching both yachts and overtaking them in the early hours of Day 3. The "racing watch" then retired to their respective bunks leaving the "cruising watch" to drop the anchor off the island and have a good read of the Sunday newspapers, or so it seems. The rested and previously contented "racing watch" returned to a dawn filled horizon with two specks on it in the form of the aforementioned Class II boats well ahead! No explanation could be proffered by the "cruising watch", but, true to form, the "racing watch" resisted all suggestions of retiring and battled on to regain our position later on as will be reported.

## DAY THREE

At 07:30 hrs. JUNO passed the Fastnet Rock and radioed in. We were on a broad reach now and bearing off more and more up the West coast which afforded our bowman plenty of 'walkman' listening time. Contrary to the crew consensus that his nickname of "the quiet man" was acquired due to the constant look of sheer fright on his general visage, I believe that Neil Power is in fact a serious music buff unable to survive without his daily fix of Nirvana, Pearl Jam, ABBA, Boyzone etc. JUNO was carrying a full main and a No. 3 Genoa at this stage and powered along on the ever increasing seas up the south-west coast. At 09;20 hrs. we passed Mizen Head. Cooking was somewhat easier now that we were coasting along off wind and Jim Newport prepared some soup and sandwiches, amply filled with assorted meats and Ballymaloe relish. A helicopter which had visited us each day appeared over the horizon and spent some fifteen minutes circling extremely low given the sea state while filming our 'Can-Can' imitations to the amusement of the cameraman, who I'm sure is convinced that offshore floating loony bins exist off our coast. At 15:15 hrs. we radioed to Inishtearaght and reduced our Genoa to a No. 4 and put a reef in the main. Our boat-speed was constantly in excess of 11 knots with a wind speed of 29 knots. Seas were increasing as previously mentioned but were relatively easy to handle given the dinghy experience among the collective helms! Dylan Murray was in his element and kept urging the skipper to increase sail. Simon finally acceded to Dylan's lust for more speed. We decided on hoisting a spinnaker having resurrected the bowman and put up the 1.5 oz. kite, thus increasing our speed to an average of 13 knots with the occasional burst of 15 knots. The log reads at this point in the race "hold onto your hat if you still have one". At 18:00 hrs. on Day 3 our position read 52.30.27 N 10.52.29 W with a course of 359 compass. At 22.00 hrs. the wind having veered and fallen off we dropped the kite and hoisted the No. 1. At this point in the proceedings we all wanted to know how we were faring as there wasn't much in sight. At 00:30 hrs. we sighted Rock Island lighthouse on Inis Mor.

## DAY FOUR

07:21 hrs. JUNO was sailing west of Clare Island heading for Black Rock with a 0.75 oz. spinnaker flying doing a steady 8 knots. "Darina" Buckley served up an Ulster fry in anticipation of the looming north of

Ireland and everyone was happy or maybe she mistook the crew's contented looks for food poisoning. The cigarette situation was fast becoming a problem and so John "Bummer" Flynn was rationed but later resumed his normal intake when he was found rolling some of Johnny Mordaunts socks in a met. chart and trying to light same. At 09:30 hrs. we were lying west of Black Rock being bombarded by continuous downpours of rain. Our bowman Neil Power discovered that his, up until then, essential Musto babygrow had in fact given him fairly nasty burns on both of his ankles. The crew having deliberated for some two hours decided to allow him stay on board and not, as was one suggestion, "toss him over the side"! As is common in the North West we were all basking in glorious sunshine at 13:30 hrs. due west of Eagle Island. Every item of clothing was hung out to dry and JUNO resembled a proverbial clothesline of the floating variety. The sea state was somewhat calm affording us plenty of cooking time. A few quiet libations were enjoyed and morale was good with plenty of slagging around. Dylan Murray was able to shave his legs and coiffeur his hair during this quiet respite. One of the navigators, John Mordaunt, decided to air the damp and reeking cabin area below by removing his boots having worn them constantly for three days leaving Jim Newport in a collapsed state on the cabin floor having overdosed on the resultant fumes. A certain party who shall remain nameless endeavoured to off-load some excess body weight suspending himself from the stern of JUNO and was most successful given the numerous clicking cameras pointed in his immediate vicinity. Mind you, I have always said that Shane is somewhat of an exhibitionist. Less of the toiletries anyhow! At 18:30 hrs. we were coasting along on a run from Eagle Island to Tory Island peeling spinnakers from the 0.5 oz. to the 0.75 oz. At 20.00 hrs. unbeknownst to the relaxed crew the wind was steadily increasing. I must mention that up until then JUNO had miraculously avoided the litany of gale warnings received over both the VHF and RTE weather forecasts! We were now steering for Tory Island in 30 Knots of wind with a full main and spinnaker, all to a man contemplating copious amounts of beer while exchanging our trials and tribulations to our fellow sailors in Wicklow Yacht Club on Thursday ! ? Our average boat speed was 13 knots at 23.00 hrs. with 23 nautical miles to reach Tory Island. At this point in the proceedings a worrying situation arose which rendered JUNO invisible to other craft. Our navigation lights were not working ! Over the VHF speaker in the cockpit came the voice of a Donegal drift-net fisherman announcing that he had 4-6 miles of drifting net out. He was unable to see us and wouldn't respond to our calls over the radio. We were now travelling at a steady 14 knots surfing occasionally at 16 knots, still with full main and spinnaker aloft. A continuous line of water gushed along the gunwales from the bow to the cockpit. Every member of the crew was giving 100% concentration to either trimming, driving or sighting a close approaching net. Our navigator "the sewer king" O'Flaherty, was frantically endeavouring to communicate with an elusive fisherman who obviously was not at all partial to his dulcet Dublin tones. Suddenly on our bow a bright light loomed and increased in intensity as we closed on it. "Steer straight for the light" were the instructions to the straining helmsman, Colm Buckley, who on seeing the light reciprocated with a string of expletives! With a fast reducing 100 metres between JUNO and our unresponsive Donegal friend, our stoical navigator announced "He wants you to leave him to your starboard". We shot past the fishing-boat with only metres to spare at a steady 15 knots, unlit, save a torch that was grabbed as there was no time to rig up our spare navigation lights. JUNO trundled on into the darkness, and ever increasing seas, not to speak of winds, made helming and trimming more demanding than ever before. A reef in the main would have been very desirable but on a dead run an impossible operation to perform and so with his shovel-like-hands and the look of a man possessed, Simon Knowles ably steered JUNO on and the atmosphere became utterly electric! During this entire drama the skippers wife, Christina, decided on trying to communicate with us shore to ship, to be politely told by the navigator Shane O'Flaherty that her husband was indisposed, so to speak, and would call her back at the first available opportunity ! Christina was however, the purveyor of good news informing Shane that we were lying in 12th place overall and 4th in our class. It was now 0130 hrs. and we had 38 knots of wind pushing us along at breathtaking speeds while surfing on big rolling seas with the occasional wave breaking on our open transom, flooding the cockpit ! Another drift net lay waiting for us 100 metres later, and having been instructed wrongly which way to leave it by one of the fishermen, we hit at a steady 15 knots and the net slowed us down momentarily while it tensioned and made its way down our keel. Luckily our rudder was never interfered with, as a sharp blade on the leading edge was there to greet any foreign objects! Without warning a gust hit us and we were thrown into a bad broach which hooked JUNO around into mountainous seas and forced her onto her side for what seemed like an eternity. Two of the crew were standing up to their knees in sea water on the side of the cockpit while the remainder clung on for dear life in the pitch darkness, until the boat finally righted herself allowing us to assess the damage. We democratically decided to lower the spinnaker and hoist a No. 4 Genoa! Tory island whizzed by us in the darkness only a couple of hundred yards away and we set a course for Inishtrahull, yet again increasing our speed and creating an adrenaline rush among the crew to surpass all previous ones. Several more nets lay ahead of JUNO in the early hours of the morning of Day 4 which were forcing us off our layline and so we made the decision to jibe! The wind strengths were strong and rather than risk dropping the mast, we decided on a more conservative tack. With everyone alert and ready, Simon brought JUNO up into the howling wind and swirling seas in order to tack. Jim Newport and John Flynn on the runners at that time noticed that the port runner had dropped to the deck, leaving the rigging in a precarious position. The mainsail then ripped under the immense pressure and we were forced to drop sails and start our engine. At the risk of the second runner falling out we, after much debate, decided reluctantly to abandon the race and so radioed Malin Head informing them of our retiral. JUNO motored up Lough Swilly to Rathmullen which took four hours against tide and wind.

## DAY FIVE

The naval ship the L.E. ORLA was docked when we arrived and there were no refusals to the invitation to have breakfast on board. We checked the mast and discovered that part of the bolt holding both runners up had obviously popped out during the broach, and that it was only a matter of time before the other half would go. Fully loaded with diesel and foddered courtesy of the Irish Naval Service, JUNO limped out of Rathmullen and through Lough Swilly under motor for the 140 mile trip back to Howth. Not much was said for the first 2-3 hours but, as had been true to the form, it wasn't long before banter and reminiscing on the trip was exchanged by all aboard ! As we motored past Dundalk Bay NISSAN ONE, the female crewed boat, caught up with us and sailed by as did BLACK TIE later on. We hugged the coast after that and not many boats were sighted from then until we berthed in Howth Marina. We all debarked a fully intact JUNO, mast intact, to be greeted by a smiling Andrew and Joan Knowles who were delighted to see us ! Everyone agreed that as a crew we worked very well together and collectively we would attempt the next Round Ireland Race subject to Andy kindly loaning us his new 60 footer !

# Keep-on-Smiling

by Tim Little

Owner-Skipper Tim Little sails at Pwllheli and Abersoch, North Wales. The crew is made up of family (son, daughter and cousin) and very keen friends. The average age is 27 years and we are very competitive. We race regularly in I.S.O.R.A. and have started three "Round Ireland's". We retired in "Keep Smiling" in 1990, finished third in class in "Keep on Smiling" in 1992 and won the trophy for the fastest Sigma.

We had twelve crew which was too many especially as we only have six offshore berths. We did manage but changes will be made for 1996. Food was prepared in advance by "The Ladies". We either heated it up on the top or in the oven. Bread with sandwich fillers, cake, cuppa soups and biscuits filled in the gaps. Water is always a problem; this time we half-filled the tanks (10 gallons) and brought 48 litres of bottled water. We took a little alcohol; whiskey, Cork Dry Gin and some beer but it was hardly touched. It all went very quickly after the finish! The bottled water was the favourite during the race.

## Wicklow to Tuskar:

We had a reasonable start and drew quickly away from the smaller boats. It was great to be started at last. The afternoon start meant that the "bad heads" from the previous evening's celebrations had almost gone! All the "400's" were fairly close at this stage and so was MAXOL UN-LEADED. We cross-tacked with her several times and nearly "T-boned" her. The crew were ready to abandon ship but we missed by a whisker. She disappeared after that.

We then had a series of disasters, all within three hours of the start:-

1. Our GPS aerial fell in the water as a result of a faulty pole fitting. It did not work for the rest of the race.
2. The leech line of our No.1 genoa (medium-heavy) broke and the back third of the sail delaminated! It was our workhorse and was made of Kevlar genesis. So that was no use. We do not carry a No.2 so had to rely entirely on the No.3.
3. Our mainsail outhaul broke. We quickly put in a reef and used a sail tie as a makeshift outhaul. This lasted the whole race but we were not able to adjust it, of course.

4. Our wind instruments went loopy. We did in the end need a new mast head unit.

I must say here that we are a well prepared boat with regular maintenance carried out but all these problems came out of the blue all at once quite unexpectedly. Our navigator did bring with him a hand-held battery-operated Garmin GPS which did help to make us not to have relied on dead reckoning completely. Batteries were in short supply however so we were only able to us it 'sporadically'.

## Tuskar to Fastnet:

We had no mishaps. Saturday night was very dark, rough and unpleasant. South of Colinbeg with wind against tide we had waves of 3 or 4m in height. Some came over the side green or black at night time. Some of the crew were sick but we sailed hard - keeping "The Smiler" well powered up to overcome the waves. Full main with the No.3 genoa was ideal. It was quite misty and we made our first landfall at Ballycotton, tacked out beyond Old Head of Kinsale then tacked back in West Cork. It was beautiful! We saw many cottages without light and wondered if they were holiday homes that were unoccupied. We reached Fastnet at 0100 Monday behind "PROSPECTOR" and in front of "JANEY MAC II".

## Fastnet to Eagle Island:

The wind was generally S to SW force 6/7, later 4/5. It was great to turn the corner and free off, but we made a mistake in going 3 miles off the rhumb line between Fastnet and The Bull. Can you believe it? We had no GPS to speak of and visibility was about 1 mile. So JANEY MAC II caught up with us. At The Bull we hoisted our 1.5oz. Spinnaker and took off! We flew it for many miles. Our fastest surf was 15.9 knots. It was a great sail! Sunshine and wind - you can't beat it!

JANEY MAC II was close by and sometimes would nearly completely disappear from view when we were both in troughs. When we both decided that we could not hold the spinnakers any longer, she goose winged her genoa but we did not, thinking that we would be too unstable. Consequently she held a course much closer to the rhumb line than we did. In retrospect I think we could have held the spinnaker all the way up the west coast. At one time the sea was a very light green with frothy white caps and the crew had perpetual grins on their faces! It was fantastic - and warm too!

Approaching Black Rock in the evening we had a beautiful view of the Hebrides silhouetted by the sunset. The colours were superb and their shape changed every minute. They must have been at least 60 miles away.

As night time came there was "JANEY MAC's" stern-light! It made helming much easier as we had a light to follow from Black Rock to Eagle Island.

## Eagle Island to Rathlin:

This was the best part of the race from the "comfort" point of view. We had a spinny run with the wind still SW about force 4/5 (no wind instruments) across Donegal Bay, past Aran Island to Tory Island. The first nets we met were off Aran Island. We came upon them very quickly and tried to reach their end but with the spinnaker up we had to broach over them. I don't think we damaged them. The fishermen did not seem to be too upset. Tory Island to Inistrahull was great! It was warm and dry, the sun was out, we had a following wind of about force 3/4 and it was warm!

We dried the boat out, dried out all our clothes, sunbathed and ate lots of food. "JANEY MAC II" was still in sight. The skipper (me) saw a silhouette of Joseph and Mary on the cliffs of Farad Head. I was amazed that no-one else could see it. I tried very hard to show everyone else where it was - in vain. Never mind, it didn't do us any good anyway!

Approaching Malin Head and Inistrahull we came across several nets. The fishermen had taken a liking to our name and they kept calling us up on channel 16 then channel 12 and having a chat. It was great because they told us where to go to avoid their nets. We didn't have to go very far out our way either. They chatted about where we came from and were particularly happy about Ireland's win over Italy in the World Cup. This was a huge change from the 1992 race when all we got from the fishermen was very vocal abuse! Inistrahull to Rathlin was a most enjoyable sail. A lovely evening, lots of wind and a very happy crew. At Rathlin the tide was against us for three hours but we had enough wind to hold our own and set course for Wicklow.

## Rathlin Island to Wicklow:

Dawn over Galloway was beautiful! We caught the S flood S of Rathlin (eventually) and in time the S ebb from the Isle of Man. The North Channel was very flat but by the time we reached South Rock Light we had force 6/7/8 wind SW i.e. "on the nose". The crew took it very well. More green stuff came over the bow but it was the home straight. It's 90 miles to Wicklow from South Rock but some of the crew thought it was much further, even so, they resolved to survive to the end! So we had a close fetch all the way to Kish, then to Wicklow. From The Bull to Dublin Bay we had followed "JANEY MAC II" and in Dublin Bay we thought we had caught up with them. We did not quite, and five miles from Wicklow we stopped!

It took us 2 hours to do the last 5 miles! Never mind, when we got ashore we had a super welcome from the people on the pier, especially those from Wales, and the bar stayed open for many hours.

As ever the WSC did us proud after our circumnavigation of Ireland.

Yacht position at 13:00 each day:

19th June   $51^0$ 45.3 N.    $07^0$ 49.2 W    Distance run - 140 nm
Av. speed - 6.08 kts.

20th June   $52^0$ 26.9 N.    $10^0$ 45.6 W.    Distance run - 175 nm
Av. speed - 7.29 kts.

21st June   $55^0$ 01.0 N.    $08^0$ 38.2 W.    Distance run - 200 nm
Av. speed - 8.33 kts.

22nd June   $54^0$ 03.0 N.    $05^0$ 33.2 W.    Distance run - 185 nm
Av. speed - 7.70 kts.

Total distance run - 765 nm. Average speed - 7.34 kts.

Final Position: 7th. Overall
                 6th. CHS - Class 1
                 3rd. Sigma 400/Sigma combined.
Crew:
Ch. Raine, Roger Pollard, James Baldwin, Ian Ridgway, Albert Vaines, Hugh Richmond, Andrew Topham, Andy Jackson, Ian Little, Andy Bale, Cath. Little.

# Marissa V111

by Jonathan Bradshaw

The Round Ireland race, once referred to as the seven hundred and five mile challenge. Head out of Wicklow, turn right, don't turn round until you come back!

## First Night

My second 'down watch', my turn to sleep. I slept on the engine cover, assisted by a maximum dose of sea sickness pills which came in a pack marked on the side: "This product may make you drowsy". Despite them I was too sick even to make the effort to get out of the protective clothing and safety equipment that four hours ago I had wrapped, crawled into, and belted around me before doing my turn at 'up watch'. It had been warm and dry then. What little resolve I might have had to remove the now cold clothing was destroyed by the certain knowledge that to hold myself almost naked in the position required to get into a bunk and warm dry sleeping bag on the upper starboard side would induce another fit of that which I had been trying to avoid.

The others had hung wet-gear and safety equipment from the roof of the boat when they had gone to their bunks. The empty suits were almost standing around talking to each other, as the boat constantly shifted, the three or four suits staggered like commuters on a train. There was no light but what was leaking in out of the instruments, behind me, or coming in through the hatch over the wash boards along with the muted voices of the 'up watch'. And it was wet. Water dripped from the roof, catching the din orange light of the low wattage bulbs which seemed hardly strong enough to light the sounds of the sea and the creak and bang of the boat as she lurched from wave to wave.

Like waking from one of my dreams . . . sitting there watching, waiting for sleep to drain away like spray from the deck above; to separate what was real from what was to be washed away only to be carried back a moment later as the drug pulled me mercifully from the breach of reality and the feeling in my now empty gut.

It was not the last time I was to spend the night on the engine cover wedged up against the chart table with my head pushed back against the bulkhead. The next time was better. I had eaten. I was still wet and cold and still doped, but I had food in my gut. One of the suits had managed to get down from the hand rail. I was alarmed that it had untied itself, hanging and moving in time with the rest I could see the lanyard, uncut and no sign of the suit. The boat lurched off one wave and crashed into the next. Everything moved, even the suit which should have been lying on the deck. I waited, my mind trying to look where I could feel the panic rising. I watched, waiting to be engulfed, and even as I did the panic disappeared along with sleep like a wave sinks into the soft beach leaving only its foamy crown.

"Yo, Frank". A hushed voice, my hushed voice, just loud and hard enough to carry over the cluck of the engine as it forced life back into the tired batteries under my feet and warmth into my legs . . . not hard enough to catch the attention of the sleeping 'down watch'. "Jonathan, how are you?" a voice from the suit, muffled by sleep, cold and dark. "Good, are you going up?" I still had not moved. I wanted to be sure that all the sleep had drained away before I started to move. "Yea . . ." the voice, sharper now, more awake, cut across the dark and wet of the cabin, "Plot a position". I turned, taking my leg of the warm cover, keeping my head down, (it seemed to help), and lifted my eyes to look at the six dancing numbers against the phosphorescent green display. I had been asked to take these numbers and turn them into a smudge on the chart in front of me. The boat lurched, my left eye tracked '53 north' my right eye reached for the horizon that it knew existed on dry land. I held my breath. "I'm getting better at this." I thought "This time yesterday that would have been the end of it." Drops fell from the roof, from my jacket and hood. I rubbed the water away before it could find its way under the parallel rule which I was pushing across the chart. The smudge got bigger. "They are doing well." I thought of the two sitting above holding the tiller, watching in the wet starless night. Crash. Another wave. Water shot past the hatch into the cockpit. Not far now and then the Fastnet and the beginning of the leg which would take us north up the west coast. Then I could say "Half way."

## Day Two

Day one had been wet. We started well enough, around the head and then a boat-destroying punch down the Irish Sea. I saw three boats head back. They passed us in the night, running before the wind . . . driven by the sea, headed back to the bright lights, the flags and the party which had been set for out departure. Back to failure. Later I saw a parachute flare aft of us floating in the sky, burning red amongst the wind, the rain and the clouds crying 'help' for those who had birthed her this night. A short, brilliant life, she floated for so long it seemed impossible, and then she died in the angry sea. The radio was alive with the voice of the calling skipper and the steadying sound of the Lifeboat Cox who drove his vessel and its crew before the wind and sea to answer her call. He was close; it was going to be all right. It was all right, the stricken boat and her crew brought safe to harbour.

"Mayday! Mayday! . . . I'm sinking", the radio cracked to life and shout-ed urgently across the sheets and warps lying wet and twisted in the bot-tom of the cockpit. We had already had our visit from the press 'chopper'. He had taken his images and moved on to find better news. It had been a good day sailing. Now it was evening and we were bedding in for the long evening watch, the 'down watch' were sleeping. "This is Rosslare Radio. . . Rosslare Radio . . . Rosslare Radio . . . would the vessel calling Mayday please identify yourself?"

Part by broken part, the radio operator extracted the necessary infor-mation from the stricken skipper. And by his manner installs calm across miles of threatening water. As a position becomes known, boats from the race put about and declared themselves as 'this distance' or 'that time' from the stricken craft. Almost impossibly soon, racing boats are alongside the sinking craft shortly to be relieved of their self-imposed watch by the men of the lifeboat. Lifeboat 1 - Racing Boats 1. As it happens, the final score, at least for this year.

## Day Three

The sound of the sail flapping like a flag in the wind. Not a good sound on a racing boat. It's early on day three, we are the 'down watch'; snuggled in warm sleeping bags. The world above is an alien place to our almost helpless bodies below. My face, warm against the lea board, soft flexible canvas which welcomes the sleeper. I hear the skipper shout above . . . "TACK!" . . . I brace myself to roll against the cold bubbling hull at my back. Instead of waiting until the sails fill and she starts to heel and then be catapulted across the narrow bunk as my side of the boat goes under the water. I choose, I roll, and the cold against my face threatens to wake me. "Quick now!" the skippers voice is sharp, "Get that sheet back on or we are going to hit the rock . . . Paddy . . . get ready to fend off . .. TACK!"

She comes head to wind; just as she starts to heel I roll . . . back against the welcome canvas. Once more sleep rises around me. I am going down, deep, I cannot see, far behind is the light of day, ahead in the depths is the light of dreams. I hear children in the distance calling, laughing, crying out to me, "Come and play". I have heard stories of the children of the sea; men have been lost answering such calls. I close my eyes, in case they have their own light by which they play, and dive harder and deeper to where I know I am safe.

I wake to the call of the 'up watch'. The outside of my sleeping bag is damp; the inside of my coat is wet. The cabin is crowded and the day light streaming through the open hatch adds to the discomfort of the transition from the warm bunk into the real world. Like a space man I force myself past the washboards onto the deck, into a bright world of wind and black, black sea. The boat pitches and rolls in the waves, water rushes past sometimes above us, sometimes below, always crowned with icing-white flecks driven by the wind. "Where are we" I ask as I land, tossed by the movement of the boat, almost head first onto the wet cold deck. "Well the Fastnet is back there, and we are making for the Bull Rock". I look at the skipper, his eyes are wide open, the sailing is good, the wind is abeam and we are making good speed helped by the sea. A soldier's wind, it's said to be so easy to steer a boat when the wind is abeam that even a soldier could do it. I wondered, could I?

'The sea is my friend, she will not hurt me'.

The boat dives into the next wave. I pitch forward grinding my shoulder into the safety bar for the third time. 'Bitch' I'm up to my knees in water, I've taken another face full and I'd swear that its gone so far up my arms that its now running down the inside of my last dry shirt into my trousers. This is about as much fun as I can take.

'The sea is my friend, she will not hurt me'

I say it like a prayer. She lurches again, this time up, I pitch forward, and again, suddenly I am clear of ocean, blowing the spray out of my face, blinking to clear my eyes, I can see the foot of the sail I am trying to clear from the deck. I jam my foot down once more pulling with both hands . . . one more kick one more pull . . . bang, I rap the side of my head on the forestay as I pitch back and then forward once more into a world of white foam and heavy driving water. 'Bitch'. That's it . . . I've had enough, someone else can have some fun for a change, It's OK for them sitting back there in the nice dry cockpit giving benign instructions like 'we need to change the headsail' . . .wap! going forward again . . . I brace myself,

'The sea is my friend, she will not hurt me'

A world of white, deeper, wetter, colder than any before. I swear he is doing this on purpose. Now I am really pissed, I lash out with my foot mindlessly into the water and the foam and I yank with all my weight. Just as the sail comes free this cool voice starts up in the back of my head "that's ¼ inch steel hook down there, you can yank all you like, it's not going to make any difference.' The voice finishes up just in time for me to land on my arse in what feels like two feet of water which is now draining-up-my legs. There is this 'I told you so' tone ringing in my ears.

'The sea is my friend, I don't think so!

I met myself that day, three times; three times I walked away from that sail, from all that water, three times I walked back to the cockpit, three times told them to do it themselves.

## Day Four

This is fifty knots of wind, I was in fifty knots of wind on Dublin Bay, and this is fifty knots of wind, easy. You know when its fifty knots of wind because the tops of the waves get chopped off by the wind and get driven along as spray. I was looking at that now, I was in a good place to see, wrapped around the boom as I was trying to keep the mainsail from going over the side. It was only a matter of time before the wind got under some part of the sail and it inflated like a parachute. In this wind, that would be a problem. Just as the skipper opened the hatch and stuck his head up to see what the hell was going on Ken screamed 'Wave'. Head down, hatch shut . . . bang! It was like something out of a cartoon sketch. It was funny right up to the point where the wave struck and I got wet.

It was early on day four, very early, it had just got bright enough for us to see a squall get up and march out of the mountains behind Malin Head. Jason took one look at the blackest cloud I have ever seen and shouted . . . 'Get them down . . . all of them . . .the sails . . . get them down now!' We were doing fine until the mainsail jammed leaving the top six or eight feet stuck in the mast. Just about then the wind and the rain hit. After that we gave up and went to bed, the other watch could have some fun for a change, and welcome to it!

Rathlin Island, the marker for the last turn for home. The beginning of the northern passage. And the most impressive lighthouse I have ever seen. Early this morning when we gave up our watch she was flashing brilliantly in the distance. Now she is silent but no less impressive. Cottage white, perched almost at the top of the stone black cliffs which mark this side of the island. If you take the time to look at the chart, it tells you that the light can be seen from 26 miles away, and its elevation above the sea is 246 feet. That is the profile of an impressive lighthouse.

We were going fast, drawn into the channel between Ireland and Scotland by the tide, pushed along by the wind and surfing down great rollers coming in off the Atlantic. The children of yesterday's winds. 14.75 knots is a little more than 16 miles per hour, it does not sound like much. Try it in a boat, skidding down the front of a wave with no brakes, then tell me it's not fast. **Something is going to break . . . something is going to break . . . I can tell", the boat is starting to sound like a piano that has just been struck with a hammer.** I'm starting to vibrate; the helmsman looks like he needs medical attention in the form of a suppository! Instead of slowing down like the last time this happened the next wave pushes us on even faster, the piano gets another belt, and I swear it's all over. If we bury our bow in that wave (the one we are catching up on at 14.75 knots) we are going to cartwheel.

The first three or four feet of the bow drive into the wave in front, Jason puts the helm over and she starts to tear her way free, I relax my grip on the hand rail and let go of the lung-full of air I have been recycling since the piano started up, maybe next time. Ken leans over me and looks at Jason, "that sail up there in the bow, it's starting to pull us down; someone is going to have to go up there and get it back".

"The sea is my friend, she will not hurt me" . . .

## Day Five

From here, on an ordinary Tuesday or Thursday evening, or a Saturday afternoon for that matter, in less than one hour I would be in the clubhouse stalking my first pint!

Unfortunately for me this is not an ordinary Thursday evening, it's very early in the morning and we are not going to be anywhere for at least four or five hours. What seems like an eternity later we are fifty metres off Greystones beach not even half way to Wicklow and the finish and I swear I can see my mother's house. I could jump ship, swim, and ten minutes after hitting the beach I could be sitting in front of her fire drinking a hot cup of tea. Imagine a hot cup of tea! I just don't seem to have the energy.

Standing in the clubhouse, admitted by a hot shower, a shave and holding my first pint I looked at the others who had managed to get through the cleansing process and be re-accepted into society. It was a strange feeling looking around at those who had gathered at the finishing line. Or as close to the finishing line as the bar in the clubhouse would permit! A bitter sweet mix of contempt, despair, respect and grim satisfaction.

Despair for those who had failed. Respect for all that had tried. And behind the mask of despair, barely concealed satisfaction. It was like having a death in the family, everybody looked deep into your eyes to see if they could see it, no one dared broach the subject in case you were one of those that had failed. Contempt that was reserved for those prancing around in uniforms the rightful owners of which were still at sea. Still watching in the wet night. Still pushing their way through the seven hundred and five miles home. I felt contempt for those who would stand in the heat and light generated to show the way home, and to warm those who were still watching in the cold, the wet and the night.

I made a vow while surveying the society created by the groupies, hangers-on and spectators who must have been frightened off the pier by the sound of the starting gun five days ago, to take cover in the clubhouse. I vowed that the next time someone asks me, "How are your fixed for the Round Ireland?" I will say, "I'm, not!" No small vow taken in the presence of one of the greater Irish institutions, a virgin, pristine, pint of Guinness, and my first since the start of the race five days ago.

Of course it's a lie. Nine months later the days will be getting longer, and while we have been trapped by winter in our cars and heated homes the bug will be incubating silently, deadly! In another twelve months, at the end of another winter, someone will say, "How are you fixed for the Round Ireland?"

The answer will be, "Are you joking, when do we start?"

Medicine may have Penicillin but it doesn't have a cure for a bug the like of the Round Ireland. And while I'm on the subject the cure for sea sickness is equally lacking. Given a choice, I would prefer it if they worked on the latter, it would make the former at least, tolerable.

*(Whatever Jonathan was on, I want some of it. It should be standard issue to all competitors. (Ed.))*

*Piet Vroon of the Netherlands was back in 2008 with the impressive Formidable*

# Nissan 1
by Siobhan Crowley

*Nissan 1 Crew Members from left Marie Ormonde, Diane Hanrahan, Daire Conway, Tricia Breen, Margaret Lehane, Siobhan Crowley (skipper), Avril*

# LOG

Sat 18th June. Race started at 1400 on the nose. So is the wind at 25-30 knots. Tide is flooding and its a beat with full main and No.2 Sun 19th June Reached the Tuskar rock at 0100 with the wind SW. Beating comfortably with full main and No.3. Mayday call at 1725 so we alter course to respond. Arrive at scene to find other CDG yachts had responded. Delay 60 minutes plus.

Mon 20th June    Wind stays S/W - 20 knots and we are back on No.2 with full main. 0930 we are abeam of the Fastnet Rock. 1535 reach the Great Skellig - running big seas.

Tues 21 June. It's Midsummer's Day! 1550 and we are abeam Achill Island in beautiful sunshine. Wind is light, S-S/E and we are flying spinnaker and full main.

Wed 22 June.          Inishtrahull abeam at 1230. Big winds of 37-40 knots with gusts of 44. Two reefs in main and a No.3. Spinnaker halyard blown in increasing winds.

Thu 23 June.          1800 Lambay Island Ahoy! Beating into S-S/E wind of 15 knots with full main and No.1. 2245 - we are under Bray Head. Wind still S-S/E

Fri 24th June.        Crossed the line at 0145. Well done everyone.

Nissan 1 arrived in Wicklow harbour for final boat preparation and the safety check. The normally quiet and colourless harbour was bedecked with bunting and battle flags and the pre-race excitement was palpable. Met up with old friends from the ISORA series, competitors, Gwawr and Megalopolis and Tir na n-Og and Poolbeg Y.C.'s Decibel. Drinks were shared with crews of Rock Adventure, STY Tailte (the Navy boys!) and Black Tie.

The CDG pre-race party proved extremely enjoyable and the crew survived generous imbibing of their 'deoch' without too much suffering on the Saturday morning. Even those with obvious hangovers rose to greet 'race-day' in bright and breezy fashion.

Family and friends, from England and the four provinces of Ireland, turned up to see us off. Pre-race nerves showed as otherwise experienced sailors moved out too quickly from the trots along the harbour wall, creating chaos, with lots of quipping and the odd four letter word. Cheers erupted from spectators on the harbour wall as each set of groupies favoured their yacht with loud and voluble send-offs.

Out of the harbour and on to a choppy sea where the L.E. Aoife waited to start the race. All the pre-race training had honed the crew and each one took up her task to get the yacht under way and ready for the gun.

We were off! Off on our, previously only imagined, 704 mile circumnavigation of our homeland. The yacht responded well and gradually we overtook our friends on Constance and Decibel of Poolbeg Y.C. and the other all-girl crew on Tropicana. It wasn't the most pleasant of starts, beating into wind and tide, but the crew quickly settled down into a watch system and though conditions remained tough for the following 48 hours, the previous cold winter and spring training proved its worth.

The first MAYDAY was an unnerving experience, coming as it did so soon after the start and in the middle of Ireland's match with Italy! The Ballycotton MAYDAY, to which we responded, was very disturbing, particularly because of the anxiety expressed in the skipper's voice as he related the scene and his sinking boat. The Ballycotton lifeboat came to his rescue and we were very relieved that they did. We had changed course to assist and stood by on Channel 16 while searching for the vessel for over an hour.

The retirement of so many yachts, almost one third of the fleet, came as a shock, particularly that of the veteran Moonduster and the other all-girl crew on Tropicana so soon into the race. Nissan, Decibel and Angel formed one of two teams from the Poolbeg Y.C. and it was disappointing to learn that Angel, having taken water, had to retire off Cork.

Crew morale was supported by the excellent cuisine of Aidan McManus of the King Sitric Restaurant (definitely to be recommended) and a little 'light' relief was provided by flicking, now and again pausing to gaze, through the pages of an X-rated male magazine (kindly presented to us by the men on Megalopolis). A special heart warming flask is a necessary accompaniment on such a voyage and the fluid in ours popped the cork every time a wave hit the boat (a special prize from our friends in the 'Brass Monkey's series in Howth, who are familiar with its contents!)

Mid-Summer Day was very special - sunshine to top up our wind burn - warmth to dry out ourselves, sleeping bags and the boat and time to enjoy a meal of fresh salmon with dill and white wine sauce. We communicated daily on the 'chat line' with Rock Adventure and Black Tie when promises were made and plans laid for the post race celebrations in Wicklow which lived up to our expectations when realised. Those Donegal men did not disappoint us!

The reception we received in Wicklow when we crossed the finish line was spectacular and most welcome. What a homecoming! We celebrated 'til dawn when one crew member took a well deserved early morning swim!

Finishing Position:     26th. Overall
                        7th. IMS Class 4
                        1st. Ladies Trophy

Skipper: Siobhan Crowley
Crew:  Tricia Breen, Daire Conway, Karen Fitzsimons, Diane Hanrahan, Christine Jeffers, Linda O'Keefe, Marie Ormond, Frances O'Shaughnessy.

# Raasay of Melfort

Raasay of Melfort, the Rival 34 from Dunmore East has now competed in more Round Ireland races than any other, and all with the same skipper, Brian Coad from Inistioge, Co. Kilkenny. It was my first time taking part but I had sailed with Brian before and though I own a Dufour 34 I was slightly hesitant in entering on my own behalf. Consequently I was delighted to accept Brian's invitation and was really looking forward to the event.

The day of the start came and we were out there with the fifty three others. The starting gun went and we got a reasonable start with the front runners in clear wind. It didn't take long though before Raasay was back towards the end of the fleet because it was one of the slowest boats to start. However we were keeping some faster boats behind us so we were happy. The two Dufours, Alpara and Tailte, were very evident and we were crossing tacks with them. Owning a Dufour myself I was curious to see their progress.

Evening time came on the first day and I informed my skipper that I was definitely going off watch to listen to the Ireland v Italy match in the World Cup. It appeared that I was the only real football fan on the boat. The other four crew members were content to ask me from time to time how things were going and there was great cheer when Ireland went ahead and won. During the broadcast it was nice to hear the RTE commentator wish all the Round Ireland race entrants the best of luck and that there were many messages of goodwill received by the radio station to broadcast during the match commentary.

It was tough sailing that first night and we managed fine with a No. 3 jib and two slabs. The heavy weather meant that cooking was difficult and Bill Colfer (Le Chef supreme) did his usual heavy weather food preparation sitting on the cabin sole keeping the ingredients together between his legs. There was some mal de mer as well but thankfully it wasn't long before everyone had their sea legs. The bravest member of our crew was Steve Hulse who had come over from his farm in Norfolk to take part. Steve had never really sailed a lot before and he was handling it very well. He was never afraid to go forward and change down a sail when the weather deteriorated and he proved a quick learner. It was just as well because with only five aboard there could not be a passenger. We rounded Tuskar Rock at 06.00 and the Coningbeg Lightship at 09.00.

Day Two brought us into home waters and Waterford Harbour Sailing Club members wished us well as we passed. We hadn't realised the number of boats who had got into trouble during that first rather wild night because Raasay is built like the proverbial brick whatsit and we had none.

Still hard on the wind and in the region of Tramore Bay we were filmed extensively by a helicopter - God they play hell with the set of your sails. At 18.30 we were off Mine Head and under full canvas. At 03.00 on Night Two of the race we met a salmon net with a Winkie light off Ballycotton and we could smell a whale. We managed to jump the net even though we were only doing about 3 knots at the time. I don't think the fisherman was very impressed but he was more concerned with what the pilot whale was doing with his net and fish. Still hard on the wind in Day Three we plodded across the West Cork coastline and regularly crossed tacks with Alpara and Tailte. A Frenchman appeared from Kinsale at 12.00 and seemed to be enjoying a race with us until he went through the Gascanane Sound and we headed for the Fastnet Rock. It was just about then that we broke a jib halyard but we had another one already rove. That was our only gear failure of the entire trip. We rounded the Fastnet at 20.30 on Monday with the wind SW 6/7 occasionally 8 and much to the relief of all aboard we were able to ease the sheets and comfort came at last as the boat straightened up. Le Chef was then able to feed us without having to use the floorboards for chopping the veg.

On Night Three we rounded the Bull Rock near Dursey Island at 04.00 in a strong tide and very little wind. As I helmed past the rock the tide seemed to draw us towards it and it was much to my relief when I felt the tide lessen its grip as we drew north of it. The wind gradually became lighter until by 08.00 we were north of the Skelligs and becalmed. This was something of a relief after the heavy weather of the past few days and we set about drying and sorting out our gear. About mid afternoon the wind began to appear again and we rounded Inis Tireach at 18.00 on Day Four. The wind at this stage was about SW 2 and Alpara had just got ahead of us. The wind continued to build during night Four and by 02.00 we were off Slyne Head with a SW 7/8 and the going was very hard. Fortunately it was off the nose but the helm was very heavy. We reduced canvas to a No. 3 and two slabs and hung on. Malin Head was recording 50 knots of wind. During the gale Tailte went ahead.

On Day Five we rounded Eagle Island at 13.15 and reported in. The wind at this stage had reduced to a westerly 4/5 so we set the spinnaker and carried it into the night. We then heard a Gale Warning for our Sea Area but skipper Brian said we should disregard it because we had already had it. He was right.

Day Six saw us rounding Tory Island at 06.00 and level with Ulysses. The wind at this stage was westerly force 2. We noticed a little problem of low battery capacity and our GPS notified us that it might not be able to operate. We had been charging the battery daily but it now seemed to be less able to hold the charge so we decided that we had no option but to charge more often for a little longer. Fortunately the starter battery on the engine was separate. At 13.00 the wind came around on the nose to a SE 4/5 and we had a battle royal with Ulysses. It was very entertaining sailing and was spiced up by salmon drift nets in our way. The fishermen asked us not to tangle their nets and we told them that if we sail over them that nothing will happen. They didn't seem very keen on us doing that and I reminded the skipper that these pleasant Donegal men sometime carry cement blocks in their boats. We didn't have to test out their diplomacy.

We heard on the VHF that Alpara was 25 miles ahead, somebody else was 20 miles ahead and Tailte is 17 miles ahead. At 14.25 Inistraill Island was abeam and we reported to the Race Office. At 23.00 we were abeam of Rathlin Island and the wind was SE 5/6. It was an unpleasant night with heavy rain. The yacht Ulysses was still in sight. At 03.00 on Night Six we found that we were being carried up on the tide towards the Mull of Kintyre. The wind was SE 5 and we decided to tack back towards Rathlin Island. I found a large scale tidal chart for the North Channel and on it we found a reverse tide along the east coast of Rathlin so we were able to get into it and out of the strong northerly set from the North Channel. By 06.00 we were under Fair Head and going well out of the strong northerly flow. At 09.30 we were sailing south and the wind dropped to SE 1/2 but by 10.30 we were becalmed. The tide was due to set north again at 12.30 and we were hoping to drop anchor at the Maidens. Brian has never done that before but the anchorage was clearly marked in the centre of the rocks. We never got to try it out because by 13.00 we were being swept back to the north again. We spent all day just drifting on the tide with no wind. It was very frustrating to lose all that hard won ground, especially when there was no one else in sight. To make matters worse we listened to the Ireland Mexico match and Ireland was beaten 2-1. This was to be our worst day.

On Night Seven the tide and a little wind allow us to cross Belfast Lough but there was a thick fog about. The Coastguard reported about 150 yards visibility off Strangford Lough. We heard a distress call from a boat called "Hard Earned" who didn't know where they were. The Coastguard advised them to drop anchor as soon as they can find the bottom. They do this and the Donaghadee Lifeboat is sent to them. The boat is found north of Belfast Lough and guided into a safe berth. Then we heard Ulysses calling the Coastguard to report a near miss with a coaster at 02.00. They had to light a flare to wake the crew up apparently. We had no difficulty with the said coaster because by the time they had come north to us they were using their fog horn almost continuously.

We managed to find the bottom near Donaghadee at 04.00 and the Coastguard said that the fog would lift soon because a NW 3/4 was expected. The Donaghadee Lifeboat came over to us on their way back from rescuing "Hard Earned" and enquired whether we were all right. We explained that we were in the Round Ireland Race and had anchored to stop drifting. He advised us not to move until the fog lifted and we assured him that we had no intention of doing so because we had no radar. By 06.30 we were under way again in reasonable visibility and, by 08.00 the wind was NW 1/3. We set the spinnaker and the sun came out. We began to feel better about life - maybe that was because some of us got a reasonable sleep during the night. We met a naval patrol vessel who wanted to know our Port of Registry and destination. Another following yacht called "Raffles" was also called. They also gave the information and then informed the Navy that they intended to dip their ensign as they passed. The naval vessel replied that they would acknowledge. The tone of voice used when this message was transmitted gave us no doubt that this was a regular game and the Navy didn't like it. The Coastguard then joined in when they were called by the Navy. They asked to go to a working channel and the Navy was reluctant to do so but they did finally. All our business had been conducted on Channel 16 which I'm sure did not please the Coastguard but we had no choice in the matter. We met and spoke to boats who were going to a Galway Hooker weekend at Strangford Lough. They all invited us to join them but we explained that we had come too far and gone through too much hardship to stop now.

On Day Eight, 11.00 hrs. saw us rounding the South Rock Light Vessel in an NW 5. The spinnaker was drawing well, our course for Wicklow was 200 degrees magnetic and we had 98 miles to go. Unfortunately by 14.00 we were becalmed again so we caught up with some more sleep and watched the seabirds. We were just off Carlingford Lough and there was another competitor nearby, probably Tailte. Finally at 21.00 the wind picked up from the SW but it was very slight.

Night Eight saw us with a healthy SW 4/5. By 03.00 we are off the Bailey Lighthouse and the tide is running south. At 04.00 we were tacking out near the Kish and had to change down to a No. 2 and put in a slab because the wind was now S 5/6. We could see Tailte nearby and were determined to stay ahead of them. By 08.30 we were tacking down the Wicklow coast and keeping in as close as possible to dodge the northerly setting tide. The wind was still S 5/6. We were tacking in so close that we had to keep the echo sounder going. This was the first time that Raasay was been involved in such a close finish to a Round Ireland. We called the Race Office and at 11.00 we crossed the finish line to a gun and a sizeable crowd to welcome us back. With relief we dropped sail finally and tied up in the harbour. There were plenty competitors around and we spent a pleasant time swapping experiences with them. Then up for a pint of creamy nectar in the Club and a slap up lunch up town.

Raasay had done it again.

## Note:

Raasay of Melfort is a Rival 34 from Waterford Harbour Sailing Club in Dunmore East and was crewed by Brian Coad (Skipper), Bill Colfer, Ken Murphy, Steve Hulse and Nicky Walsh. Total distance logged for the race was **863.4 miles.**

### Raasay of Melfort

| Year | Elapsed Time Hour:Min:Sec | Corrected Time Hour:Min:Sec |
|------|---------------------------|-----------------------------|
| 1980 | 147:37:44 | 124:53:43 |
| 1982 | 217:53:18 | 191:44:30 |
| 1984 | 143:39:48 | 127:05:56 |
| 1990 | 175:24:59 | 155:25:08 |
| 1992 | 162:31:53 | 142:22:38 |
| 1994 | 189:05:52 | 165:04:56 |

*Brian Coad was amazed to learn he had won the 1980 race on handicap.*

## Sty Tailte

by Lt. Willie Roberts

The Naval Service normally provides a ship to act as the outer marker for the start line and a platform for the racing committee. This year the duty was performed by the L.E. Aoife, which left the area in quite a hurry immediately after the start . . . something to do with a soccer match - well, every man to his own sport. Yes, for those of you who haven't figured it out yet, the organisers planned the race to coincide exactly with Ireland's first game in the World Cup!

This was a piece of information that did nothing to inspire a prospective crew member to join up. However, after some hiccups the crew was got together. As very few of the team were shore-based training for the event consisted of sailing from the quayside in Wicklow to the start line, by any standards not to be recommended, however, having quickly mastered the art of shouting instructions such as 'slip the guy . . . yes, the red one' we proceeded with the race instructions which some understanding and anonymous individual mailed to me for my attention. . . It went as follows . . . Go to Wicklow, leave the quay on the 18th. June and go out to the grey ship. When you hear a bang, proceed and, keeping the land on the right, keep going until you arrive back where you started. . . p.s. Do not use the engine. Couldn't be simpler, you might imagine.

Well enthused by those few words we were on our way and straight into the first problem. The wind and tide were from the south. With a weather forecast for southerly gale conditions for the first 48 hours we had prepared Tailte for the worst. During this part of the race the Class 01 boats were devastated by gale conditions and eight of the big names were out of the race, including Moonduster which has a large proportion of its crew drawn from the Naval Service.

As we passed Cork early on the second morning the VHF was alive with traffic detailing the weather ahead and the damage it had inflicted on the bigger boats. I looked around Tailte and double-checked every fitting and shackle, including the exact location of the bolt cutters, which would be required in a hurry if we had a rigging failure, which could lead to losing the mast. This had already occurred to one of the competitors.

When I awoke it was midday, the sun was beautiful and Eddie Mulligan shouted down to me, "Caught the Alpara". Alpara is an identical yacht to Tailte, based at Kinsale Y.C. This was great news as the crew were less than happy with the previous night's decision to go offshore in long tacks while the opposition stayed inshore on shorter tacks. The rest of the afternoon saw Tailte, Alpara and Raasay duelling for position in moderate to light airs towards Cape Clear.

It was late evening, the visibility was closing in and the wind was freshening quickly from the SW as we left the shore to round Fastnet. In an hour the visibility was appalling and the wind was reaching gale force. These next few hours were to prove to be very testing conditions which would ultimately mould the crew into a cohesive team and prepare us to meet the challenge that the race presented. However, for the moment, hesitant feet groped forward to reef the mainsail while waves crashed over the decks. It was now dark and fog surrounded the yacht. The navigator was shouting course and distances to run to me from the plot in cables. Where was this rock? . . . Christ - the lights big enough! We did not want to join the rest of the yachts that had made this rock infamous.

Then the VHF was sounded, "Tailte sunray Aisling" with the usual pleasantries observed and, having satisfied himself that we were safe, Aisling proceeded to a safe anchorage. There were those onboard who were too keen to follow at that point but, with the reassurance that things would improve as we rounded and turned to run before the gale, we pushed on. Well, it was drier, but running before gales provides its own difficulties, not least of which is helming. It is tremendously reassuring for any yachtsman in a gale to know he has help near at hand should fate choose that moment to be unkind. Many thanks to the crew of the L.E. Aisling for providing a great confidence boost, just at the right time.

I read the log when I was called for my watch at midnight and one of the entries from the previous watch read, "Wet - Wet - Wet rollercoaster ride to Hell". The wind dropped as quickly as it had come up and there on the starboard bow 1/4 cable off was the Alpara - not a nav light to be seen. We challenged this dangerous activity on VHF 16 as we passed and for the first time in the race took the lead from Alpara. All in all not a bad watch.

By morning we were off Dingle, three yachts drifting in still conditions. Attempts to play the spinnaker ended in disaster with it torn and wine-glassed around the forestay. This was a costly mistake so early in the race and one we could have done without. Alpara, like many of the other yachts, was already thinking of retiring, having considered the long range forecast which offered little in the way of wind. Alpaca's skipper called me and proposed we retire to Dingle. With the next Ireland game in the group due you could have heard a pin drop onboard when I declined.

That afternoon we were still drifting - the fog cleared about 1500 and Tom Griffin the Mate was busy drying out the boat. Then dark clouds appeared to the SW and within 30 minutes we were sailing. By nightfall the crew were reefing and changing headsails with a confidence not previously enjoyed.

The next three watches were to be the highlight of the race. Tailte was surfing down huge seas in the height of a gale and she was loving it! We carried the number 2 headsail with 2 reefs in the main. Several times during the course of the watch Tailte was to experience the speed clock showing full scale deflection and never fall below 8 knots. The hull noise was almost deafening. The adrenaline was pumping as we fought to helm in these conditions. The exuberance of the moment was electrifying. As we were being hurtled by the gale up the west coast being chased by seas that I am glad I had my back to for most of the watch. As daylight came and the watch was handed over we were able to proudly write in the log 30 NM covered averaging 7.5 knots. By the end of the day the west coast had come and gone.

The one funny moment during this gale, if funny moments occur during gales, was while listening to Belmullet radio the following morning with Raasay close astern. Belmullet had just got through explaining how a gale was due any moment when the skipper of Raasay invited him to look out of his window and promptly informed him that the gale had arrived 10 hours earlier. Well done Raasay. We were soon reaching across Donegal Bay and gone were the thoughts of long hours beating down the east and south coasts against tide and wind. Now it was sunny and the wind was fresh and on the quarter. By the time we had reached Tory Island the wind was gone and with a gennaker set on the spinnaker pole we slowly picked our way past salmon net after salmon net during the night and day.

We fought against 5 knot tides to cross from Loch Foyle to Rathlin Island. Never before had I sailed a boat so hard for so long and get nowhere! I had never seen tides like these . . . and we had to arrive at the wrong time of day. When eventually the tide turned it was nearing darkness and with wind against tide the rounding of Rathlin battered Tailte hard as the yacht surged forward. The crew became painfully aware of the hurt being inflicted on the fibreglass hull as she slammed into every wave with unrelenting fury.

Then the coast of Scotland was ahead 3 NM and we tacked back across Red Bay in Northern Ireland as the wind was dropping quickly and the tide was due to turn shortly. As we slowly entered the bay we could just begin to make out shore installations and other boats but the depth was still over 60 metres - too deep to anchor. Then the impossible happened . . . the wind died and the yacht was swept back out to sea and back towards Rathlin. The temptation to motor those last few yards and anchor was enormous . . . but, after coming so far under sail, and as the crew were being so critical of the competition, whom they firmly believed to be motoring. . . I released the engine starter with a very itchy finger.

The next few days we drifted from Larne to Dundalk - back and forth at the whim of the tide - the frustration at being so close to the finish and yet so far was at times unbearable. A petition to go in and see the last game in Ireland's World Cup was proposed and rejected. Crew men who were due back on duty worried they would not be back in time to sail on patrol.

Link calls were made to reassure Naval Base and family that everything was OK. . . . and still we drifted. Belfast Coastguard, being aware of our location, even used us to update their weather forecasts!

Eventually we got underway as the wind came up from the south once more and we passed on down into Dublin Bay. It was still Saturday night.

An entire week had passed and we were still making our way around Ireland. It had now been three days since the first yacht crossed the finishing line.

Sunday morning and the finishing line was in sight. We had achieved our goal of completing the race under sail and had pushed the boat for all it was worth in doing so. A great sense of achievement was realised when we heard cheering crowds as we approached the finish line.

We went alongside quickly to receive recognition from the waiting crowds. We felt our legs buckle as they struggled to cope with a platform that was stationery. It was the first time that we Salty Sailors truly understood what was meant by sealegs. Unfortunately we quickly received the bad news that we were the last to finish as seventeen boats behind had retired. Well you can't win them all!

It should be pointed out that while we were having all this fun on the west coast news reached us that Virgin City Jet with Lt. Bob McCarthy onboard was taking line honours at Wicklow. Just goes to show what a few million pounds worth of boat and the latest in technology can do. This was the message that came to back to haunt me when Lorna Siggins, sailing correspondent with the 'Irish Times', reviewed our performance under the headline, "Naval Cinderella turns into pumpkin". Somewhat unkind Miss Siggans. However the point she made was correct. Tailte was described as a Model T Ford when it came to racing yachts and question why the Air Corps could be provided with a Sigma 38 for the race while naval yachtsmen must crew civilian yachts to compete at this level. The **Brime** it is hoped will give even more Naval Service personnel the chance to experience ocean passages under sail. Plans are already being hatched to ensure the Naval Service has at least one Sigma 38 available to it for the next race in '96.

Finally it would be to sell ourselves short not to congratulate Capt. Tom O'Connor and his crew on Air Corps 1 who, sailing a Sigma 38, were the winners of that class and put in a performance to be proud of. Well done.

# St. Christopher

by Sandy Mitchell

**W**ell before the crews taking part in this Summer's Cork Dry Gin Round Ireland race had cast off their mooring ropes in Wicklow harbour, the competition had become ruthless. The hard men of Virgin City Jet glare icily from behind mirrored sunglasses. The even harder men of Maxol Unleaded let rumour spread among the fleet of 54 yachts that, although they were prepared to fit a cooker and a lavatory especially for this race, they would never be such sissies as to attach a motor to their ultra-light craft. Some resorted to intimidating pennants: dragons snorting fire, a devil shaking his trident.

Built of wood, and a matronly 24 years older than the most modern of her fellow racers St. Christopher was by far the comeliest contestant. However, aboard we had not quite melded into that synchronised unit other crews had visibly become after months of pre-race training: we had never sailed together. One or two of us had barely been to sea. It seemed that most of our last-minute preparations involved double-checking the dosage on the back of jumbo-packs of seasickness pills. Yet we were embarking on a race rated Category Two by the Royal Ocean Racing Club, the same as the Fastnet.

It was thanks to George Fairhurst, owner/skipper of St. Christopher that we were there. Thanks also to two misapprehensions in my case. I misheard the invitation over the telephone, and was expecting to compete in the "round the island race", a quick spin about the Isle of Wight. "Actually, I said the Round Ireland Race," corrected the cheery voice of Christine Fairhurst, "It will take six days, at least." It was too late to pull out.

I was aboard the yacht, tacking frenetically up to the starting line of Wicklow before I understood the scale of the second error. "We will divide into three watches: red, blue and white. Night watches are three hours long, day watches four. When you are off watch, you sleep, cook and clean the heads," shouted the skipper. Only at that moment did I realise that we would be racing nonstop, and would be canned in this 50ft by 12ft 9in space until the ripple of Wicklow's green hills appeared over the bows.

The course, say the official rules, involves "leaving Ireland and all her islands to starboard". Simple, it sounds. Only, racing adds a fourth dimension to the tide, wind and rocks. My contribution to the subtleties of trimming sails, plotting course and calculating sea changes to the minute was limited to pulling on ropes as we beat into the Force 5 wind towards the outcrop of the Tuskar Rock, our south west turning point. Others were much more useful. One, a young professor of orthopaedics, quickly took up position at the navigation table, charts and dividers to hand. Also on board were several who owned their own yachts and some who were able to help in changing the monstrously heavy sails, understanding the yelled commands to swop the "blade" for the "number one" which meant nothing to me.

*Just in case the skipper had missed it, a crewman on St. Christopher points out the Fastnet Rock.*

To my astonishment, however, I soon began to swell with pride at winding my winch until shoulders nearly gave out and the foresail sheet had snapped tight. "Grind! Grind! Grind!" The skipper screamed each time. (One is left groping for a better word to describe this endlessly repeated routine.) That first night's watch was bleak, pitch black and freezing even when cocooned in full hooded oilskins, and thawed with occasional cups of tea. Early on, the radio interrupted the crash of waves: Coastguard, this is Jackabout. We have a Mayday situation. **Mayday, Mayday, Mayday.** *Our keel is wobbling from side to side. The water lapping in the cabin is not too bad at the moment, but you can hear the structure breaking. We have the crew on deck in life-jackets and life-raft ready."* We listened in silent sympathy as Jackabout's skipper tried to sail towards land, until one of our crew poked his head into the cockpit: "Skip," he said to George. "We are taking water ourselves. The port head is awash." Unruffled, the skipper left the helm and immediately fixed the faulty stopcock, instructing us to use the only other head - exposed to view, and more of a saucer than a throne. The last message we heard was from the lifeboat coxswain, in a creamy Cork accent, to his controller on the way back to harbour. . . Jackabout was saved, we assumed

Day two: the wind is still on our nose and the sky spitting cold rain. The boat is canted permanently at a 30 deg-45 deg angle; only the side to which she leans is varied. Down below there is a shriek from the head. Jo our only female crew member, yet another medic, has discovered when taking down her oilskin trousers that her legs are covered in dark blotches. Too soon for scurvy. The diagnosis is chronic bruising from being thrown across the cabin each time the boat lurches.

At the end of the day, the professor is hunched alone over his table, which he seems not to left since we left harbour. A man of quiet and incisive thought, he confesses: "I have my own boat, and I sail a lot, but I have never, until now, asked myself why." Despite her exotic new skin colouring, Jo is still managing to laugh. "I see this as a marathon. I'm not doing it to win. I'm doing it to survive." George is alert to his crews mood, and encourages us with the thought that once we pass the Fastnet rock we will be on a reach, and the boat steady on its course. "These races come down to tenacity in large part," he admits to me. "Especially once you are on the west coast. When you turn the corner, it is like walking into a dark room. You hear and see nothing. No boats, no lights, no radio talk."

We had a day becalmed - midsummer itself - where there was nothing to do but lie on deck and drink the race-sponsor's tipple with a dash of bitters. That night caught us off Galway. Gales had been forecast for several days, and they finally hit us, building to Force 9, gusting almost 50 knots, accompanied by waves rising above 30ft, their tops smoking with spray. "If we hit a gale, we'll give it a go," the skipper had promised earlier. We surely did. Just before the wind rose, St. Christopher was sluicing elegantly along under full foresail and mainsail. It was decided to add a thin spinnaker, the "chicken chute", to eke every last ounce of force from the wind.

At first, all went smoothly; except for those of us below trying to cook tuna stew for a dozen crew on a bucking stove. (Seasickness was a long forgotten luxury.) After dinner, the off-watch tied themselves into their bunks with canvas sheeting and waited, unable to sleep for the banshee storm. From below, we could hear the voice of the helmsman bellowing out the boat's sped: "Fourteen knots . . . Fifteen knots! . . . Sixteen!" The wind had become too strong to pull down the chicken chute. Suddenly, with a clap like thunder, it shredded; the boat began to slow. And all I could care about was the delicate embrace of sleep.

The skipper shook me awake at 0430 for the dawn watch. The waves were more massive, but the wind had eased a little, and when the boat rose to a crest, it surfed smoothly to the trough. "I'm going below for some rest. Take over at the helm, will you? All you need do is turn the bows down the wave if one looks like swamping you. Otherwise we will broach." Now George knew I had never steered a yacht, and certainly never in the tail-end of a gale in monstrous swell. For my part, I knew he was inviting me to test my own limits, at some risk to his own splendid craft. I took his challenge, and for half an hour, as the sun rose over the sea, I was alone on deck, frequently terrified, more often thrilled. It felt like soaring on wings.

Meanwhile, other boats were faring less happily than St. Christopher. We passed one with barely a sail on the mast and with all her crew on deck in survival suits. Several yachts were pooped numerous times, their cockpits filling with green ocean.

On past Achill Island, Rathlin, Antrim in the dark, leaving grey Belfast behind, and down finally to Dublin's lights, where the wind ran out with only an hour or two's daylight left, given a decent breeze to Wicklow. The tide was for us though, and by two in the morning we could see the final headland. Several hours later, we were 75 yd. from waves breaking on the shore, George having to rely solely on the ebb, as we were sucked towards the narrow finish line, unable to steer for lack of wind. We were placed halfway up the field, a good third of the starters having failed to complete the course. The snug of the tiny WSC had stayed open all night waiting for us, and before we left it at least two crew members had booked their berths for the next race, another pair had fallen fast asleep on their bar stools. Sometime during that morning I wandered off down the quay, back to my bunk, my legs unsure whether they were on land or at sea. Mostly though, I think I was walking on air.

# TIR na nOg

## by Fiac O'Brolchain

Tir na nOg is a Sadler 32 belonging to the Irish Ministry for Defence and which is leased to the **Asgard Support Group** for IR1 a year.

Tir na nOg is used as a sail training vessel whose purpose is to enable and encourage people to gain their Yachtmaster Certificate. So the reason for entering the 'Round Ireland' was twofold, first to get the vessel up to R.O.R.C. standard and secondly to give the experience of offshore racing to four people who would be unlikely to be offered a berth on the race. The crew were a mixed bag of four men and two women with an age group of 18 to 60+ and a variety of experience ranging down to very little in racing terms.

In retrospect what stopped us from completing the race was the time taken in getting the vessel up to standard. This meant that not enough time was spent in exposing the crew to the sort of conditions that we met on the race. Four weekends spending at least 24 hours beating to windward would have got the crew the vessel deserved. In fact the first time the full crew were on the vessel at the same time was 1100 on the morning of the start of the race!

Our last minute Channel Number put us as one of the slowest vessels taking part; we were sandwiched between Sean Whiston's two vessels, Tjaldur and Angel. This was a greater handicap to an inexperienced crew than I had imagined. They had been told that they would see very little of the other participants after a few hours, which is true in any vessel, but it was hard to convince them that we were not hopelessly behind. Physically the vessel was well prepared, all our food was vac-packed (courtesy of Franco's Restaurant in Enniskillen), we got extra stores from Siobhan and the gang from **Nissan**, even a last minute repair was carried out by one of the crew of **Taillte**. As we were not too worried about weight we did not stint ourselves and even carried a crate of beer. Our start was within a few seconds of **Moonduster**, good enough, and the long beat down the Irish Sea began. **This was a beating session which was to last for 68 hours** - which was what eventually wore us down. Combined with this was the fact that two crewmen were very seasick. The first time we considered retiring was after only 30 hours, when we were of Dunmore East, as one of the crew was in danger of becoming dehydrated. A watch in the bunk cured him but the other victim was very slow to recover.

On Tuesday morning we were 12 miles east of the Fastnet, there had been a weather forecast that said that there would be plenty of wind on the nose till we got round the rock and that then the wind would continue to be on the nose becoming a northwester. We had had enough of beating, we could, with our last energy get around the Fastnet but the thought of not freeing-off at that stage did us in. We set a course for Kinsale and radioed in that we were retiring, the second-last of the drop-outs. The rest of the week was wonderful. We romped into Kinsale running before a 25 knot wind. Then sailed back to Ringsend via Helvick, Kilmore Quay, Arklow and Wicklow.

We had entered under the burgee of the Poolbeg Yacht Club who had a fine variety of mixed fortunes. Their best result was from Jim Ryan and **Joliba** and this was made into an excuse for a fine party. Thanks are due to the Club for all their help.

Fiacc OBrolchain
Seamus Kerrigan
Breda Murphy
Jonathan McGuinness
Michelle Sweeney
Paul Ryan

*Dive! Dive! Dive! Calyx Voice & Data (Eamonn Crosbie) finds a deep hole at the start of the 2004 race. One of the smallest boats in the race and a new design she went on to win the race on handicap.*

# Tropicana

by Jill Sommerville

## THE SPONSOR

The project began with chit chat during the '92 sailing season. The success of previous women's crews in the Round Ireland race and the push for further achievements made the possibility of putting a crew together an exciting and challenging prospect. The search for a sponsor started in early September '93 and continued until January '94. During that time Jill and a core part of the team put endless hours of work into drawing up a professional sponsorship proposal that would attract the right type of sponsor; mailing and following up leads; and meeting with interested parties. The group went through the process of having deals

*Tropicana. It all started out so well.*

almost at a conclusion only to uncover a problem and have the whole thing brought to a standstill again. Finally in December '93 they met the perfect match in a company called New Age Beverages which was distributing and promoting "Tropicana Pure Premium" orange juice which they had recently introduced to the Irish market.

"Tropicana" had not yet been involved in any large above the line advertising spend and was already 50% above targeted profit in its first year. The opportunity to get involved with a sport like sailing was the perfect vehicle to promote a high quality, totally natural orange juice to a target market of active, health and environmentally conscious people. The fact that the crew were all women was an added advantage in that the numbers of women actively involved in sport at a high level is growing rapidly in Ireland and this group would therefore have a keen interest in the project, and it is also women who hold approximately 80% of domestic purchasing power in the country. The match was perfect.

*Tropicana 1994 Two of the crew struggle to secure a reef in atrocious conditions*

## PREPARATION

Once finance had been secured the project could go ahead and look for a suitable boat to compete in and select a crew. Initially the choice of boat was whittled down to either a Sigma 400 or an IMX 38. The Sigma 400 was a relatively new design which had proved itself in the '92 Race in the form of "Keep on Smiling" from Pwellhi. It was hoped to have four or five competing in the '94 Race. The IMX 38 was a new design and was proving very fast and exciting to sail, it was also hoped that there would be a similar number racing. It turned out to be impossible to find a Sigma 400 which would be available for the race while after many trips to the UK to visit various brokers and boatyards the charter of an IMX 38 was finally secured at the end of March.

Crew trials started in Howth over the second weekend in April. In all over 30 women trialed out and a core crew had been selected by mid May.

The sailors were chosen for their extensive sailing experience and the individual expertise each one could bring to the project. The final selection formed a formidable crew many of whom had represented Ireland in International sailing events many times and who between them had logged thousands and thousands of miles offshore. By the end of April the media campaign had also started to role with photo shoots and interviews with the daily and Sunday newspapers and a number of magazines. The crew were now on the water two to three times a week and were also involved in professional coaching sessions. For the initial trials and training the crew used a number of different boats including a Tripp 40, J 39 and Sigma 38 which were all kindly lent to the project by their owners. This was but one example of the huge support the project received from all corners throughout.

The official launch of the project came in the form of a Press Reception held in Howth Yacht Club at 12pm on May 8th. The reception was a huge success and resulted in write ups in The Irish Independent, The Irish Press, The Evening Herald, The Evening Press, The Star, The Sunday Tribune and the Sunday Independent. Both "Tropicana" and the crew were delighted with the response and gratified with the positive results from a lot of hard work. Articles in "Afloat", the 'RTE Guide', "Woman" and "Checkout" magazine were to follow as were subsequent articles in the daily and evening newspapers.

## JUNE '94

The boat charter began on June 1st so at 12pm that day the crew assembled on the quay at Weymouth where the boat was lying. All the race crew were there bar the owner's representative whose place for the delivery trip was being filled by a gentleman called Maurice Wilkinson. Maurice was most helpful in showing us where everything was stowed and explaining the specific quirks which every boat has. (When a crew description was given during a TR with Weymouth Coastguard on departure the coastguard's reaction was "Hmm, lucky fellow". I suppose we'd have to ask Maurice how he felt about that). The boat was well equipped with Autohelm mast and hull instruments, a Philips Decca, Streamline GPS and Yeoman Chart Plotter. There would be no slacking on the helm or trim without it being instantly noticed!

The delivery trip was characterised by a foggy flat calm passage as far as The Lizard, a super midday kite run round Land's End and then a gale of up to 55 knots from the South for 13 hours as far as Milford Haven. After a stop over there we had a very enjoyable sail to Dun Laoghaire and tied up to the Royal Irish Yacht Club pontoon at 9pm on the 5th. With the boat in home waters the training became more intense during the weeks before the race. Each crew member had a number of jobs besides their slot on deck in order to cover everything needed to prepare a boat well for a RORC race. We competed in the Howth Regatta the weekend before the race and in a long windless sail around the Kish won our class beating hot favourite "Camp Freddie", the Rocket 31 renamed "Maxol" for the Round Ireland. During training the deck fittings and spars were thoroughly checked. There was now one other IMX 38 definitely entered in the race, Richard Burrow's "Prospector". Her set up was different in that she had fitted a babystay to lend extra support to the top of the mast. After consultation with the owner of the IMX we had chartered, he decided not to fit a babystay to his boat as it involved some major work and was not necessary for his use of the boat in the Solent. Other than this the boats were almost identical and the crews were looking forward to some close boat to boat racing.

On Thursday the 16th "Tropicana" was delivered to Wicklow looking splendidly white having been 'wallpapered' with the Tropicana logo (It had taken over a day to cover the blue hull with white PVC stickers and put the sponsor's name on top). The official safety check was passed with a compliment from the officer about the orderliness of the equipment on board, which was nice feedback at the start of a five day race. On Friday all the crew assembled and the boat was provisioned. Pre cooked dinners for twelve people for four days takes plenty of stowing. Our sponsors kindly supplied us with Aquaporte bottled water which also had to be stowed carefully. The sails were flaked and left ready and by then it was time to watch one of our interviews on RTE Television and for the Cork Dry Gin party. After a few hours good crack the crew were tucked up in their B&B to get a good night's sleep before the big day.

## THE RACE

Saturday dawned calm humid and a bit grey. However the forecast was for fresh southerly winds strengthening to gale force and going west as the fleet was expected to round the corner and head off along the south coast. Nobody was under any illusions about the weather; it was likely that we would be beating at least as far as Cork. The crowd on the pier continued to grow as the boats filed out of the harbour. Someone on the pier was heard to say that the best bit of the Round Ireland was watching the start from the top of Wicklow Head - I expect he secretly wished he was heading off himself. The best bit of the Round Ireland Race would be hard to pinpoint but those on "Tropicana" who had done the race before were dying to start this one. Offshore sailing is a strange animal; a superior breed.

The gun went at 1430h and about half the fleet squeezed a tight spinnaker reach around the Head. "Camp Freddie" showed some early flair and gave "Virgin Atlantic", 40 feet longer than her, a run for her money. Once around the head the long beat began, in close along the shore. Some diehard supporters left Wicklow in their cars and followed the race along the coast as far as Curacloe Strand. After several headsail changes "Tropicana" found her groove and continued to build good boat speed and establish a healthy place in the fleet "Virgin" was out ahead as expected and the Sigmas were enjoying close racing behind.

By 1800h the weather had closed in with the wind as forecast at about 25 knots true and still on the nose. The dinner was on and the crew were well established on the rail - home for the next few days. At about that time we heard that "Camp Freddie" [Maxol Unleaded] had broken her forestay and had to retire. Also by this time we had established that the boat was very wet to windward and there was a fundamental design fault with the water gushing down the closed hatch with every big wave crossing the deck. Everyone was wet and enjoying the comfort of their thermals. Dinner was a delicious tuna and pasta bake and went down a treat. The antics getting it in and out of the oven were a sight to behold as we beat our merry way down the coast. Food is foremost on the rail in the cold and wet. At this stage it was probably drier on deck than below what with wet sails and the continuous waterfall down the hatch.

By 2200h the sea had become quite confused off the south east coast and "Jackabout" the J 120 from the UK had issued a Mayday. Her keel bolts were loosening and she was taking on a lot of water. The crew were just able to contain the flow with the bilge pump and buckets but they had their life raft and flares etc on deck ready in case they were needed. They liaised with Rosslare lifeboat and accompanied by "Aqualina" the Sigma 400 from Arklow managed to return safely to Arklow. Also by that time Emircedes had retired with rigging problems. At 2330h we were passing Tuskar and still heading south. The seas were more confused and had taken their toll on "Hesperia IV" who had lost her mast. She also headed back to Arklow. As the first watch were sleeping we began to notice problems with our own rig. The mast was inverting badly as we came off each big wave.

The boat was sailing fast and steady and was not over canvassed. With all the halyards including the topping lift leading from the top of the mast they were useless in trying to reinforce it. We could lead a rope from just above the top spreaders to a fitting forward on the deck, but there were no fittings on the foredeck at all, not even a bow roller. There was no way to stop the mast flexing in the conditions we were experiencing. The mast set up was sufficient for the Solent but not for racing off the south west coast of Ireland. The boat was perfect but for the unforeseen and without the knowledge of hindsight it would have been impossible to foresee the likelihood of such a problem. At the risk of losing the rig and with the forecast set to remain the same for the next twelve hours at least, after much discussion we decided to retire into Dunmore East. With heavy hearts that the race had ended so prematurely, but sure in the knowledge that we had acted in the safest and most responsible manner, we had a very quiet breakfast at 7.30 am on Sunday the 19th in Dunmore East.

## THE WRAP UP

We arranged a Minibus to ferry ourselves and our gear back up to Wicklow, settled the boat at the quay and headed up to the race office to officially retire. Everyone had put so much into the project that we felt cheated at the thought of a nice cosy bed for the night. Over the next few days we travelled up and down to Dunmore East taking the logo of the hull and generally getting the boat ready to hand her over to the delivery crew who were to take her back to the UK at the end of the week. They had decided to risk sailing her back as the forecast was favourable and would mean she could reach quietly home to have the mast repaired. On our travels up and down we kept a close eye on the race dropping in to Wicklow at least once a day. We were there on the Wednesday night to cheer a lot of the boats across the line and congratulate the winners. That's where the chit chat about the '96 race started. Once the Offshore bug has bitten there's little chance of recovery and many if not all the crew of "Tropicana" will be back for more in June '96.

*Alburn (Robbie Milhench and Kenny McCullough) It was good to have an entry from Ballyholme Yacht Club. The first round Ireland race was organised by this club in 1975 although it was not a non-stop race.*

# Ulysess

by Frank Maher

*Ulysses. Enjoying a rare moment of relaxation. (Clockwise) Josephine Browne, Peter Hoare, Willie Fearon, Greg Potterton and Frank Maher*

The idea resulted from 1992 when Pat McArdle went on a spectator boat to the start of the Round Ireland Race. He was busy at this stage extending his experience in off shore sailing and felt that there were enough salt water sailors in the Mullingar club and area to make participation in the next race possible. In November '93 he decided to air the idea and press-gang a crew. He even used the month to his advantage insisting that commitment given while "on the dry" could not be broken.

He was lucky to have club member Peter Hoare, the owner of three conventional yachts and one folk boat, as a near neighbour. Willie Fearon - a member of Wicklow S.C. for many years - and now Mullingar based, was recruited as were Frank Maher, Edmund O'Donnell, Dave Hogan and Greg Potterton all from Mullingar. The final crew member Josephine Browne from Donegal joined later. Poolbeg Y.A.B.C. members are advised that if given enough provisions (and provocation) she can cook.

Despite W Nixon's comments our qualifying race was not held on the Royal Canal. From March onwards the crew availed of every opportunity to sail. In May/June we sailed the ISORA races from Holyhead to Wicklow and from Dun Laoghaire to Phwelli.

On the Wednesday before the race Peter and Frank sailed Ulysess to Wicklow for safety checks - and socialising. The weather was fine and the craic was good. When the safety checks were complete the facilities and entertainment provided by Wicklow S.C. were much appreciated.

Before the start line we again declined offers to disembark Josephine to a Poolbeg boat - who offered to swap her for someone who could cook. Listening to the RT did not give any reassurance on our trip down the coast. Calls for assistance from Jackabout and other traffic helped our concentration on the long beat to the Fastnet which we reached on Monday evening. Our seasick crewman at this stage began to take an interest in life again and even to enjoy himself. Listening in to the RT calls to other boats we heard of gas explosions, broken dusters? And shelter in Cape Clear. Raasay and Brian Coad were again beside us in the wet and heavy conditions.

The next day brought a complete change. Calm and bright sun, a chance to dry out all the gear. Then the wind arrived getting to force 7 during the evening and night. High seas, wind, bright moonlight, lightning, caused Greg Potterton to exclaim "great bloody special effects". It was almost too much for lake sailors. The Atlantic gave us our most enjoyable sailing taking us from Mizen Head to Malin in two days. It also gave us our only injury when Willie was thrown heavily against the chart table as Ulysess plunged down a high wave. The ship's doctor must have done a good job of treating himself because on shore X-rays revealed a broken scapula.

It took three hours to round Malin Head against the tide. Rathlin at midnight and again missed the tide - cruising in the lee to 04.00 - then good progress to the Maidens in six hours and then becalmed to 15.00 Friday. It has to be said that the conditions did not have a calming effect on our skipper. Nautical commands like "Get out of my sight" "Throw it over the side - NOW!" were sometimes heard. He also developed an aversion to lentil soup.

Another tide gate was missed and we were becalmed in fog off Belfast Lough. The night watch equipped with flares had a busy time and one very close encounter. We were glad to depart under spinnaker and made good progress to Dundalk Bay where we again became becalmed. This stop- go progress continued for the day. Visions of reaching the bar in Wicklow before closing time faded. After nightfall the wind finally increased and we reached the finish line at 04.30 on Sunday.

The crew wish to thank Wicklow S.C. and the committee for their support, hospitality and great good humour. We enjoyed the race and hope to be back. Pat is looking for a major sponsor and at least a Sigma 38 for '96 - we need a longer boat to escape from Brian Coad.

Crew:
Pat. McArdle, Edmund O'Donnell, Josephine Browne, Willie Fearon, Dave Hogan, Frank Maher, Greg Potterton, Peter Hoare.

# VSOP

For the crew of VSOP the months of preparation were now over and the real thing was about to start. Everyone was in good shape on Saturday morning and feeling well, mainly because skipper John Godkin had steered us away from the Gin Traps of Wicklow the night before and seen to it that we had a reasonably early night and a comfortable bed. The hours before the start seemed endless, with just a few jobs to do and several hours in which to do them. The boat had been sailed from Kinsale a few days earlier, by Bill Sheane, who was returning to his native Wicklow. He had been accompanied by crew members Mel O'Donovan and John O'Connell, plus a few first class passengers who enjoyed the sunshine, the food and the wine. John stayed with the boat and sampled Wicklow's hospitality as well as seeing the boat through the safety scrutiny.

Now at last we were waiting for the 10-minute gun and checking the wind, getting transits for the starting line etc. . . . .Soon the minutes had ticked away and the starting gun sounded. We had chosen to start approximately half way along the line afraid that the land would interfere with the wind near the shore. This was mistake number one, as the boats nearer the pier head proved.

The skipper said we would have no trouble carrying the spinnaker and just after the start the reacher was hoisted. Mistake number two! What a twist! In four years of racing on VSOP no one could remember anything like it. Our moment of glory was soon turning to embarrassment and frustration as the foredeck crew attempted to break out the 'hourglass'. When it did open it wasn't helping us so it was soon dropped and the No.2 genoa re-hoisted.

After Wicklow Head we settled down to a good windward contest with several other boats, crossing ahead on starboard and dipping sterns on port tack. Our own Club mates 'Mad Bull' and 'Imp' were giving us a hard time. We give them both time on handicap and although we led them pass Brittas Bay they had gained the advantage by Arklow and both were ahead of us. A change to the No.3 genoa in these heavy conditions made sure that on the foredeck Jimmy Murphy and Ralph Godkin didn't stay dry for long. The choppy sea had meant a very wet boat and we seemed to be up to our knees in water down below decks as well. It was discovered that we were taking water through the galley sink when on port tack and through a hand basin in the heads when on starboard. The appropriate seacock's were quickly turned off, but still we couldn't get rid of the water until we found that the bilge pump hose had been removed from the bilge sump and all that was happening was that we were sucking air through the pump. Hour after hour of tacking is hard work for trimmers like Martin Gowran and John O'Connell but their fitness was evident by the end of the day when they collapsed into their bunks exhausted!

Thinking the tide had turned we left the shore and ventured out to sea before our rivals. Mistake No.3! This lost us considerable ground to 'Mad Bull' and by now 'Imp' was really going higher and faster into the failing light. The radio informed us of difficulties experience by other yachts and we were very sorry to see 'Moonduster' limping along having lost her forestay and almost her mast.

Our first hot meal nearly turned into a disaster. Much discussion during the week before the race had focused in whether we should bring a supply of spuds for our daily hot meal. The skipper was in favour of bringing pasta or rice which is light to carry and high in energy. A compromise was reached - spuds for 2 days, pasta or rice from there on. Tonight was chicken casserole and spuds! John Penwell put aside his navigator's cap and began his other duties as Chef. He lit the oven and in went the casserole to heat. However as the boat pitched in the choppy sea, the contents of the dish spilled over the gas burners at the back of the oven and completely blocked all the jets. From then on all casseroles became stews being dumped into a saucepan and heated on the top burners. Despite the spillage there was plenty of food to go around as several appetites were somewhat dampened by the heavy conditions.

That night was very dark as we beat down the coast passing Tuskar about midnight and on towards Conningbeg. Very few boats were seen and by daybreak we had no idea where the opposition was. We could just make out a yacht about a mile or two ahead of us in the mist. It wasn't until we reached Youghal that we recognised her as 'Mad Bull' - but where was 'Imp'? With the wind still on the nose we tacked along the coast past Cork and down to our home waters off Kinsale. By now there were only a couple of boat lengths between us and we could see another yacht a few miles ahead. Dinner of baked ham and spuds with butter was devoured eagerly.

The wind moderated and we were using our No.1 genoa. Through the night and down the familiar coast towards the Fastnet. Some good navigating by John Penwell who is more used to the comfort of the cockpit of a Boeing 747, found us rounding the rock at 4 a.m., just ahead of 'Mad Bull', and there was 'Imp' ahead by approximately a mile. Visibility was poor as we eased sheets for the first time since leaving Wicklow and then headed up the west coast. A fast two sail reach past Mizen Head and up to the Bull Rock. 'Imp', who was still ahead, hoisted her kite and seemed to be carrying it without difficulty. We tried a small heavy weather reacher but found it difficult to maintain our course and experienced a few exciting broaches. Suddenly, out of the mist, loomed 'Skellig Michael', 'Imp' was very low on her course and had to harden up considerably and lost a lot of ground to us. The seas were very broken with big rollers and square cross-seas on top. We decided that in these conditions it was not suitable for a spinnaker so we boomed out our No.2 to port and set off in pursuit of 'Imp' who was a couple of hundred yards ahead carrying the same rig. 'Mad Bull' however hoisted her mini-tri and to our surprise never appeared to be in any difficulty.

An hour or so later they were abeam of us with the crew smiling from ear to ear as they passed to leeward, surging down the waves at a reported 17 knots. Our battle was now to stay in touch and wait for more favourable conditions, but more problems now arose. Something was coming loose in the steering. The constant correcting of course in the heavy seas was causing a problem. The steering system has a bronze quadrant at the top of the pedestal which is turned on a cog from the shaft of the steering wheel. The Quadrant had worked loose from the bolts which are holding it in place. This was a job for Billy Long, better known as 'Billy Fix-it'. Out came the tools; off came the compass and the top of the steering housing. The loose bolts were clearly visible but as the quadrant turned with each change of direction, the bolts were covered and exposed in rapid succession. By steering closer to the wind the effect was to create more pressure on the helm which meant that one bolt was exposed for a few seconds longer. In these few seconds Billy got the spanner on to the bolt, turned it a fraction and removed the spanner before the quadrant swung back and jammed everything. Perhaps twenty times this exercise was done, demanding coordination between helmsman and spanner-man. Now one bolt was tight. To do the same on the other bolt meant we would have to jibe and create the windward pressure on the other side. So, to 'Imp's' amazement, and for no obvious reason, we jibed off on to starboard. Another twenty times the spanner darted in and out of the quadrant until the steering gear was secure. Every boat should have a 'Billy Fix-it'!

By now we were looking at 'Mad Bull' approximately five miles ahead of us and not feeling too comfortable about our position, but the gods smiled on us and as the wind moderated we hoisted the kite and later, when it veered further west, we were in the right place to benefit. Beef Casserole/ Stew with rice was a great reward for a difficult day.

That night we sailed under spinnaker in light to moderate conditions. We had managed to get ahead of 'Imp' and later when 'Mad Bull' blew out their light spinnaker we took over the lead in our private race. By 0100 Thursday morning we were rounding Eagle Island and later that day we saw the sun shining on the Donegal coast as we sailed past under spinnaker, peeling from the reacher to the runner off Tory Island. 'Imp' who had not been seen all day now appeared over the horizon to join us approximately a mile behind - much too close!

Not to our surprise we encountered nets in this area. While talking to a fishing boat about the position of his nets we sailed straight over another net which didn't seem to have anyone with it. However we managed to avoid two other nets off Lough Swilly. As darkness descended we gybed off Malin Head and headed for Rathlin Island. It was an exciting shy spinnaker reach with several broaches to keep the adrenaline running. Later, as the wind freshened and the possibility of running into Scotland seemed to loom large, the spinnaker was replaced by the No.2. It was now 0200 Wednesday morning and we had first hoisted the kite at 2200 on Monday - 28 hours earlier! Constant trimming by Mel and Martin had paid great dividends as we had now opened a gap on our two rivals. Then round Rathlin Island, the place we had often dreaded because of those foul tides which can hold you back for hours. But not this time. We were doing approximately 13 knots over the ground, with the favourable tide pushing us towards the Maidens, which we passed at about 0800. The south west wind was still very fresh and we were having trouble holding the No.2 genoa in the squalls.

A change to the No.3 and we were going faster and more comfortable too. We had 'Imp' in sight all along the Antrim coast and we should have been 40 minutes ahead to be holding our time. Our rough timing put her about 30 minutes behind which meant she was beating us and seemed to be doing well. We still had a job to do and every ounce of speed was needed. A powerful sail down passed Mew Island and on towards South Rock. We seemed to be doing well and looking back had made a substantial gain on 'Imp'. At the time we didn't know that a navigational error at the Maidens had cost them dearly. She was now in a boat for boat race with 'Mad Bull'. We rounded South Rock just after noon in sunshine and at last could set a course for Wicklow still 90 miles away.

It was difficult to settle down to windward sailing having been off the wind for so long, but as the wind eased we had a wonderful sail down towards Howth. Our last hot meal was served off Skerries and everyone's appetite was back to full strength to make quick work of the Irish stew and rice. Off Howth at around 2130 that evening the wind moderated further and the reaching spinnaker was flown. The navigator looking knowledgeably at the sky commented that the wind might die away later but hopes were high that we would be in Wicklow before closing time. No one was going to their bunks now even though their bodies were tired and energy was in short supply. We were due to finish in a few hours and excitement was evident. Jokes were told and bets were made on how long it would take to drink the first pint. The No.1 genoa had replaced the spinnaker as lights on shore replaced the fading daylight. We still had a good breeze on a close reach and a strong tide helping us along. Now we could see the lights of Wicklow pointed out to us by local Bill Sheane. Local knowledge is, as everyone knows, a great advantage. Bill had spent his youth (many years ago) sailing along this coast so when the navigator said we were not heading for

Wicklow he was told to go and check again. He did and confirmed that we were in fact heading for Greystones not Wicklow! So much for local knowledge - but to be fair, at night, and from a distance, the lights do look alike! It was now apparent the wind was getting lighter, much lighter. The problem now was to ensure that the south going tide wouldn't bring us past the limit mark at the finishing line. All of a sudden the wind disappeared. Gone. Flat calm. No jokes were being cracked now. Would we spend the night becalmed within sight of the finish line as so many boats had done in the past? But someone up in the Wicklow mountains opened a door and a draught came off the shore, just enough to fill our lightest spinnaker. The wind came and went as we drifted along within a few yards of the shore. Now we were really looking at Wicklow. Through the binoculars we could see people along the quay, but where was the finishing line. No sign of the outer limit mark. All eyes strained to find that miserable flashing torch-light. We were now within half a mile of the finish and very close to the shore. Relief at last as the strobe light was spotted and we sailed or drifted slowly across the finishing line. The overwhelming feeling was relief, and the pleasure and satisfaction at having completed the course.

It was 0150 and we had spent several hours doing those last few miles. Now the question was, where was 'Mad Bull' and 'Imp'? Had they avoided the calm? Would they finish within 50 minutes? Nothing we could do now. Only time would tell if we had done enough. Well time ran out for the others. The light winds which we had tasted settled over the area and several hours passed before 'Imp' and 'Mad Bull' sailed slowly across the line.

Now for that pint! It was 0200 and surely all the bars would be closed. As we came alongside the pier head, a voice from heaven, or was it a member of WSC, shouted out. "The bar will be open for another 20 minutes, if you hurry." Suddenly energy flowed into every muscle as the sails were dropped, fenders and warps tied up and the ship abandoned in a state of chaos as the crew headed for our first drink in five days. The 20 minutes for a pint turned out to be 6 hours and the hospitality received was something which we will all remember with pleasure.

What was it someone said "been there - done that - never do it again!" - Well, maybe not until 1996.

Finishing Position:    6th. Overall
                          1st. CHS Class 2
                          Winner (with Imp and Mad Bull) Team Prize.

Crew:
John Godkin, Mel O'Donovan, Bill Sheane, Ralph Godkin, John Penwill, John O'Connell, Martin Gowran, Jimmy Murphy, Bill Long.

*Where am i going to put the crew?
Simon Greenwood, skipper Wicklow
Racing, 1998*

*. . . and the answer is, 'On the rail',
Adam Drew finds a comfortable perch on
the starboard quarter.*

# 1994 CLASS RESULTS

## CHS - CLASS 1- 1994

| Place | Yacht | Entered By | CHS/TCF | Elapsed | Corrected |
|-------|-------|-----------|---------|---------|-----------|
| 1 | Bridgestone | Peter Wilson | 1.046 | 4:06:38:19 | 4:11:21:36 |
| 2 | Prospector | Richard Burroughs | 1.064 | 4:06:39:18 | 4:13:13:30 |
| 3 | Corwynt | Gwilym Evans | 1.061 | 4:07:40:05 | 4:13:59:31 |
| 4 | Janey Mac II | A Lee | 1.064 | 4:07:40:05 | 4:14:18:10 |
| 5 | Megalopolis | Urban Taylor | 1.119 | 4:02:35:15 | 4:14:19:10 |
| 6 | Keep On Smiling | Tom Little | 1.065 | 4:08:11:48 | 4:14:58:10 |
| 7 | Beamont Spirit | Roy Dickson | 1.169 | 4:01:45:45 | 4:18:17:04 |
| 8 | Stormbird | Ciaran Foley | 1.268 | 3:23:46:57 | 5:01:27:08 |
| 9 | Aquelina | James Tyrrell | 1.062 | 4:18:50:30 | 5:01:57:43 |
| 10 | Virgin City Jet | Dix/Power/Barrington | 1.414 | 3:16:30:33 | 5:05:09:07 |
| | Moonduster | Denis Doyle | 1.154 | | |
| | Elusive | John Sisk | 1.098 | | |
| | Maxol Unleaded | G. Peck & K. Jameson | 1.121 | | |
| | Comanche Raider | Roy Hamilton | 1.125 | | |
| | A.I.B. Sailing | A.I.B. Sailing Club | 1.156 | | |
| | Tropicana | Jill Somerville | 1.064 | | |
| | Constance | Clem Kelly | 1.065 | | |
| | Jackabout | Andrew Hall | 1.108 | | |

## CHS - CLASS 2 – 1994

| Place | Yacht | Entered By | CHS TCF | Elapsed Time | Corrected Time |
|-------|-------|-----------|---------|--------------|----------------|
| 1 | V.S.O.P. | John Godkin | 1.03 | 4:11:40:57 | 4:14:54:47 |
| 2 | Imp | George Radley Jnr. | 1.019 | 4:14:55:59 | 4:17:02:27 |
| 3 | Mad Bull | Olaf Sorensen | 1.028 | 4:15:26:31 | 4:18:33:44 |
| 4 | Marissa VIII | Frank Elmes | 0.992 | 5:00:51:58 | 4:23:53:57 |
| 5 | Air Corps I | Tom O'Connor | 1.011 | 4:22:39:36 | 4:23:57:55 |
| 6 | Hobo V | John Bourke | 1.011 | 4:22:47:29 | 5:00:05:53 |
| 7 | Duel | Michael Fleming | 1.017 | 4:22:17:57 | 5:00:18:37 |
| 8 | Gwawr | Anthony Jones | 1.014 | 4:22:59:03 | 5:00:39:00 |
| 9 | Spirit of Mayo | Robin Smith | 1.011 | 5:00:45:17 | 5:02:04:59 |
| 10 | Rock Adventurer | Daniel Gallagher | 1.011 | 5:09:34:06 | 5:10:59:37 |
| 11 | Black Tie | Frank Jackson | 1.011 | 5:11:17:30 | 5:12:44:09 |
| 12 | Nissan I | Siobhan Crowley | 1.011 | 5:11:44:36 | 5:13:11:33 |
| 13 | St. Christopher | C.G. Fairhurst | 1.026 | 5:14:39:56 | 5:18:10:01 |
| 14 | Arthur | Robin Kay/ G. Dempsey | 1.011 | 5:18:22:21 | 5:19:53:41 |
| 15 | Darramy | Brian Wallace | 1.011 | 5:23:07:17 | 6:00:41:45 |
| 16 | Spirit of Ringsend | Purcell/Daly/Crowley | 1.023 | 6:17:44:13 | 6:21:27:25 |
| | Estrellita | Bernard Freyne | 0.966 | Retired | Retired |
| | Juno | Simon Knowles | 0.998 | Retired | Retired |

## CHS - CLASS 3 – 1994

| Place | Yacht | Entered By | CHS TCF | Elapsed | Corrected |
|---|---|---|---|---|---|
| 1 | Deerstalker | Michael Taylor-Jones | 0.911 | 5:01:58:00 | 4:15:06:42 |
| 2 | Amazing Grace | Anthony Kingston | 0.973 | 4:23:47:31 | 4:20:33:27 |
| 3 | Witchcraft of Howth | Nixon/Wheeler/Whelehan | 0.97 | 5:00:48:03 | 4:21:10:37 |
| 4 | Samaki | John Buckley | 0.91 | 6:00:49:39 | 5:11:47:35 |
| 5 | White Rooster | James Donegan | 0.981 | 5:18:14:53 | 5:15:37:17 |
| 6 | Joliba | James Ryan & A. Murray | 0.94 | 6:01:34:10 | 5:16:50:07 |
| 7 | Alpara | B & M Carroll | 0.92 | 7:09:20:57 | 6:19:09:40 |
| 8 | Raasay of Melfort | Brian Coad | 0.873 | 7:21:05:52 | 6:21:04:56 |
| 9 | Ulysses | Par McArdle | 0.908 | 7:14:35:51 | 6:21:47:55 |
| 10 | Sty Tailte | Lt. William Roberts | 0.928 | 7:22:17:10 | 7:08:35:08 |
| | Emircedes | P. Ryan & M. Hogan | 0.906 | | |
| | Trailblazer | Roy Conway | 0.952 | | |
| | Tjaldur | Sean Whiston | 0.88 | | |
| | Pink Panther | Dr. Seamus Moneley | 0.921 | | |
| | Angel | Gerard Whiston | 0.896 | | |
| | Juno | Simon Knowles | 0.998 | | |
| | Golden Gryphon | John O'Regan | 0.909 | | |
| | Tir Na nog | Asgard Group | 0.883 | | |

## IMS - CLASS 4 – 1994

| Place | Yacht | Entered By | Elapsed | Corrected |
|---|---|---|---|---|
| 1 | Bridgestone | Peter Wilson | 4:06:38:19 | 3:12:39:42 |
| 2 | Janey Mac II | A Lee | 4:07:40:05 | 3:15:19:17 |
| 3 | Marissa VIII | Frank Elmes | 5:00:51:58 | 3:22:59:19 |
| 4 | Stormbird | Ciaran Foley | 3:23:46:57 | 3:23:46:57 |
| 5 | Hobo V | John Bourke | 4:22:47:29 | 4:00:29:10 |
| 6 | Black Tie | Frank Jackson | 5:11:17:30 | 4:10:48:48 |
| 7 | Nissan I | Siobhan Crowley | 5:11:44:36 | 4:11:05:06 |
| 8 | Arthur | Robin Kay/ G. Dempsey | 5:18:22:21 | 4:15:25:37 |
| 9 | Spirit of Ringsend | Purcell/Daly/Crowley | 6:17:44:13 | 5:12:44:53 |

## IMS - CLASS 6 – 1994

| Place | Yacht | Entered By | Elapsed | Corrected |
|-------|-------|------------|---------|-----------|
| 1 | White Rooster | James Donegan | 5:18:14:53 | 5:18:14:53 |
| 2 | Joliba | James Ryan & A. Murray | 6:01:34:10 | 5:18:35:14 |
|  | Emircedes | P. Ryan & M. Hogan |  |  |
|  | Juno | Simon Knowles |  |  |

## CLASSIC – 1994

| Place | Yacht | Entered By | CHS TCF | Elapsed | Corrected |
|-------|-------|------------|---------|---------|-----------|
| 1 | Deerstalker | Michael Taylor-Jones | 0.911 | 5:01:58:00 | 4:15:06:42 |
| 2 | Joliba | James Ryan & A. Murray | 0.94 | 6:01:34:10 | 5:16:50:07 |
| 3 | St. Christopher | C.G. Fairhurst | 1.026 | 5:14:39:56 | 5:18:10:01 |
| 4 | Raasay of Melfort | Brian Coad | 0.873 | 7:21:05:52 | 6:21:04:56 |
| 5 | Ulysses | Par McArdle | 0.908 | 7:14:35:51 | 6:21:47:55 |
|  | Tjaldur | Sean Whiston | 0.88 |  |  |
|  | Angel | Gerard Whiston | 0.896 |  |  |

## ISORA – 1994

| Place | Yacht | Entered By | CHS TCF | Elapsed | Corrected |
|---|---|---|---|---|---|
| 1 | Corwynt | Gwilym Evans | 1.061 | 4:07:40:05 | 4:13:59:31 |
| 2 | Janey Mac II | A Lee | 1.064 | 4:07:40:05 | 4:14:18:10 |
| 3 | Megalopolis | Urban Taylor | 1.119 | 4:02:35:15 | 4:14:19:10 |
| 4 | Keep On Smiling | Tom Little | 1.065 | 4:08:11:48 | 4:14:58:10 |
| 5 | Witchcraft of Howth | Nixon/Wheeler/Whelehan | 0.970 | 5:00:48:03 | 4:21:10:37 |
| 6 | Marissa VIII | Frank Elmes | 0.992 | 5:00:51:58 | 4:23:53:57 |
| 7 | Duel | Michael Fleming | 1.017 | 4:22:17:57 | 5:00:18:37 |
| 8 | Gwawr | Anthony Jones | 1.014 | 4:22:59:03 | 5:00:39:00 |
| 9 | Stormbird | Ciaran Foley | 1.268 | 3:23:46:57 | 5:01:27:08 |
| 10 | Aquelina | James Tyrrell | 1.062 | 4:18:50:30 | 5:01:57:43 |
| 11 | Samaki | John Buckley | 0.910 | 6:00:49:39 | 5:11:47:35 |
| 12 | Darramy | Brian Wallace | 1.011 | 5:23:07:17 | 6:00:41:45 |
| 13 | Ulysses | Par McArdle | 0.908 | 7:14:35:51 | 6:21:47:55 |
|  | Emircedes | P. Ryan & M. Hogan | 0.906 |  |  |

## IOR - CLASS 8 – 1994

| Place | Yacht | Entered By | IOR TMF | Elapsed | Corrected |
|---|---|---|---|---|---|
| 1 | Hobo V | John Bourke | 0.9939 | 4:22:47:29 | 4:22:04:00 |
| 2 | Gwawr | Anthony Jones | 0.9941 | 4:22:59:03 | 4:22:16:56 |
| 3 | White Rooster | James Donegan | 0.9261 | 5:18:14:53 | 5:08:01:53 |
| 4 | Nissan I | Siobhan Crowley | 0.9939 | 5:11:44:36 | 5:10:56:23 |
| 5 | Joliba | James Ryan & A. Murray | 0.9063 | 6:01:34:10 | 5:11:53:47 |
| 6 | Spirit of Ringsend | Purcell/Daly/Crowley | 0.9328 | 6:17:44:13 | 6:06:52:06 |
|  | Emircedes | P. Ryan & M. Hogan | 0.8763 |  |  |
|  | Angel | Gerard Whiston | 0.8897 |  |  |

## Sigma 38

| Place | Yacht | Entered By | Type | Elapsed | Corrected |
|-------|-------|------------|------|---------|-----------|
| 1 | Air Corps I | Tom O'Connor | Sigma 38 | 4:22:39:36 | 4:23:57:55 |
| 2 | Hobo V | John Bourke | Sigma 38 | 4:22:47:29 | 5:00:05:53 |
| 3 | Spirit of Mayo | Robin Smith | Sigma 38 | 5:00:45:17 | 5:02:04:59 |
| 4 | Rock Adventurer | Daniel Gallagher | Sigma 38 | 5:09:34:06 | 5:10:59:37 |
| 5 | Black Tie | Frank Jackson | Sigma 38 | 5:11:17:30 | 5:12:44:09 |
| 6 | Nissan I | Siobhan Crowley | Sigma 38 | 5:11:44:36 | 5:13:11:33 |
| 7 | Arthur | Robin Kay/ G. Dempsey | Sigma 38 | 5:18:22:21 | 5:19:53:41 |

## Sigma 400

| Place | Yacht | Entered By | Type | Elapsed | Corrected |
|-------|-------|------------|------|---------|-----------|
| 1 | Corwynt | Gwilym Evans | Sigma 400 | 4:07:40:05 | 4:13:59:31 |
| 2 | Janey Mac II | A Lee | Sigma 400 | 4:07:40:05 | 4:14:18:10 |
| 3 | Keep On Smiling | Tom Little | Sigma 400 | 4:08:11:48 | 4:14:58:10 |
| 6 | Aquelina | James Tyrrell | Sigma 400 | 4:18:50:30 | 5:01:57:43 |

## Sigma's Combined

| Place | Yacht | Entered By | CHS TCF | Elapsed | Corrected |
|-------|-------|------------|---------|---------|-----------|
| 1 | Corwynt | Gwilym Evans | 1.061 | 4:07:40:05 | 4:13:59:31 |
| 2 | Janey Mac II | A Lee | 1.064 | 4:07:40:05 | 4:14:18:10 |
| 3 | Keep On Smiling | Tom Little | 1.065 | 4:08:11:48 | 4:14:58:10 |
| 4 | Air Corps I | Tom O'Connor | 1.011 | 4:22:39:36 | 4:23:57:55 |
| 5 | Hobo V | John Bourke | 1.011 | 4:22:47:29 | 5:00:05:53 |
| 6 | Aquelina | James Tyrrell | 1.062 | 4:18:50:30 | 5:01:57:43 |
| 7 | Spirit of Mayo | Robin Smith | 1.011 | 5:00:45:17 | 5:02:04:59 |
| 8 | Rock Adventurer | Daniel Gallagher | 1.011 | 5:09:34:06 | 5:10:59:37 |
| 9 | Black Tie | Frank Jackson | 1.011 | 5:11:17:30 | 5:12:44:09 |
| 10 | Nissan I | Siobhan Crowley | 1.011 | 5:11:44:36 | 5:13:11:33 |
| 11 | Arthur | Robin Kay/ G. Dempsey | 1.011 | 5:18:22:21 | 5:19:53:41 |

# Round Ireland '94 – Retirals

| Cork Dry Gin Round Ireland 1994 - Overall Results | | | |
|---|---|---|---|
| Retirals | | | |
| Estrellita | Bernard Freyne | 0.966 | Retired |
| Emircedes | P. Ryan & M. Hogan | 0.906 | Retired |
| Trailblazer | Roy Conway | 0.952 | Retired |
| Tjaldur | Sean Whiston | 0.880 | Retired |
| Pink Panther | Dr. Seamus Moneley | 0.921 | Retired |
| Moonduster | Denis Doyle | 1.154 | Retired |
| Elusive | John Sisk | 1.098 | Retired |
| Maxol Unleaded | G. Peck & K. Jameson | 1.121 | Retired |
| Comanche Raider | Roy Hamilton | 1.125 | Retired |
| A.I.B. Sailing | A.I.B. Sailing Club | 1.156 | Retired |
| Tropicana | Jill Somerville | 1.064 | Retired |
| Angel | Gerard Whiston | 0.896 | Retired |
| Juno | Simon Knowles | 0.998 | Retired |
| Golden Gryphon | John O'Regan | 0.909 | Retired |
| Constance | Clem Kelly | 1.065 | Retired |
| Tir Na nog | Asgard Group | 0.883 | Retired |
| Jackabout | Andrew Hall | 1.108 | Retired |

| Wind Speed and Direction, Coastal Stations | | | | | | | | | | | |
|---|---|---|---|---|---|---|---|---|---|---|---|
| 22-Jun-94 | | | | | | | | | | | |
| Time | Dublin | | Rosslare | | Cork | | Valentia | | Belmullet | | Malin Head | |
| Hour | Kts. | Dir. | Kts. | Dir. | Kts. | Dir. | Kts. | Dir. | Kts. | Dir. | Kts. | Dir. |
| 00:01 | 10 | 260 | 07 | 270 | 06 | 260 | 11 | 250 | 16 | 230 | 20 | 230 |
| 01:02 | 12 | 240 | 09 | 260 | 05 | 250 | 12 | 250 | 20 | 230 | 21 | 230 |
| 02:03 | 12 | 240 | 10 | 260 | 06 | 240 | 10 | 240 | 20 | 240 | 23 | 230 |
| 03:04 | 12 | 230 | 09 | 250 | 08 | 230 | 12 | 250 | 22 | 240 | 26 | 250 |
| 04:05 | 14 | 230 | 10 | 240 | 08 | 240 | 11 | 240 | 22 | 250 | 27 | 250 |
| 05:06 | 15 | 230 | 12 | 240 | 08 | 240 | 11 | 240 | 23 | 250 | 29 | 260 |
| 06:07 | 16 | 250 | 13 | 240 | 07 | 250 | 13 | 250 | 22 | 250 | 30 | 250 |
| 07:08 | 19 | 250 | 15 | 250 | 13 | 260 | 08 | 270 | 21 | 250 | 30 | 250 |
| 08:09 | 20 | 250 | 13 | 240 | 15 | 270 | 07 | 270 | 22 | 250 | 31 | 250 |
| 09:10 | 20 | 260 | 14 | 250 | 11 | 290 | 09 | 270 | 21 | 260 | 31 | 260 |
| 10:11 | 22 | 260 | 15 | 240 | 13 | 290 | 09 | 280 | 19 | 250 | 29 | 260 |
| 11:12 | 21 | 260 | 17 | 240 | 12 | 280 | 08 | 280 | 18 | 260 | 28 | 260 |
| 12:13 | 19 | 260 | 17 | 240 | 10 | 280 | 07 | 280 | 18 | 250 | 26 | 270 |
| 13:14 | 19 | 260 | 17 | 230 | 09 | 290 | 07 | 280 | 17 | 250 | 26 | 260 |
| 14:15 | 16 | 270 | 15 | 240 | 08 | 290 | 06 | 280 | 16 | 250 | 26 | 270 |
| 15:16 | 14 | 270 | 14 | 230 | 08 | 280 | 05 | 280 | 16 | 250 | 25 | 260 |
| 16:17 | 13 | 260 | 14 | 240 | 06 | 280 | 04 | 270 | 14 | 250 | 24 | 280 |
| 17:18 | 12 | 260 | 13 | 240 | 05 | 300 | 03 | 280 | 14 | 250 | 22 | 280 |
| 18:19 | 12 | 260 | 13 | 250 | 05 | 270 | 01 | 280 | 12 | 250 | 21 | 270 |
| 19:20 | 09 | 260 | 09 | 240 | 04 | 290 | 00 | ... | 11 | 250 | 19 | 270 |
| 20:21 | 07 | 250 | 07 | 230 | 03 | 320 | 01 | 110 | 08 | 250 | 15 | 270 |
| 21:22 | 05 | 260 | 06 | 230 | 04 | 020 | 01 | 170 | 06 | 260 | 13 | 280 |
| 22:23 | 05 | 250 | 05 | 230 | 03 | 040 | 02 | 160 | 02 | 240 | 13 | 260 |
| 23:24 | 05 | 240 | 05 | 250 | 01 | 120 | 01 | 060 | 02 | 230 | 12 | 270 |

# BMW Round Ireland 2006

Simon Johnson

It was a dramatic start for all, though after the first 24 hours of sailing in the BMW Round Ireland Yacht Race, all 38 boats have safely passed the Tuskar Rock on Ireland's South-eastern corner. Light winds have befallen the entire coastline as far as the famous Fastnet Rock off West Cork and are proving testing for many race hopefuls.

The race began as the gunshot from Committee boat; the L.E. Aoife marked the start of the race. Unfortunately, Lascar was recalled as she got into difficulties with her jib wrapped around the forestay, which unfortunately put her across the line before the start gun. She came back around the stern of the Committee Boat, where she re-started and joined the fleet four and a half minutes later.

The biggest yacht ever to compete in the race continues to lead the fleet with a tactical start; Konica Minolta Zana called in at the Fastnet mandatory radio check-in at 1615 this afternoon, just over 24 hours since the start of the race at Wicklow.

Moderate winds are forecast from the south-west corner off the County Kerry coastline and at 98 feet overall, the New Zealand leader should be able to make a fast getaway from the becalmed pack astern.

Based on handicap corrected times at the Tuskar Rock, Konica Minolta Zana was leading overall while Roy Heiner on his VO60 footer chartered to Lyons Solicitors of Dublin was in second place.

Current Round Ireland record holder JP Chomette on Solune was in third place in a repeat of the 2004 BMW Round Ireland Race that saw similar conditions on the second day slow his progress.

Nevertheless, there is a real prospect of a slower race than normal. Limerick entry Altana Chieftain reported total calm off the Old Head of Kinsale and was surrounded by smaller boats at 1800 today. The crew of the Cookson 50 provisioned for four days but based on current progress, their finish could be later than Wednesday. Ireland's West, the Galway entry skippered by Aodhan Fitzgerald came within three miles of Chieftain before tacking out to sea in search of breeze.

Defending title holder Eamon Crosbie on Teng Tools was within sight at that time but placed mid-fleet on corrected handicap time.

Two of the 39 boat fleet have retired from the competition as the event moves onto the Atlantic Ocean. Both are competitors in the two-handed division and were in the leading positions in their class before retiring. Yannick Monnier and Michael Greely on Southbound.ie broke a key fitting on their mainsail that cannot be repaired at sea. Ironically, the pair were close to their home port of Dingle where they have arrived this evening (Monday).

Mike Jacques of Nunatak has also retired as slow progress in the light headwinds would not allow them sufficient time to reach the finishing-line at Wicklow before the weekend when the crew have prior commitments.

Meanwhile, Konica Minolta Zana continues to lead the fleet on the water and was enjoying 22 knot north-easterly winds this afternoon (Monday) as they passed the Eagle Island mandatory radio check-in point off the County Mayo coast.

Speculation is growing that the New Zealand entry may be able to set a new course record but must finish before 4pm on Tuesday to realise this target.

The actual race for the overall trophy is being dominated by smaller entries racing on IRC handicap. Based on the Fastnet Rock check-in times, defending title holder Eamon Crosbie on Teng Tools and Aodhan Fitzgerald's Galway team on Ireland's West were both covering each other as light winds hampered progress of the Kerry coastline.

Sunday night also provided an additional bonus to the fleet when passing the West Cork coast. A spectacular display of phosphorescence was witnessed by the crew Pepperbox who reported a school of up to six dolphins who played with their yacht for 20 minutes during the night, escorting the Howth YC team on their race towards Innistearacht.

After three full days racing in the BMW Round Ireland Yacht Race, un-typically light winds around the 704-mile course have presented additional challenges to the 37 boats in the competition. While gear failure and retirements due to rough weather have been avoided, the race is set to last longer than most boats have planned for.

The first 'casualty' of the conditions has been Stuart Thwaites' Konica Minolta Zana, the 98-footer from New Zealand that has led the fleet from the outset on Saturday afternoon at Wicklow. Just six knots of wind passing Malin Head, County Donegal the most northerly point of Ireland meant the super-maxi missed the crucial tidal gate at Rathlin Island.

Meanwhile, the battle for the overall win on handicap corrected time is being fought out by several smaller boats. Eamon Crosbie's, "Teng Tools" that is defending the 2004 title continues to feature in the latest provisional standings along with Aodhan Fitzgerald's Galway entry Ireland's West.

Dun Laoghaire yacht Jeronimo is also on the top of the results and has the added edge of 1996 winner Michael Boyd on board with skipper Niall Dowling. Anthony Richards' Minnie the Moocher from the UK is in the hunt. In the 2004 event, Richards saw his hopes of overall victory end on the final approach to the finish due to rudder bearing problems.

However, even these contenders may be disappointed as fresh winds forecast to reach those still at sea on Thursday morning may bring the back-markers up the course in faster time. Such an outcome might see Eric Lisson's Cavatina repeat her 2002 result when the Royal Cork YC boat won overall.

With little or no wind on the Irish Sea, progress south towards the finishing line of the BMW Round Ireland Race has been painfully slow for Konica Minolta Zana. The 98-footer passed the Mew Island radio check-in point 110 miles from the finish at 00.30 on Wednesday morning. Some 18 hours later, she was on final approach to Wicklow and expected to achieve line honours at dusk.

Winds have been untypically light through the race so far. Normally a mixture of light to fresh or strong winds can be expected but headwinds have been a dominant factor since the start four days ago.

While several boats have reported running low on food supplies, there was good news for the smaller boats still only reaching the halfway stage. Force five winds from the south-west veering westerly are expected on the west from Thursday morning and will remain favourable until the weekend.

The fresher conditions reaching the fleet from behind spells bad news for the mid-sized entries. Although dominating the provisional handicap results to date, they now stand to lose out to the back-markers in what may prove to be a classic Round Ireland Race about turn in the results.

Up to half a dozen boats have been in contention since the weekend: defending champion Eamon Crosbie on "Teng Tools"; Aodhan Fitzgerald and his Galway Bay team on Ireland's West; Anthony Richards' Minnie the Moocher from the UK; George Radley's 1980 classic Imp and Niall Dowling's Jeronimo from Dun Laoghaire.

Shortly before nine o'clock on Wednesday evening, Stuart Thwaites' 98 foot Konica Minolta Zana from Wellington, New Zealand crossed the finishing-line at WSC to win line honours in the BMW Round Ireland Yacht Race.

With line honours safely secured by Konica Minolta and no records broken, the battle for the overall victory in the most testing of races remains wide open and it may be the weekend before final results are confirmed.

After four days and almost five hours at sea, headwinds tracked the fleet leader for the entire 704-mile course and denied the super-maxi either the course or race record.

Depending on breeze over the next 24 hours, Konica Minolta may emerge winner of Class Super Zero though the latest forecast calls for freshening weather to arrive from the south-west overnight which could aid the other big boats.

"We tried to push all the headlands rather than go 100 miles offshore to hunt for breeze and we did see 25 knots at one stage," said navigator Steve Hayles. "The last stage (south down the Irish Sea) was frustrating but all in all, it was awesome and I really enjoyed it."

The course record remains at 57 hours set in 2005 by JP Chomette on City Jet Solune of France, (This record was set outside the constraints of the race) while Colm Barrington's 1998 race record of 76 hours and 23 minutes is also unbeaten.

Currently, 36 boats remain at sea racing and the next group of boats are expected to finish from mid-day on Thursday while it is likely to be Saturday before the overall winner can be confirmed.

Competitors in the BMW Round Ireland Yacht Race have started arriving in steady stream of finishers just as fresher winds have arrived for those yachts still racing. After days of near calm conditions, the new breeze has spelt the end of the prospects of a big boat win for the fourth consecutive race.

The remaining five class super zero arrived en masse 15 hours later. The group have been in close contact since converging at Tory Island on the north-west coast.

The longer than expected race proved more testing for some than others. Ger O'Rourke's Cookson 50 footer Altana Chieftain menu was reduced to freeze-dried food and muesli mixed with orange juice.

Meanwhile, crew on rival entry Whisper Faimente, a 35-tonne Reichel Pugh 78 footer reportedly sent them mobile phone pictures of their steak with rosemary jús evening fare. Nevertheless, O'Rourke has emerged overall winner of the class on provisional results.

The fresh winds have brought further uncertainty to the standings of the smaller boats in open contention for the overall trophy. While there is every possibility of a shock turnaround when the slowest boats reach the finish over the weekend, a battle royal is being staged on the Irish Sea overnight.

Defending title-holder Eamon Crosbie on his 32-foot Teng Tools has been locked in a match race with Galway's Aodhan Fitzgerald on Ireland's West, a Beneteau 40.7 as the pair are within sight on one another and enjoying a fetch from Mew Island southwards to Wicklow and expected shortly after dawn.

Once ashore, stories of exceptionally light conditions were being told in Wicklow SC and while records have stood intact in this race, the slowest speed claimed to date stands at an excruciating 35 miles in 20 hours.

The outcome of the BMW Round Ireland Race was hanging by a thread last night (Friday) after more than six days of racing on the 704-mile course. More than half the 39-boat fleet had arrived back at WSC by nightfall but all eyes were turned seawards in anticipation of one finisher.

This started with a cluster of yachts that arrived with new wind that had been so desperately missed by the fleet since starting at Wicklow last weekend and while the breeze was welcome, it was of little use to the biggest boats racing who were heavily penalised for their slow race.

That shifted the emphasis towards the smaller entries and onto a group of half a dozen crews which had all featured prominently on provisional standings calculated at key check-in points around the coast.

Niall Dowling's Jeronimo from the Royal Irish Yacht Club in Dun Laoghaire and Anthony Richard's Minnie the Moocher from Britain arrived in the early hours of the morning, both keenly aware of the pursuing pack. Then it was Aodhan Fitzgerald's Galway team on Ireland's West that finished at 8.15am.

But it was defending course champion Eamon Crosbie on the 32 footer Teng Tools that held the unofficial 'clubhouse' leader since 9.14 am as the handicaps repositioned the finishers in corrected time order. For a time after Crosbie finished, expectation was running high that George Radley's 1980 classic 40-footer Imp would reach Wicklow by lunchtime to take over the handicap lead. But a foul tide denied the Glandore Harbour crew the honour and once again, the calculators and spread sheets were busy.

Having enjoyed the new wind at the back of the fleet and benefiting too from a low handicap, 2002 race winner Eric Lisson on Cavatina had the assembled crowd at WSC holding a collective breath late last night.

A deadline of 3.15am on Saturday morning must be beaten for Crosbie to be beaten. By tea-time, Cavatina had yet to make its report at the Rockabill Lighthouse, some 40 miles from the finish. Then at one minute to seven came the report - 40 miles to go.

However, the last stage is against the wind and effectively longer than 40 miles. Plus there is a foul tide to battle as well. Lisson may yet emerge overall winner of the BMW Round Ireland Race 2006 but this result will come down to the wire - and the second hand sweep of the countdown clock.

After more than six days at sea, Eric Lisson and the crew of Cavatina reached the finishing-line at WSC and are expected to be confirmed overall winners of the BMW Round Ireland Yacht Race. The Cork yacht completed the 704-mile course shortly after 1.15am today (Saturday).

Lisson and Cavatina are set to enter the record book alongside the late Denis Doyle and the famed Moonduster for winning the circumnavigation of Ireland twice.

What was expected to be a nail-biting finish to beat the handicap time deadline ended with just two hours to spare for Lisson as fresh winds and the last of a favourable tide swept his Granada 38 footer southwards from the Rockabill Light off Skerries. Co. Dublin.

Waiting in anticipation was defending course champion Eamon Crosbie on Teng Tools, the 'clubhouse leader' since early on Friday morning. In turn, this Dublin skipper watched as several key rivals failed to beat their own handicap deadlines leaving just Cavatina as the main threat to his title.

Most of the remaining competitors still at sea will reach Wicklow by this evening or tomorrow morning when final overall results will be announced.

The BMW Round Ireland Race was drawing to a close this evening (Saturday) as the final competitor approached Wicklow on the eighth day of racing around the 704-mile course. Just one crew remains at sea and is expected to cross the finishing-line around mid-night tonight.

In the early hours of this morning (Saturday), Eric Lisson and the crew of Cavatina reached the finishing-line at WSC and are expected to be confirmed overall winners of the BMW Round Ireland Yacht Race.

The Cork yacht completed the 704-mile course shortly after 1.15am, two hours ahead of the handicap deadline needed to beat defending title holder Eamon Crosbie on Teng Tools that finished the course some 16 hours earlier.

Forecast south-east gales have yet to arrive and the crew on Sarnia from the National Yacht Club will be 37th and final finisher of the 14th edition of the race.

Untypically light winds for almost all the race ensured that victory would go to a smaller, lower handicapped entry as the overall win is decided on IRC handicap. Headwinds resulted in a slow slog for all 39 starters of which 36 completed the course.

Late on Saturday night after more than a week at sea, the last competitor sent a message to the WSC Race office notifying the organisers of his intention to retire. Facing a southerly gale for the final 90 miles and in an area known for its seven metre waves in such conditions, Mick Creedon pulled into Carlingford after reefing gear failed on his SandS 36 footer.

This year's race will be remembered by all 400 competitors as one of the toughest sailing tests for many years - but for different reasons than the usual mountainous seas and harsh weather. Light winds dominated the 704-mile course, delaying the boats with the result that several ran out of food and almost starved.

*2006. Stuart Thwaites Accepts the Line Honours trophy from WSC Commodore John Johnson.*
Photo: Richard Nairn

# BMW 2008 RACE

by Charlie Kavanagh
(This was Charlie's blog on the WSC website)
(As well as being Commodore of WSC Charlie maintains the club website and what follows is his account of the 2008 race as it unfolded.

The bigger boats compete for top honours and for the race record, which is held by Colm Barrington who skippered Jeep Cherokee to victory in 1998 in a time of 76 hours 23 minutes and 57 seconds, breaking the previous record by a massive eight hours. The 2004 winner was a 32' one off design built in Ireland for Eamon Crosbie called Calyx Voice and Data ("Voodoo Chile") and the 2006 Race was won by a previous winner, Eric Lisson's "Cavatina" (2002), a Grenada 38 classic GRP yacht.

*2008: the view from LE Aoife. Galileo (IRL 1944), Ocean Spirit of Carlingford (IRL 1207), Lee Overlay Partners (IRL 5005), Nadie (IRL 4600) and Dinamite Tee (GBR 7753T) cross the starting line.*
Photo: Richard Nairn

March 2008 **Round Ireland 2008 Update** -There is already great interest in this year's race with entries from France, the UK and Ireland. The **Two Handed** class is also looking very interesting with many enquiries but as usual a lot of people are playing their cards very close to their chest. Good news is that past winners **George Radley** and **Eric Lisson** (who is looking for a third win in Cavatina) are both entered. We also have **four Prima 38s** from the UK. If there are any more Primas out there, do come along. We will give class prizes if we get enough entries of any class as the Sigma entries have been getting less each year. To all you sailors out there that missed out or had to retire from the **Fastnet** race in 2007 come to Wicklow and take part in the Round Ireland. It's a great race.

Colm Barrington's race record will yet again be under threat as **Mike Slade** who broke the Fastnet record in **ICAP Leopard 3** is coming to do the race. ICAP Leopard 3 will then be returning to the UK to do the Round the Island race.

13th May 2008 - interest is hotting up with 17 fully confirmed entries and another 20 or so in the works - looks like the 2008 BMW Round Ireland will be a bumper race with between 40 and 50 boats expected to start. ICAP Leopard will have stiff competition with a strong possibility of at least one Volvo 70, state of the art 80 footer as well as a few other biggies talking about entering. 10th June 2008 - We now have 46 entries with possibly another 4 due before the final deadline of Thurs 17th June. There is a real international flavour to this race including Kingspan, a shared entry between Howth YC and St Petersburg Sailing Union, with love from Russia in this wonderful race.

16th June 2008 - Only 5 days to go, we now have 47 entries, most of whom will be in Wicklow Harbour from Wed/Thur creating a wonderful pre-race spectacle for interested observers to drool over and interact with the sailors before the off on Sat 21st. Race day will see a feast of boats large and small (100' - 30') all jockeying for position on our start line and as always, we won't be sure of the winner until the last boat is in - could Cavatina be the first to win 3 races, might ICAP Leopard 3 carry the favourites tag around in record time, is there a surprise package waiting in the wings, will a 2 hander embarrass the fully crewed boats? There are loads of possibilities and a few surprise entrants still have to show their hands.

Entries range from a 9.2m Ker yacht up to a state of the art 30m Farr OD "ICAP Leopard 3" and all sizes in between, with eleven 2 handed boats, a particularly tough task taking on the unpredictable weather around this little island of ours. The excitement is building as the off approaches and our visitors and townsfolk will be treated to a wonderful spectacle on Saturday afternoon as the boats jockey for position before the off and on out past Wicklow Head as they leave Ireland and all its islands to starboard - next stop Wicklow.

**The GPS Tracking System** is Supplied by RORC and powered byOC Technology. It will be available at the time of the race.

17th June 2008 - Down to 4 days now - the race boats are starting to dribble in to Wicklow Harbour, the excitement is building as the club dusts itself off for the week of festivities before the off. Our main bar area has been redecorated and will be unveiled to our members, visiting sailors and public on Wednesday 18th to compliment the improvements to our Round Ireland room. Thanks to David

Branigan of Oceansport it now has all the previous winners' photographs and a wonderful map of Ireland with all the lighthouses around our coast complete with flashing lights and the race call in points (sponsored by JBS Ashford Ltd). The map was designed and created by Latitude Kinsale.

21st June 2008 - Due to a Gale force 8 to strong Gale 9 S-SW forecast, the Race Director, Dennis Noonan, has taken advice and has delayed the Race start until 1000hrs Sun 22nd June, when the worst of the weather should have gone through. Our sailors are tucked up nicely in Wicklow Harbour and Dun Laoghaire waiting for the off in miserably wet conditions which are soon to have strong winds also. The pre-race atmosphere was wonderful at the Sailors reception on Friday evening with live music and complimentary drinks and food. Let's hope all will be well and our sailors have a safe and enjoyable race.

**22nd June 2008 - BMW Round Ireland** got under way at last at 1200hrs, started by Race Organiser Dennis Noonan from the LE Eithne. All boats made a clear start but unfortunately without 5 entered yachts - Mc Connells Chieftain, Alegre, Uluha, IRL 107L and Voador. For the first time the progress of yachts could be followed on our tracker on the Race website.

22nd June 2008 - 1530hrs - we expect ICAP Leopard to round the Tuskar Rock in the next 15 minutes or so - he is on track to smash the 10 year record of Jeep Cherokee by up to 24 hours, a phenomenal achievement if they can manage it. Big winds are boosting all of the fleet down the Irish Sea and we would hope all the fleet will be around the first mark by nightfall. Safe sailing to all our sailors.

23rd June 2008 - 0435hrs - Manning the Race office this morning watching the dawn come up we have our dedicated Junior crew of Sean Doyle, Jonathon Flood and Liam Knight - who I guess will all be on the next Wicklow boat to do the race. All our Race boats are on the south coast and making a beeline for the Fastnet Rock into a decreasing Westerly headwind - ICAP Leopard is just about favourite to get there first (in about 7 hours time at present speed) but hot on his heels are Formidable 3 and Lee Overlay Partners. In the 2 handers, Cheetah Cub is absolutely flying and if he keeps up his present form, they could be challenging seriously for the handicap overall honours. First of September had a leak problem and some sail damage which they took time out to repair at Cahore and are now catching up fast on the tail enders, boosted by the ebbing tide no doubt around Tuskar Rock. Winds are starting to slacken but another weather system in the Atlantic should arrive overnight to help shoot the fleet up the West coast.

23rd June 2008 - 1030hrs - ICAP Leopard 3 is now doing 13 knots abeam of Mizen Head, having rounded the Fastnet Rock at 0808hrs (must have got a big wind shift to lift them), with Formidable 3 and Lee Overlay Partners his nearest pursuers. But now that almost all the boats GPS trackers are switched on, we can see the wily Cork duo of Cavatina and MccarthyMotors.ie are in hot pursuit to win the overall trophy, as both are well placed and moving in the "sailaton". We can confirm 3 retirals at this stage - Legally Brunette, Inis Mor and Mighty Max 2 all with gear failure of one sort or other

*POWERFUL BEAST!*
*2008: ICAP Leopard 3 (Mike Slade) set a new race record time of*
*2 days 17 hours 48 minutes and 47 seconds*

*ICAP Leopard seems to be on a collision course with the LE Aoife at the 2008 start.*

*ICAP Leopard 3. Jubilation! Mike Slade holds aloft the 2008 Line Honours Trophy to the delight of his crew.*

and the Race Office are trying to contact Joker and Aqualina to ascertain their position, as their trackers do not seem to be functioning. The tail enders seem to have found a dead wind hole while the leaders are enjoying a fresh breeze - ces't la vie in your average Round Ireland - you win some, lose some.

23rd June 2008 - 1330hrs - ICAP Leopard is half way up the Kerry coast, Formidable 3 is chasing hard having rounded the Fastnet and Lee Overlay Partners is just off our SW turning point as I write. With S-SE winds due to strengthen over the day bringing possible gales tonight, the whole fleet will be well positioned to make this the fastest Round Ireland for both first and last boats home - another record to be broken, we hope. Out of our 46 entrants, we still have 39 racing and its fingers crossed all will make it home in one piece.

23rd June 2008 - 1600hrs - Now off Dingle Peninsula, the Mega Cat is doing 15 knots at which speed we would expect them in Wicklow in 30 hours time, but this forecasted gale could shorten that time considerably - possibly even lunchtime Tuesday. The chasing fleet are all moving well and if they keep these winds all round, the small boats will be in the hunt for glory again. It's anyone's guess who will win but if ICAP Leopard stays sound he will win line honours and trounce the old record - with several other boats likely to be inside the old 1998 mark also.

23rd June 2008 - 2100hrs - All but one of the Super Zero and Zero class boats are now around the Fastnet, with White Tiger the odd one out. Leopard is now about half way around, making 13 kts but still no sign of the promised gale to drive him onwards to glory - another 27hrs to the finish at this average speed. At the back of the fleet Lascar, Sarnia and Cassiopea are in light airs but hopefully will get a morale boosting lift shortly - if the forecast pans out, they will enjoy a fast trip up the West coast.

24th June 2008 - 1350hrs - Sorry for the delay in update - catching up on sleep deprivation and had to clear the memory to allow more inputs. Looks like Leopard will definitely break the record barring some disaster but the strong winds behind favour the smaller boats for the handicap overall winner. More retirals are WSI, Lascar, Star Dancer and we think First of September and Ruffian, both of whom are stopped but not declared retired. From the tracker, most of the boats are past Inishtearacht but very few have been recorded by Valencia Radio on mandatory call-ins.

25th June 2008 - 0000hrs - Leopard is now in the Irish Sea and charging towards the finish, ETA Wicklow 0600hrs. The record is within his grasp now and we expect a good turnout for the finish. The real race is taking place mid-fleet where Cavatina, McCarthymotors.ie and Ireland West are in a dog fight for the overall honours and it looks as if these will be dicing it out right down to the wire.

25th June 2008 - 0800hrs - At last, ICAP Leopard 3 finally crossed the finish line, taking the gun from Race Organiser Dennis Noonan at c.0548hrs, watched by a good crowd including County Chairman, Cllr Derek Mitchell and Wicklow Town Mayor, Cllr. Denis Teevan. Needless to say, owner Mike Slade was delighted to have achieved the record, taking nearly 11 hrs off Jeep Cherokees 1998 record and setting a new standard for future campaigns to aim at - expect more mega yachts in the future trying to further reduce this new benchmark. He came ashore with 15 of his crew for the traditional post race photo call, trophy presentation, champagne reception, breakfast and a few well earned pints. Back at the end of the fleet, classic S&S 36 yacht, Sarnia, has had a casualty due to a main track accident causing rib damage to one of their crew, who is being evacuated to Galway. We wish him/her a speedy recovery. The rest of the fleet are being whooshed along by strong winds, which is bad news for most of the big boats out near the front who never got far enough ahead to establish time in hand to give them handicap advantage - mid-fleet is the place to be, despite all the expensive mega yachts in the vanguard.

25th June 2008 - 1700hrs - With the first boat home and a new record in the bag, all eyes are on the rest of the fleet to see who will succeed Cavatina (if not retained by her) as the 2008 BMW Round Ireland winner. Peter Finnegan's Ocean Spirit of Carlingford has provisionally put the north east in the frame as they approach the Irish Sea, just ahead of McCarthymotors.ie and Cavatina, giving ordinary club boats a very strong hand against the cream of international high tech yachts. We expect the next 3 maxis to finish before midnight tonight and the core of the "sailaton" will be arriving over the next 24hrs after a fast and very tough 2008 race. In the 2 hander class, current leader Mumbo.ie from Malahide SC is provisionally in fourth place overall just a few places ahead of Jalfrezi, a phenomenal performance by these shorthanded crews in very testing and energy sapping conditions. Of local interest, Kelly Spillane would like you all to know that local man Alan Murphy is navigator on yacht Gallileo, which has been putting in a good performance.

Our race is about giving all sailors of competent abilities the opportunity to match their wits and sailing skills against the top professional crews and consistently they have stepped up to the mark to enhance the egalitarian nature of this wonderful event. Long may Irish and other regular club sailors give this race the thumbs up and we look forward to welcoming them every two years. The level of interest in the race is phenomenal with **12,936** visits yesterday (24/6/08) to our dedicated race website with hits from all over the world checking on progress of the yachts - not bad for a small club situated on the East coast of Ireland. Thank you our yachting public for your support and interest - maybe many of you will aspire to be on the start line in 2010.

26th June 2008 - 2000hrs - Having spent most of the day berthing in the spilling rain, I am finally getting around to giving our 20,000 fans an update - thank you for keeping an eye on our wonderful event - you have been a great audience. With c.18 boats finished, we have another 12 still out there, but only one of those can now possibly win the overall race - you guessed right, Cavatina. By my rudimentary calculations and they're only that, I reckon he needs to finish c.0100 hrs Fri 27th June to beat Ireland West who is the leader in the clubhouse and feeling confident as the forecasted strong winds have still not materialised. McCarthymotors.ie have lost out in the light airs having been a strong contender up to early afternoon but the old nemesis of foul tides and light airs finally frustrated them - they did remarkably well anyway - well done George and crew. Mumbo.ie has been the long time provisional leader in the 2 hander class, but needs those strong winds immediately if he is to beat clubhouse leader Jalfrezi - as they say it's not over until the fat lady sings! Back at the tail end of the fleet Casiopeia is off the Co. Down coast chasing his nearest neighbour Persistence, both of whom we expect in Friday - winds will dictate and as usual, tides might have a say too. The last boat home has to be here before **1109hrs Friday 27th** to claim the dubious title of **fastest last boat** - come on guys and gals, we're rooting for you! From the crews we have spoken to, they have enjoyed the experience enormously despite the very tough conditions and will be back for more. Bravo.

Congratulations.

26th June 2008 - 2100hrs - Watching the Spain v Russia European semi final (3 - 0) as I ate my dinner of spring lamb, spuds and veg washed down by a glass of red wine and followed by strawberries and cream, my thoughts went out to the Russian crew on Kingspan who provisionally are the class 0 winners - they had their post race pints and grub and headed off up the town this afternoon in the rain looking for a steak dinner - what was Matt Davis feeding the poor sods on that boat? I'm sure they'll be back to soak more of the post race atmosphere and our traditional drink of "black vodka with the white head"! It was a great boost to our event to attract sailors from St Petersburg and let's hope we see many more in the future. We wish Evelyn Noonan (wife of Dennis, mother of Jacky) well as she recovers from a turn last night.

Race Postscript - For the romantics in our midst, an event of a truly romantic nature occurred on board Ocean Spirit of Carlingford as they crossed the finish line. Crew member Peter Eagleson went down on bended knee and asked his sweetheart and fellow crew member Emma Finnegan to marry him. To his (and all the watching crew's) relief, she accepted. A champagne celebration was held afterwards in the clubhouse and they were feted by fellow competitors and WSC members alike. We wish them well.

27th June 2008 - 2230hrs - All good things must come to an end sometime and boy, did I need to see the end of this non-stop event/party after 2 weeks. As with the best Round Ireland tradition, the biggest cheer and warmest welcome was for the last boat home - this year the honour fell to Cassiopeia at 16.31hrs on Fri 27th, representing the Royal St George YC. They were about 5 hours outside the fastest last boat - a record still to be broken.

All our returning sailors said it was a wonderful experience despite the sometimes horrendous conditions and the safety record of our biannual event remains 100% intact, despite 11 starters not completing the course. Our RORC tracker system has been a huge hit and has brought the Round Ireland to a whole new audience and hopefully interested future competitors. Our club members played a blinder in keeping the show on the road 24/7 but the real heroes are the participants themselves, who pit themselves against the elements in a truly testing offshore event that is the BMW Round Ireland Yacht Race.

[For sheer grit, determination and dedication the prize has to go to Peter McIntyre and Emma Nutt who entered in the two-handed class in their Sigma 36, Ruffian. Members of Scarborough Y C in Yorkshire. They sailed Ruffian all the way up the east coast of England and Scotland, down the Caledonian Canal, the Inner Isles, the North Channel and then the Irish Sea just to arrive at Wicklow.

And then they were forced to retire!

And then they had to sail all the way home. Ed.]

*At the other end of the scale the introduction of the two-handed class proved very popular. This is Moontiger (A. Bell) in 2006*

# TIPS FOR ROUND IRELAND SUCCESS

The Round Ireland Race is one of the classic middle distance offshore yacht races of the world and over the years the challenging, interesting and beautiful race course has attracted world class sailors and their boats. It's also a great race for the avid club sailor because if you successfully negotiate the tides and the weather and get your sail changes right you will be in with a great chance of picking up some silverware. There are ways and means of ensuring that your boat and crew are not only, prepared for the race down to the last detail, but also fit and in the right place at the right time to take best advantage of every opportunity as it presents itself.

## Preparation

There is no substitute for practice. So try to do as many offshore races as possible in the months leading up to the race. The Irish Sea Offshore Racing Association (ISORA) and the Royal Ocean Racing Club (RORC) both run middle distance offshore races. These races typically vary from 80 to 150 miles and can normally be completed in a weekend. They also provide a valuable opportunity to size up the opposition.

Make sure to double-check all equipment and fittings. Spend time inspecting blocks, winches and load bearing fittings. Do a rig check, looking for any hairline fractures at key stress points. Take all the tension off the rig as this is when some cracks may become apparent. Very importantly, ensure that the rig is tuned. If possible sail against an identical boat to match your speed. Have the engine serviced.

On the morning of the race scrub the bottom. This is important and many crews overlook this. One tenth of a knot gained can translate into minutes over a 700 miler.

## Safety

The Round Ireland Race falls under ISAF Offshore Special Regulations, Category 2. Year after year boats fall suspect of the high standards imposed by the official inspectors and, unlike the Fastnet Race, every boat is inspected without fail in the Round Ireland. The first inspections take place on the Thursday before the race and if you have studied the Special Safety Regulations and prepared your boat before arrival then, when your boat is inspected, you may have little extra preparation to ensure compliance allowing time to relax and plan the race. Do not under any circumstances alter equipment after the inspection. All Safety Regulations are there for good reason and may well save your life. For example, there is one stipulation that requires there to be a strop down below, anchoring the mast heel to the boat. If the mast breaks, then, in heavy seas, the bottom of the mast remaining down below can fly around, injuring the crew or damaging the craft. This has happened in offshore races before and is why this rule exists. Remember your boat must comply with the ISAF Offshore Special Regulations to permit you to race. So spend time reading up on these and prepare your boat accordingly. Ensure your tracking device is on and working. It's a great modern day tool that adds to the excitement of the race for all ashore as well as being a useful safety tool.

## Personal Safety

Make sure no crew members suffer from illnesses that you aren't aware of. If they do, ensure that they can be treated at sea and that these crew members will not be a liability to themselves or the crew. When on deck at night the following should be adhered to strictly: always wear a lifejacket, be clipped on with a safety harness and carry a personal light. A good quality waterproof head torch is essential for sail changes at night. There are long periods of inactivity during this race so safeguard against hypothermia by getting into warmer clothes sooner rather than later.

## Provisions

It is very important to strike a balance between feeding the crew well and not taking too much food. Options range from freeze-dried food to full on cooking. The former isn't exactly the most palatable while the latter is simply just too much hassle. The best way we have found is to prepare one hot meal per day in a tinfoil baking tray. This simply needs to be reheated in the oven or in a pot. For other meals make sandwiches and have soup. Bring chocolate for energy and fruit for health. It is very easy to bring too much food. Sit down and work out what the requirements will be for the expected duration of the race. Do not throw in extras for good measure or get tangled up in what if scenarios, such as getting becalmed. Many boats have retired from this race in the past but none from starvation. If you have to go without food for a day; so what? It just makes finishing the thing even better. And please, ask around to make sure that the whole crew will like the food that they are going to be eating. This is one area where democracy should be taken seriously on a boat.

Remove as much packaging as possible before the race. For example, do not bring a bag of sugar, empty it and put the sugar in a plastic container. Likewise, with items such as soup sachets, teabags etc.

Try to get your drinking water requirements right. This can be hard to gauge sometimes but one litre per person per day in these temperate latitudes is generally ample. To minimise weight, don't bring ice - just freeze your drinking water. This will melt gradually in an icebox throughout the race, keeping the ready-made-meals fresh while satisfying the vessel's drinking water requirements.

## Clothing

Here is my recommended wardrobe for the race:

- Sea Boots and thick socks
- Breathable Base and mid layers
- Shorts
- Breathable foul weather gear
- Balaclava / woolly hat
- Sunglasses
- Gloves

The above list caters for all the varying weather conditions that will be experienced on the race. All oilskin manufacturers have offshore or ocean ranges. These are getting a lot lighter than they used to be and less restrictive. If you wear all the above clothing underneath then the outer layer needs only to be waterproof and breathable. Each crew member requires only one set of clothes with maybe a spare pair of socks.

No member of the crew needs to have a bag for this race. There should be one bag for the whole crew where they can put a toothbrush or a camera etc. This bag could also hold spare clothes in case somebody gets wet. If you want to do well in this race do not allow iPods' and mobile phones or other creature comforts, which only tend to clutter below decks and serve as a distraction. Off watch, any crew member giving it 110% on deck will only want to bother with sleep.

## Sleeping Arrangements

Hot bunking is best. If your boat has eight crew, only take four sleeping bags to save weight and clutter. Crew must be woken and moved to windward bunks if necessary. Keep the weight to weather and amidships when beating in heavy airs and to leeward in light airs. When surfing in heavy airs keep the weight aft and to weather. Otherwise when running in light airs, try to keep the weight out of the ends. When sailing in really light conditions, keep the centre of gravity low, by sending as many of the crew as possible down below.

## Stowing Gear

Minimise it and keep it low, as near to the keel as possible. Keep it away from the ends too. Do not stow sails or gear in the cockpit. Remember, you can keep one spare sail on deck. If on a long fetch or reach, this is worth doing. Stow all sails on the floor in the main living area. Stow all safety gear such as flares, bolt-croppers, etc. within easy reach in an emergency. It's no use having to dig these out from under mounds of gear if danger is imminent.

## Navigation

Before the race map all way-points into the chart plotter. Make sure you map these in as close as possible to each headland. There is no sense in putting these way-points a mile off a headland if you do not need to go that far away from it. Having said that, it is worth remembering that it may well be worth giving a headland a wide berth either for safety's sake or because it's fast.

Passage plan the whole trip bearing in mind the tides over the whole course. Make sure you know the tidal vectors for any part of the race course at any time. Know the tidal gates such as Tuskar Rock or Rathlin Island and be aware of how these can benefit you or disadvantage you. It is important to always know HW Dover as this is your starting point for all calculations. So write down HW Dover for each day of the race, and then you can reference it quickly. Be aware of the effects of tide over banks. Sometimes a fair tide will be faster over a bank. Sometimes the opposite is true depending on the contours of the seabed. Look closely at the water, especially off the south coast where you will see corridors or rivers within the sea where the tide is stronger. These can push your vessel along faster.

Try to establish what tides are doing at headlands. These are marks of the course and we all know that in any race mark rounding is a key skill. The tide at a headland may be stronger in close or indeed there could be a back eddy under the cliff. Indeed there may well be a counter current on the exit from the headland. So be alive to all these possibilities.

In general, stay as close to the rhumb line as possible. Never stray off looking for wind. This is a serious gamble and rarely pays off. Play wind-shifts constantly especially in light conditions to keep your apparent wind speed high. Above all, work hard and push relentlessly. Even if you have made a mistake and are beginning to feel out of the frame, continue to push as hard as ever.

## Weather

Before the race get a long-range forecast and use this to estimate when you will reach key areas and at what time.

For weather forecast times type up a quick reference card which you can laminate and stick to the navigation station. Forecasts are available from RTE, BBC and Coast Radio Stations. Get every available forecast and keep a weather log to see if the trends/changes you are hearing are actually happening. If you have a system that accepts grib files this is fast becoming the preferred option for up to the minute meteorology. Use the weather reports from the series of met buoys and coastguard stations around the course. Keep a good watch on the VHF for boats reporting in, as they will give a good indication of conditions ahead or behind. Bring a small AM/FM receiver in addition to the boat radio.  Useful weather websites are:

www.met.ie
www.xcweather.co.uk
www.winguru.cz
www.eurometeo.com

Be prepared for heavy weather. Make sure storm sails are accessible and you know how to rig them. Ensure that the crew are well fed and rested before the onset, as these basic human requirements could be difficult to fulfil in extreme conditions. Keep a good lookout and maintain a radio watch. If surfing downwind, it is very important to wear the correct canvas to keep the boat sailing at the right speed. Too much, and the boat will broach; too little and it will become engulfed by the following sea. In these conditions it may well be necessary to temporarily alter the watch-keeping arrangements. For example, with a crew of eight it may well become necessary to run a system of six on and two off. Above all look to safety. Know your ports of refuge wear safety harnesses and lifejackets and don't take any unnecessary risks. Don't forget though that you are still racing and it's often in these types of conditions, where if you have the nerve and the skill, you can make hay.

## Double Handed

I can't profess to having any great knowledge of the double handed Round Ireland but I do know that in this type of sailing your sleep patterns are essential and your ability to make measured and not too hasty decisions together with preparing for the onset of changing weather conditions are paramount to maintaining speed and consistent momentum over the race course.

## ...and Finally

Enjoy this epic race. Imagine a Formula One motor racing circuit with no corners. Add the twists and bends into it and you have an exciting and varied course. Indeed, the same is true of the Round Ireland, which has so many turning points, providing for a range of diverse weather and tidal conditions that serve up a cocktail of complexity for the offshore racer. Whether you sail a 30ft cruiser/racer or an 80ft maxi you will find this race a challenge that is unrivalled amongst any middle distance offshore race the world over. If you have not contemplated doing the Round Ireland, or you are thinking about it but are undecided, I urge you to take the plunge and go for it. I guarantee you won't be disappointed.

*Tim Greenwood is a graduate of the WSC junior training 'academy'. He comes from a family with salt water in their veins. He is a much respected figure in the Irish sailing community*

*The Start. They don't take long to disappear over the horizon.*

# ENTRANTS AND RESULTS OF ALL ROUND IRELAND RACES

## 1980 - 2008

**Round Ireland Yacht Race**

**Summary 1980 - 2008**

| Year | Started | Finished | Line Honours | Elapsed Time | Winner | Elapsed Time | Last to Finish | Elapsed Time |
|------|---------|----------|--------------|--------------|--------|--------------|----------------|--------------|
| | | | | d:hh:mm:ss | | d:hh:mm:ss | | d:hh:mm:ss |
| 1980 | 16 | 10 | Force Tension | 5:15:02:27 | Raasay of Melfort | 6:03:37:44 | Tjaldur | 8:01:43:36 |
| 1982 | 17 | 13 | Moonduster | 4:03:45:25 | Moonduster | 4:03:45:25 | Raasay of Melfort | 9:01:53:18 |
| 1984 | 21 | 17 | Moonduster | 3:16:15:43 | Moonduster | 3:16:15:43 | Raasay of Melfort | 5:23:39:48 |
| 1986 | 27 | 27 | Mazda Drum | 4:03:35:43 | Spirit | 5:02:49:19 | Crazy Jane | 7:12:06:01 |
| 1988 | 52 | 48 | Moonduster | 4:20:15:46 | Lightning | 5:13:27:46 | Lady Shamrock | 7:12:08:06 |
| 1990 | 61 | 35 | Rothmans | 3:12:56:06 | Rothmans | 3:12:56:06 | Raasay of Melfort | 6:11:24:59 |
| 1992 | 46 | 33 | Whirlpool | 4:00:43:06 | Whirlpool | 4:00:43:06 | Raasay of Melfort | 6:18:31:53 |
| 1994 | 53 | 36 | Virgin City Jet | 3:16:30:33 | Bridgestone | 4:06:38:19 | Sty Tailte | 7:22:17:10 |
| 1996 | 56 | 55 | Bridgestone | 3:15:58:59 | Big Ears | 4:11:27:27 | Quest of Lytham | 7:08:53:50 |
| 1998 | 26 | 24 | Jeep Cherokee | 3:04:23:57 | Jeep Cherokee | 3:04:23:57 | Pandanova | 5:17:23:42 |
| 2000 | 28 | 26 | Fenix | 5:12:41:10 | Imp | 6:04:05:16 | Damp Store | 9:05:57:05 |
| 2002 | 28 | 24 | Team Tonic | 3:11:35:50 | Cavatina | 4:15:24:11 | Endeavour | 4:23:09:30 |
| 2004 | 47 | 37 | Team Spirit | 3:04:48:39 | Calyx Voice & Data | 4:05:38:33 | Enshalla | 6:18:16:16 |
| 2006 | 39 | 36 | Konica Minolta Zara | 4:04:57:30 | Cavatina | 6:09:20:20 | Quite Correct | 7:11:09:41 |
| 2008 | 44 | 28 | ICAP Leopard | 2:17:48:47 | Ireland West | 4:00:01:57 | Cassiopeia | 5:04:31:14 |
| Total | 561 | 449 | | | | | | |

| Place | Yacht | Entered by | CHS TCF | Elapsed Time | Corrected Time |
|---|---|---|---|---|---|
| | **Wm. Egan & Sons and Irish Boats and Yachting Round Ireland 1980** | | | | |
| 1 | Raasay of Melfort | B. Coad | 0.846 | 147:37:44 | 124:53:43 |
| 2 | Red Velvet | D. J. Ryan | 0.926 | 139:50:10 | 129:29:18 |
| 3 | Crazy Jane | B. Murphy | 0.926 | 149:22:37 | 129:59:21 |
| 4 | Orbih | B. Hayes/G. Wardell | 0.87 | 153:25:06 | 133:46:51 |
| 5 | Feanor | J. Poole | 0.966 | 139:19:19 | 134:35:06 |
| 6 | Force Ten-Sion | A.J. Vernon/J.S. Morris | 1 | 135:02:27 | 135:02:27 |
| 7 | Partizan of Emsworth | D.H.B. Fitzgerald | 0.987 | 137:14:04 | 135:27:01 |
| 8 | Bataleur | I. Campbell | 0.926 | 146:27:49 | 135:37:31 |
| 9 | Crazy Jane | S. Gallagher | 0.926 | 147:12:18 | 136:18:43 |
| 10 | Tjaldur | E. Doran | 0.913 | 193:43:36 | 196:52:51 |
| | Garter Star | J.R. Hall | 0.859 | Retired | Retired |
| | Tango | B. Siggins | 0.872 | Retired | Retired |
| | Iolar Mara | C. Kelly | 0.906 | Retired | Retired |
| | Tam O' Shanter | J.C. Butler | 0.985 | Retired | Retired |
| | Snowball | A. Cooper Ball | 0.973 | Retired | Retired |
| | Crystal Clear | P. A. Farrelly | 0.966 | Retired | Retired |

| Place | Yacht | Entered by | CHS TCF | Elapsed Time | Corrected Time |
|---|---|---|---|---|---|
| | **Irish TV Rentals Round Ireland 1982** **Results** | | | | |
| 1 | Moonduster | D. Doyle | 1.1274 | 099:45:25 | 112:27:58 |
| 2 | Storm Bird | C. Foley | 1.0131 | 118:52:34 | 120:26:00 |
| 3 | Feanor | J. Poole | 0.9018 | 138:13:07 | 124:38:44 |
| 4 | Wild Goose | S. Gallagher | 1.0258 | 124:47:53 | 128:01:04 |
| 5 | Shanaghee | T. McCauley | 1.0013 | 141:30:44 | 141:41:46 |
| 6 | Red Velvet | D. Ryan | 0.8950 | 164:44:37 | 147:26:44 |
| 7 | Korsar | R. Mollard | 0.8856 | 173:25:25 | 153:35:02 |
| 8 | Crystal Clear | A. Farrelly | 0.8948 | 172:45:09 | 154:34:44 |
| 9 | Finndabar of Howth | P. Jameson | 0.9587 | 174:04:37 | 166:53:15 |
| 10 | Partizan of Emsworth | D. Fitzgerald | 0.9529 | 177:55:02 | 169:32:14 |
| 11 | Emircedes | L. Shanahan | 0.8917 | 192:12:28 | 171:23:30 |
| 12 | Crazy Jane | B. Murphy | 0.8988 | 195:00:22 | 175:16:17 |
| 13 | Raasay of Melfort | B. Coad | 0.8800 | 217:53:18 | 191:44:30 |
| | Starry Starry Night | D. Blacklaws | 0.9263 | DNS | DNS |
| | Stratus | D. Harte | 1.0320 | Retired | |
| | William Tell | P. O'Donovan | 0.9839 | Retired | |
| | Challenge | I. Firth | 0.8694 | Retired | |
| | Midnight Oil | R. Gill | | Retired | |

| Place | Yacht | Sailed By | TCF | Elapsed | Corrected |
|---|---|---|---|---|---|
| | **Cork Dry Gin Round Ireland 1984** | | | | |
| 1 | Lightning | Kertesz/Poole | 0.9369 | 108:49:50 | 101:57:48 |
| 2 | Hamburg | M. Westphal | 1.0598 | 97:44:43 | 103:35:26 |
| 3 | Hesperia III | R. Gomes & B. Law | 1.1029 | 95:09:08 | 104:56:36 |
| 1 | Tearaway | P.J. O'Reilly | 0.953 | 110:07:12 | 104:56:40 |
| 4 | Born Free | N.Cordiner & D. Kensett | 1.1274 | 93:24:44 | 105:18:47 |
| 2 | Andante | M.J. Hall | 0.9729 | 112:20:02 | 109:17:23 |
| 1 | Irish Mist II | J. McCarthy | 1.0335 | 106:06:05 | 109:39:21 |
| 2 | Silver Shadow | I. Firth | 0.922 | 120:29:14 | 111:05:21 |
| 1 | Crystal Clear | A. Farrelly | 0.8911 | 126:05:26 | 112:21:33 |
| 3 | Lady Shamrock | B. Lyster | 0.8896 | 129:18:58 | 115:02:23 |
| 2 | Baron | S. Gallagher | 1.037 | 111:40:14 | 115:48:09 |
| 3 | Black Panther | J.J. Kelleher | 0.9771 | 119:04:59 | 116:21:22 |
| 3 | Lady Ruth | G.J. Moran | 0.9186 | 130:17:17 | 119:40:57 |
| 2 | Raasay of Melfort | B. Coad | 0.8847 | 143:39:48 | 127:05:56 |
| 4 | Marissa VI | F. Elmes | 0.9249 | 138:12:07 | 127:49:23 |
| 4 | Greased Lightning | R. Coffey & Britannia S.C. | 0.9659 | 142:17:45 | 137:26:37 |
| 1 | Moonduster | D.N. Doyle | 1.232 | 88:15:43 | 99:08:09 |
| | Imp | M. O'Leary & T. Sinstaden | | | Retired |
| | Stormbird | C. Foley | | | Retired |
| | Live Wire | D. O'Brien | | | Retired |
| | Rapparee II | Kelly/O'Coineen | | | Retired |

Baron had 25 minutes deducted from elapsed time for time lost in investigating flares.

| | Cork Dry Gin Round Ireland 1986: Results | | | | |
|---|---|---|---|---|---|
| Place | Yacht | Entered By | TMF | Elapsed Time | Corrected Time |
| 1 | Spirit | R. Burrows | 0.9369 | 126:49:19 | 118:49:10 |
| 2 | Lightning | L. Shanahan | 0.9339 | 129:14:54 | 120:42:18 |
| 3 | Demelza | N. Maguire | 0.8803 | 138:28:01 | 121:53:33 |
| 4 | Crystal Clear | P. Farrelly | 0.8816 | 138:42:14 | 122:16:52 |
| 5 | Tearaway | P. O'Reilly | 0.9473 | 129:10:02 | 122:21:36 |
| 6 | Seren Wib | William Humphries | 0.9354 | 131:09:31 | 122:41:09 |
| 7 | Madame | P. Watson | 0.9018 | 136:46:07 | 123:20:17 |
| 8 | Glider II | J. Poole | 0.9038 | 136:57:12 | 123:46:42 |
| 9 | Philips Innovator | D. Nauta | 1.225 | 100:50:59 | 124:32:58 |
| 10 | Musketeer II | B. Ivans | 0.9104 | 138:07:19 | 125:44:46 |
| 11 | Sunspot | G.R. Haggas | 0.9088 | 138:38:34 | 125:59:55 |
| 12 | Scenario | A.J.M. Jones | 0.9087 | 138:55:50 | 126:14:46 |
| 13 | The Famous Grouse | D. Cullen | 1.0494 | 120:57:16 | 126:55:47 |
| 14 | Imp | Roy Dickson | 1.0067 | 126:12:41 | 127:03:25 |
| 15 | Popje | T. Wormington | 0.9069 | 140:20:17 | 127:16:21 |
| 16 | White Rooster | James Donegan | 0.9311 | 137:42:31 | 128:13:14 |
| 17 | Moonduster | Denis Doyle | 1.1112 | 116:15:05 | 129:10:43 |
| 18 | Marissa VI | Frank Elmes | 0.9163 | 143:31:00 | 131:30:16 |
| 19 | 'Smagic of Lleyn | C.H. Peters | 0.9545 | 138:06:14 | 131:49:13 |
| 20 | Live Wire | D.D. O'Brien | 0.9642 | 138:02:14 | 133:05:44 |
| 21 | Trail Blazer | Barnard Barker | 0.9771 | 138:25:54 | 134:51:16 |
| 22 | Born Free | Norman Cordiner | 1.1139 | 121:19:57 | 135:09:08 |
| 23 | Mazda Drum | M. O'Leary/T. Power | 1.3727 | 99:35:43 | 136:42:52 |
| 24 | West Coast Cooler | G. O'Neill | 1.0031 | 138:31:12 | 138:56:58 |
| 25 | Electra | G.D. Taylor | 1.0027 | 138:37:04 | 138:59:31 |
| 26 | Baron | Seamus Gallaher | 1.0231 | 138:31:11 | 141:43:10 |
| 27 | Crazy Jane | B. Murphy | 0.8816 | 180:06:01 | 160:36:48 |

| | Cork Dry Gin Round Ireland 1988 | | | | |
|---|---|---|---|---|---|
| Place | Yacht | Entrant | TCF | Elapsed Time | Corrected Time |
| 1 | Lightning | Liam Shanahan | 0.9345 | 5:13:27:46 | 5:04:43:16 |
| 2 | Canterbury | A.J. Vernon | 1.0203 | 5:5:26:25 | 5:07:59:12 |
| 3 | Moonduster | Denis N. Doyle | 1.105 | 4:20:15:46 | 5:08:15:46 |
| 4 | Scenario Act II | William Humphries | 0.9343 | 5:17:47:40 | 5:08:44:29 |
| 5 | Europlex Deja Blue | Peter Wilson | 0.9361 | 5:17:35:07 | 5:08:47:37 |
| 6 | Crystal Light | Peter A. Farrelly | 0.9363 | 5:17:44:59 | 5:08:58:30 |
| 7 | Imp | | 1.0015 | 5:10:16:55 | 5:10:28:38 |
| 8 | Shooting Star | Eugene Casey | 0.9275 | 5:20:56:26 | 5:10:43:20 |
| 9 | Woodchester Challenger | B.W. Buchanan | 1.129 | 4:21:07:44 | 5:12:14:19 |
| 10 | Comanche Raider | Norbert and Patrick Rielly | 1.0555 | 5:05:42:25 | 5:12:41:01 |
| 11 | Megalopolis | Jim Poole - U.C, Taylor | 0.9795 | 5:15:30:15 | 5:12:43:35 |
| 12 | Blue Oyster | Barry J. Ord | 0.9761 | 5:17:49:20 | 5:14:31:42 |
| 13 | A.I.B Sports Club | Mark Mansfield | 0.98 | 5:17:32:45 | 5:14:47:41 |
| 14 | Poolbeg | Clem Kelly/Sean Whiston | 0.9991 | 5:15:04:18 | 5:14:57:01 |
| 15 | Penner | Bernie Pope | 0.9952 | 5:17:32:34 | 5:16:52:57 |
| 16 | Born Free | Michael O'Leary | 1.1054 | 5:03:54:16 | 5:16:57:50 |
| 17 | Corwynt Cymru | Gwylim F. Evans | 0.9952 | 5:17:45:16 | 5:17:05:35 |
| 18 | Greased Lightning | Bernard J. Cox | 0.9911 | 5:18:31:03 | 5:17:17:05 |
| 19 | Humphrey-Go-Cart | Vincent Farrell/Tony Fox | 0.901 | 6:09:18:08 | 5:18:07:31 |
| 20 | UFO III | Maurice Keating | 0.9123 | 6:06:54:30 | 5:19:29:54 |
| 21 | Milky Way | Edward Gerald Hudson | 0.9965 | 5:20:03:03 | 5:19:33:38 |
| 22 | Demelza | N.D. Maguire | 0.8762 | 6:16:56:09 | 5:21:00:43 |
| 23 | Finndabar of Howth | Kieran Jameson | 0.9565 | 6:05:37:28 | 5:23:06:57 |
| 24 | Emircedes | Peter Ryan | 0.8807 | 6:18:33:12 | 5:23:09:38 |
| 25 | Sunshine 101 | Romaine Cagney | 0.9346 | 6:09:17:17 | 5:23:15:47 |
| 26 | Firanjo III | Brian Ingham/Graham Hirst | 0.9888 | 6:01:48:48 | 6:00:10:49 |
| 27 | Fiona | Patrick Coyne | 0.8771 | 6:21:08:45 | 6:00:50:58 |
| 28 | Eliminator | John Roger Hall | 0.8834 | 6:20:17:57 | 6:01:08:41 |
| 29 | Andromeda of Dee | Dr. A.L. Stead | 0.9022 | 6:17:08:42 | 6:01:23:06 |
| 30 | Simply Red | Dale Kirk | 0.905 | 6:17:02:13 | 6:01:44:19 |
| 31 | Crazy Jane | | | 6:20:40:55 | 6:02:16:14 |
| 32 | Spirit of Bangor | David Craine | 1.048 | 5:20:26:07 | 6:03:10:34 |
| 33 | Hustler | | 0.9192 | 6:17:02:14 | 6:04:01:31 |
| 34 | Tearaway | F.J. Hughes | | 6:05:36:32 | 6:04:15:44 |
| 35 | Jubilee B | Maurice Homes | 0.9173 | 6:17:55:51 | 6:04:32:21 |
| 36 | Cork Dry Gin | Cork Dry Gin | 1.079 | 5:17:48:19 | 6:04:41:31 |
| 37 | Marissa VII | Frank Elmes | 0.9015 | 6:20:57:54 | 6:04:42:58 |
| 38 | Zag Zig | David Edgar Griffith | 0.9247 | 6:18:38:41 | 6:06:23:51 |
| 39 | Moonraker | Michael D. McGrath | 0.9747 | 6:10:25:20 | 6:06:30:55 |
| 40 | The Charelisa | Charles McDonnell | 0.8817 | 7:03:02:18 | 6:06:48:16 |
| 41 | Lady Shamrock | Paul K. Clandillon | 0.8781 | 7:12:08:06 | 6:14:10:35 |
| 42 | Twenty/Twenty | Jim Mackey | | 6:17:50:25 | 6:18:50:25 |
| | Sceolaing | Dermod Ryan | 0.9559 | Retired | |
| | Nyala | Martin G. Crotty | 0.9519 | Retired | |
| 45 | Jimi The Fink | Bernard Barker | 0.9305 | Retired | |
| | White Rooster | James D. Donegan | 0.9274 | Retired | |
| | Red Velvet | Michael O'Rahilly | 0.8973 | Retired | |
| | White & Mackay Drum | Sponsor/Harold Cudmore | 1.3137 | Retired | |
| | Marling Barracuda | Peter Minnis | 1.172 | Retired | |
| | Traffic | Gerald J. Moran | 0.912 | Retired | |

| \multicolumn{5}{c}{**Cork Dry Gin Round Ireland 1990 - Overall Results**} |

| Place | Yacht | Entered by | Elapsed | Corrected |
|-------|-------|------------|---------|-----------|
| 1 | Rothmans | Laurie Smith | 84:56:06 | 110:36:39 |
| 2 | NCB Ireland | Joe English | 86:16:38 | 112:34:28 |
| 3 | Mylene V | H. Mirlesse | 95:46:12 | 124:36:58 |
| 4 | Woodchester Challenge | Brian Buchanan | 104:10:09 | 132:46:26 |
| 5 | Decibel | Philip Watson | 142:57:45 | 133:18:45 |
| 6 | Comanche Raider | Norbert & Patrick Reilly | 129:46:47 | 136:40:16 |
| 7 | Shadowfax | N.J. Thistleton | 147:31:30 | 136:45:20 |
| 8 | Megalopolis | U.C. Taylor | 132:46:46 | 139:18:15 |
| 9 | Hill Samuel Offshore | Roy Dickson | 138:40:47 | 141:13:03 |
| 10 | Moonduster | Denis Doyle | 131:38:19 | 144:51:19 |
| 11 | Racal Chubb | B.W. Buchanan | 134:31:55 | 144:57:29 |
| 12 | Marissa VII | Frank Elmes | 162:02:14 | 147:05:32 |
| 13 | Imp | Roy Hamilton | 142:17:34 | 147:24:55 |
| 14 | Country Girl | T. Oliver Sheehy | 165:39:24 | 147:58:52 |
| 15 | Penner of Clontarf | E.F. Chandler | 145:26:50 | 148:30:06 |
| 16 | X-Cavator | Barry O'Loughlin | 144:33:12 | 148:53:24 |
| 17 | Preying Mantis | Thomas E. Crosbie | 146:03:52 | 149:07:55 |
| 18 | Greased Lightning | Bernard Cox | 141:50:13 | 149:32:34 |
| 19 | Corwynt Cymru | Gwylim F. Evans | 147:13:15 | 150:18:45 |
| 20 | Duel | Michael Fleming | 146:22:27 | 151:03:29 |
| 21 | Escapade | Vincent Farrell/Tony Fox | 162:15:06 | 151:38:25 |
| 22 | Springtime | Stuart Kinnear | 163:35:44 | 151:49:00 |
| 23 | Ringsend Challenge | Michael Purcell | 147:50:55 | 151:58:05 |
| 24 | Cuileann | Cormac Twomey | 145:49:45 | 153:24:44 |
| 25 | Raasay of Melfort | Brian P. Coad | 175:24:59 | 155:25:08 |
| 26 | The One & Only | Gerry O'Neill | 144:54:42 | 156:12:53 |
| 27 | Elusive | John & George Sisk | 144:20:18 | 157:45:43 |
| 28 | White Rooster | James D. Donegan | 163:41:46 | 160:25:20 |
| 29 | Nyala | Peter Cullen/Martin | 163:37:14 | 161:39:26 |
| 30 | Krystal | Bernard Pope | 163:41:24 | 161:54:26 |
| 31 | Malahide Tearaway | James M. Molihan/Des Nolan | 166:14:41 | 164:44:55 |
| 32 | Lady Irene | Oliver Farrell | 165:34:36 | 168:23:29 |
| 33 | Flying Formula | John D. Reilly | 166:34:00 | 170:03:52 |
| 34 | Aquelina | James S. Tyrrell | 167:42:51 | 171:14:10 |
| 35 | Spirit of Galway | Enda O'Coineen/John Killeen | 142:44:15 | 195:24:28 |

| Place | Yacht | Entered by | TCF | Elapsed time | Corrected time |
|---|---|---|---|---|---|
| | **Cork Dry Gin Round Ireland 1992 - Overall Results** | | | | |
| 1 | Whirlpool | C.Barrington | | 4:00:43:06 | 5:03:14:29 |
| 2 | The Youth Challenge | M. Humphries | 1.085 | 4:19:21:13 | 5:05:09:31 |
| 3 | Irish Mist | A. O'Leary | 1.078 | 4:20:37:05 | 5:05:42:51 |
| 4 | Imp | G. Radley | 1.028 | 5:02:35:31 | 5:06:01:28 |
| 5 | Keep on Smiling | J.T. & J.I. Little | 1.083 | 4:20:34:33 | 5:06:15:05 |
| 6 | Bootlegger | P. Wilson | 1.116 | 4:17:46:17 | 5:06:58:07 |
| 7 | Shadowfax | N.J. Thistleton | 0.991 | 5:08:11:02 | 5:07:01:48 |
| 8 | Be Careful Please | D. Cullen | 1.017 | 5:05:11:31 | 5:07:19:12 |
| 9 | Daisy Belle | O. Sorensen | 1.041 | 5:03:12:13 | 5:08:15:17 |
| 10 | Wet 'N' Wilde | A.H. Wilde & A .J.M. Jones | 1.095 | 4:21:14:30 | 5:08:22:46 |
| 11 | Emircedes | P. Ryan & M. Horgan | 0.916 | 5:20:17:09 | 5:08:30:06 |
| 12 | Witchcraft of Howth | W. Nixon et al | 0.985 | 5:10:44:17 | 5:08:46:37 |
| 13 | Krystal | B. Pope | 0.987 | 5:11:01:22 | 5:09:19:10 |
| 14 | Cornix II | R.J. Raven | 1.017 | 5:07:13:20 | 5:09:23:05 |
| 15 | Incitatus | E.F. Chandler | 1.017 | 5:08:01:21 | 5:10:11:55 |
| 16 | Madame X | V. Delaney et al | 1.034 | 5:07:07:17 | 5:11:26:36 |
| 17 | Samakai of St. Helier | J. Buckley | 0.911 | 6:01:01:26 | 5:12:07:00 |
| 18 | Blue Diamond | R. & V. Dickson | 1.118 | 4:22:35:51 | 5:12:35:31 |
| 19 | Moonduster | D.N. Doyle | 1.152 | 4:19:10:18 | 5:12:40:39 |
| 20 | Megalopolis | U. Taylor | 1.15 | 4:19:41:23 | 5:13:02:35 |
| 21 | Elysia | A. Vernon & M O'Leary | 1.157 | 4:19:10:43 | 5:13:15:41 |
| 22 | Sarah Mercedes | L Shanahan | 1.032 | 5:09:53:58 | 5:14:03:22 |
| 23 | Mayhem | J. Killeen | 1.044 | 5:10:13:07 | 5:15:56:53 |
| 24 | White Rooster | J.D. Donegan | 0.984 | 5:18:36:28 | 5:16:23:24 |
| 25 | Crystal Light | A. Farrelly | 1.008 | 5:16:07:30 | 5:17:12:50 |
| 26 | Janey Mac | R.P. Lee | 1.017 | 5:16:06:39 | 5:18:25:28 |
| 27 | Aquelina | J.S. Tyrrell | 1.017 | 5:18:30:46 | 5:20:52:02 |
| 28 | Pandanova | P.C. Boyle | 1.017 | 5:18:43:47 | 5:21:05:07 |
| 29 | Duel | M. Fleming | 1.024 | 5:18:28:31 | 5:21:47:55 |
| 30 | Bandersnatch | K. O'Grady | 0.947 | 6:05:44:49 | 5:21:48:37 |
| 31 | Hideaway | F.J. Hughes | 1.024 | 5:18:42:37 | 5:22:02:21 |
| 32 | Raasay of Melfort | B.P Coad | 0.876 | 6:18:31:53 | 5:22:22:38 |
| 33 | Ringsend Challenge II | M. Purcell et al | 1.028 | 5:21:43:10 | 6:01:41:15 |
| | With Integrity | J. Menton | 1.328 | 4:23:46:33 | 6:15:03:44 |
| | Star Wars | J.D. McEvoy | | | Dsq. |
| | Elusive | J. & G. Sisk | 1.106 | | Retired |
| | Tring Challenge | J. Reilly | 1.031 | | Retired |
| | Koala | P. Cullen & M. Crotty | 1.03 | | Retired |
| | Mystique of Malahide | R. & R. Michael | 1.002 | | Retired |
| | Marissa VIII | F. Elmes | 0.995 | | Retired |
| | Pacesetter | D. Nesbit | 1.028 | | Retired |
| | Draig O'R Mor | G. R. Haggas | 1.024 | | Retired |
| | Confusion | B. Scanlon | 0.964 | | Retired |
| | Boomerang | P. Kirwan | 0.91 | | Retired |
| | Live Wire | S. Dunn | 0.974 | | Retired |
| | Billy Whizz | D. Meagher | 0.979 | | Retired |
| | Kamakura V | C. Geoghegan | 0.984 | | Retired |

| Place | Yacht | Entered By | TCF | Elapsed | Corrected |
|---|---|---|---|---|---|
| | **Cork Dry Gin Round Ireland 1994 - Overall Results** | | | | |
| 1 | Bridgestone | Peter Wilson | 1.046 | 3:16:30:33 | 4:11:21:36 |
| 2 | Prospector | Richard Burroughs | 1.064 | 3:23:46:57 | 4:13:13:30 |
| 3 | Corwynt | Gwilym Evans | 1.061 | 4:01:45:45 | 4:13:59:31 |
| 4 | Janey Mac II | A Lee | 1.064 | 4:02:35:15 | 4:14:18:10 |
| 5 | Megalopolis | Urban Taylor | 1.119 | 4:06:38:19 | 4:14:19:10 |
| 6 | V.S.O.P. | John Godkin | 1.030 | 4:06:39:18 | 4:14:54:47 |
| 7 | Keep On Smiling | Tom Little | 1.065 | 4:07:40:05 | 4:14:58:10 |
| 8 | Deerstalker | Michael Taylor-Jones | 0.911 | 4:07:40:05 | 4:15:06:42 |
| 9 | Imp | George Radley Jnr. | 1.019 | 4:08:11:48 | 4:17:02:27 |
| 10 | Beamont Spirit | Roy Dickson | 1.169 | 4:11:40:57 | 4:18:17:04 |
| 11 | Mad Bull | Olaf Sorensen | 1.028 | 4:14:55:59 | 4:18:33:44 |
| 12 | Amazing Grace | Anthony Kingston | 0.973 | 4:15:26:31 | 4:20:33:27 |
| 13 | Witchcraft of Howth | Nixon/Wheeler/Whelehan | 0.970 | 4:18:50:30 | 4:21:10:37 |
| 14 | Marissa VIII | Frank Elmes | 0.992 | 4:22:17:57 | 4:23:53:57 |
| 15 | Air Corps I | Tom O'Connor | 1.011 | 4:22:39:36 | 4:23:57:55 |
| 16 | Hobo V | John Bourke | 1.011 | 4:22:47:29 | 5:00:05:53 |
| 17 | Duel | Michael Fleming | 1.017 | 4:22:59:03 | 5:00:18:37 |
| 18 | Gwawr | Anthony Jones | 1.014 | 4:23:47:31 | 5:00:39:00 |
| 19 | Stormbird | Ciaran Foley | 1.268 | 5:00:45:17 | 5:01:27:08 |
| 20 | Aquelina | James Tyrrell | 1.062 | 5:00:48:03 | 5:01:57:43 |
| 21 | Spirit of Mayo | Robin Smith | 1.011 | 5:00:51:58 | 5:02:04:59 |
| 22 | Virgin City Jet | Dix/Power/Barrington | 1.414 | 5:01:58:00 | 5:05:09:07 |
| 23 | Rock Adventurer | Daniel Gallagher | 1.011 | 5:09:34:06 | 5:10:59:37 |
| 24 | Samaki | John Buckley | 0.910 | 5:11:17:30 | 5:11:47:35 |
| 25 | Black Tie | Frank Jackson | 1.011 | 5:11:44:36 | 5:12:44:09 |
| 26 | Nissan I | Siobhan Crowley | 1.011 | 5:14:39:56 | 5:13:11:33 |
| 27 | White Rooster | James Donegan | 0.981 | 5:18:14:53 | 5:15:37:17 |
| 28 | Joliba | James Ryan & A. Murray | 0.940 | 5:18:22:21 | 5:16:50:07 |
| 29 | St. Christopher | C.G. Fairhurst | 1.026 | 5:23:07:17 | 5:18:10:01 |
| 30 | Arthur | Robin Kay/ G. Dempsey | 1.011 | 6:00:49:39 | 5:19:53:41 |
| 31 | Darramy | Brian Wallace | 1.011 | 6:01:34:10 | 6:00:41:45 |
| 32 | Alpara | B & M Carroll | 0.920 | 6:17:44:13 | 6:19:09:40 |
| 33 | Raasay of Melfort | Brian Coad | 0.873 | 7:09:20:57 | 6:21:04:56 |
| 34 | Spirit of Ringsend | Purcell/Daly/Crowley | 1.023 | 7:14:35:51 | 6:21:27:25 |
| 35 | Ulysses | Par McArdle | 0.908 | 7:21:05:52 | 6:21:47:55 |
| 36 | Sty Tailte | Lt. William Roberts | 0.928 | 7:22:17:10 | 7:08:35:08 |

| **Cork Dry Gin Round Ireland 1994 - Overall Results** | | | | |
|---|---|---|---|---|
| Retirals | | | | |
| Estrellita | Bernard Freyne | 0.966 | Retired | |
| Emircedes | P. Ryan & M. Hogan | 0.906 | Retired | |
| Trailblazer | Roy Conway | 0.952 | Retired | |
| Tjaldur | Sean Whiston | 0.880 | Retired | |
| Pink Panther | Dr. Seamus Moneley | 0.921 | Retired | |
| Moonduster | Denis Doyle | 1.154 | Retired | |
| Elusive | John Sisk | 1.098 | Retired | |
| Maxol Unleaded | G. Peck & K. Jameson | 1.121 | Retired | |
| Comanche Raider | Roy Hamilton | 1.125 | Retired | |
| A.I.B. Sailing | A.I.B. Sailing Club | 1.156 | Retired | |
| Tropicana | Jill Somerville | 1.064 | Retired | |
| Angel | Gerard Whiston | 0.896 | Retired | |
| Juno | Simon Knowles | 0.998 | Retired | |
| Golden Gryphon | John O'Regan | 0.909 | Retired | |
| Constance | Clem Kelly | 1.065 | Retired | |
| Tir Na nog | Asgard Group | 0.883 | Retired | |
| Jackabout | Andrew Hall | 1.108 | Retired | |

## Cork Dry Gin Round Ireland 1996 - Overall Results

| Place | Yacht | Entered by | TCF | Elapsed | Corrected |
|---|---|---|---|---|---|
| 1 | Big Ears | Michael Boyd | 1.048 | 4:11:27:27 | 4:16:36:56 |
| 2 | Beaumont Spirit | Roy Dickson | 1.115 | 4:06:20:58 | 4:18:07:11 |
| 3 | Silk 2 | Jocelyn Waller | 1.144 | 4:04:07:02 | 4:18:32:03 |
| 4 | Sarah J | Cormac Twomey | 1.077 | 4:11:07:40 | 4:19:22:36 |
| 5 | Mad Bull | Olaf Sorensen | 1.093 | 4:09:46:09 | 4:19:36:21 |
| 6 | Securon IV | B.B. Archer | 1.004 | 4:19:30:00 | 4:19:57:43 |
| 7 | Keep on Smiling | Tim Little | 1.061 | 4:13:45:38 | 4:20:07:36 |
| 8 | Ragtime III | Geoff Whittaker | 1.069 | 4:12:59:04 | 4:20:30:16 |
| 9 | Jackdaw | David K Walters | 1.090 | 4:11:20:58 | 4:21:00:39 |
| 10 | Mobil I | Tim Corcoran | 1.093 | 4:20:51:28 | 4:21:19:31 |
| 11 | Imp | George Radley Jr. | 1.027 | 4:19:29:14 | 4:22:36:19 |
| 12 | Kinsale & Kilmacsimon | A.J. Kingston | 1.044 | 4:19:22:32 | 5:00:27:07 |
| 13 | Paddy Garibaldi | J.A. Twomey | 1.058 | 4:18:48:00 | 5:01:27:30 |
| 14 | Changeling | K. Jameson/A. McManus | 1.005 | 5:01:10:10 | 5:01:46:31 |
| 15 | Moonduster | Denis Doyle | 1.151 | 4:10:31:24 | 5:02:36:30 |
| 16 | Janey Mac II | Adrian F Lee | 1.061 | 4:19:41:43 | 5:02:45:10 |
| 17 | Torbellino | Thomas J. Duggan | 1.004 | 5:02:27:08 | 5:02:56:31 |
| 18 | Pandanova II | Daniel Gallagher | 1.004 | 5:02:32:34 | 5:03:01:59 |
| 19 | Joggernaut | Donal Morrissey | 0.984 | 5:05:10:28 | 5:03:10:18 |
| 20 | Mayo Naturally | Robim Smith | 1.073 | 4:19:13:27 | 5:03:38:08 |
| 21 | Midnight Express | Tommy Murphy | 1.013 | 5:02:38:22 | 5:04:14:02 |
| 22 | Sorcery | Jake Wood | 1.419 | 3:16:15:02 | 5:05:13:39 |
| 23 | Jackhammer | Andrew Hall | 1.089 | 4:19:12:57 | 5:05:28:12 |
| 24 | Sigmagic | Roger K. Dobson | 1.060 | 4:23:29:11 | 5:06:39:20 |
| 25 | Phoenix III | Simon Knowles | 1.004 | 5:06:36:12 | 5:07:06:35 |
| 26 | DMYC Challenge | Theo Phelan | 1.004 | 5:06:42:55 | 5:07:13:20 |
| 27 | Canterbury | Joe McCarthy | 1.077 | 4:22:17:58 | 5:07:24:31 |
| 28 | Aseco | Harry Harbison | 1.004 | 5:07:39:48 | 5:08:10:26 |

| Place | Yacht | Entered by | TCF | Elapsed | Corrected |
|-------|-------|------------|-----|---------|-----------|
| | **Cork Dry Gin Round Ireland 1996 - Overall Results - Continued** | | | | |
| 29 | Greased Lightning | Bernard Cox | 1.021 | 5:07:37:58 | 5:10:18:47 |
| 30 | Mullingar Adventuror | Pat McArdle | 1.004 | 5:10:45:32 | 5:11:16:55 |
| 31 | Gwawr | A.J.M. Jones | 1.004 | 5:10:57:58 | 5:11:29:24 |
| 32 | Equity & Law II | Peter Gabriel | 1.303 | 4:06:55:28 | 5:13:27:33 |
| 33 | Bridgestone | Michael Slade | 1.519 | 3:15:58:58 | 5:13:38:45 |
| 34 | Joliba | Jim Ryan | 0.928 | 6:00:24:30 | 5:14:00:39 |
| 35 | White Rooster | James E Donegan | 0.978 | 5:18:00:38 | 5:14:58:28 |
| 36 | Boomerang | Paul Kirwan | 0.902 | 6:05:38:36 | 5:14:58:42 |
| 37 | Valkyrie | Stewart Hunter | 1.004 | 5:14:41:20 | 5:15:13:40 |
| 38 | Aquanox Thais | C. Fitzgerald | 0.901 | 6:06:29:23 | 5:15:53:32 |
| 39 | Aquelina | James S. Tyrrell | 1.060 | 5:09:42:00 | 5:17:28:55 |
| 40 | Team Builder | Mike Moloney | 1.004 | 5:18:55:37 | 5:19:28:58 |
| 41 | Garda Debut | Martin Landers | 1.004 | 5:19:43:33 | 5:20:17:05 |
| 42 | Cosmic Dancer III | Len Arnold | 0.981 | 5:23:17:40 | 5:20:34:19 |
| 43 | Aenigma | B.E. Woodhouse | 1.014 | 5:18:51:28 | 5:20:48:06 |
| 44 | Alpara | Carroll Bros. | 0.925 | 6:09:05:15 | 5:21:36:21 |
| 45 | Tiara | John R. Derham | 0.981 | 6:01:42:07 | 5:22:56:01 |
| 46 | Sasha | Frances O'Shaughnessy | 1.004 | 5:23:17:40 | 5:23:52:03 |
| 47 | Norvantes | Mel Bendon | 0.992 | 6:01:06:26 | 5:23:56:47 |
| 48 | Estrellita | Bernard Freyne | 0.964 | 6:07:32:57 | 6:00:09:55 |
| 49 | Arbitration | Lawerence McGivern | 1.020 | 6:00:29:25 | 6:03:22:48 |
| 50 | Deja Blue | Noel foley | 1.000 | 6:04:05:16 | 6:04:05:16 |
| 51 | Quest of Lytham | C.W. Yarwood | 0.849 | 7:08:53:50 | 6:06:11:09 |
| 52 | Golden Gryphon | John O'Regan | 0.908 | 6:21:33:48 | 6:06:19:53 |
| 53 | CQuest | Martin McKeever | 1.033 | 6:03:30:21 | 6:08:22:25 |
| 54 | Trailblazer | Francis Kelly | 0.949 | 6:17:05:50 | 6:08:52:53 |
| 55 | Creightons Naturally | David Leigh | 1.322 | 5:00:55:13 | 6:15:51:24 |

### Round Ireland Yacht Race

### Summary 1980 - 2008

| Year | Started | Finished | Line Honours | Elapsed Time | Winner | Elapsed Time | Last to Finish | Elapsed Time |
|------|---------|----------|--------------|--------------|--------|--------------|----------------|--------------|
| | | | | d:hh:mm:ss | | d:hh:mm:ss | | d:hh:mm:ss |
| 1980 | 16 | 10 | Force Tension | 5:15:02:27 | Raasay of Melfort | 6:03:37:44 | Tjaldur | 8:01:43:36 |
| 1982 | 17 | 13 | Moonduster | 4:03:45:25 | Moonduster | 4:03:45:25 | Raasay of Melfort | 9:01:53:18 |
| 1984 | 21 | 17 | Moonduster | 3:16:15:43 | Moonduster | 3:16:15:43 | Raasay of Melfort | 5:23:39:48 |
| 1986 | 27 | 27 | Mazda Drum | 4:03:35:43 | Spirit | 5:02:49:19 | Crazy Jane | 7:12:06:01 |
| 1988 | 52 | 48 | Moonduster | 4:20:15:46 | Lightning | 5:13:27:46 | Lady Shamrock | 7:12:08:06 |
| 1990 | 61 | 35 | Rothmans | 3:12:56:06 | Rothmans | 3:12:56:06 | Raasay of Melfort | 6:11:24:59 |
| 1992 | 46 | 33 | Whirlpool | 4:00:43:06 | Whirlpool | 4:00:43:06 | Raasay of Melfort | 6:18:31:53 |
| 1994 | 53 | 36 | Virgin City Jet | 3:16:30:33 | Bridgestone | 4:06:38:19 | Sty Tailte | 7:22:17:10 |
| 1996 | 56 | 55 | Bridgestone | 3:15:58:59 | Big Ears | 4:11:27:27 | Quest of Lytham | 7:08:53:50 |
| 1998 | 26 | 24 | Jeep Cherokee | 3:04:23:57 | Jeep Cherokee | 3:04:23:57 | Pandanova | 5:17:23:42 |
| 2000 | 28 | 26 | Fenix | 5:12:41:10 | Imp | 6:04:05:16 | Damp Store | 9:05:57:05 |
| 2002 | 28 | 24 | Team Tonic | 3:11:35:50 | Cavatina | 4:15:24:11 | Endeavour | 4:23:09:30 |
| 2004 | 47 | 37 | Team Spirit | 3:04:48:39 | Calyx Voice & Data | 4:05:38:33 | Enshalla | 6:18:16:16 |
| 2006 | 39 | 36 | Konica Minolta Zara | 4:04:57:30 | Cavatina | 6:09:20:20 | Quite Correct | 7:11:09:41 |
| 2008 | 44 | 28 | ICAP Leopard | 2:17:48:47 | Ireland West | 4:00:01:57 | Cassiopeia | 5:04:31:14 |
| Total | 561 | 449 | | | | | | |

### Wicklow Sailing Club Round Ireland 2000

| Place | Yacht | Entrant | TCF | Elapsed | Corrected |
|-------|-------|---------|-----|---------|-----------|
| 1 | **Imp** | **G. Radley** | **1.024** | **6:04:05:16** | **6:07:38:31** |
| 2 | Galliver | G. McConnell | 0.995 | 6:08:29:57 | 6:07:44:12 |
| 3 | Wavesweeper | D. Lee | 1.056 | 6:00:55:55 | 6:09:02:53 |
| 4 | Greased Lightning | B. Cox | 1.011 | 6:08:13:30 | 6:09:53:58 |
| 5 | Janey Mac | Adrian Lee | 1.056 | 6:02:57:22 | 6:11:11:08 |
| 6 | Psipsina | J. Loden | 1.043 | 6:05:06:21 | 6:11:31:03 |
| 7 | ADC TopCar | T. & P. Kingston | 1.077 | 6:00:37:30 | 6:11:45:40 |
| 8 | Joker | T. Mayberry | 0.995 | 6:13:02:20 | 6:12:15:13 |
| 9 | Highland Dancer | Carroll Bros. | 0.992 | 6:14:14:39 | 6:12:58:42 |
| 10 | Cracklin' Rosie | R. Dickson | 1.095 | 5:23:31:31 | 6:13:09:37 |
| 11 | Changeling | K. Jameson | 0.994 | 6:14:21:25 | 6:13:24:24 |
| 12 | Great Bear | B. Stewart | 1.085 | 6:01:08:10 | 6:13:28:22 |
| 13 | Ragtime | G. Whittaker | 1.042 | 6:08:27:00 | 6:14:51:10 |
| 14 | Aquelina | J. Tyrell | 1.075 | 6:05:04:53 | 6:16:15:45 |
| 15 | Mary P | N. Prendeville | 1.085 | 6:04:02:36 | 6:16:37:37 |
| 16 | Cutting Edge | M.J. Lawson | 1.079 | 6:05:34:29 | 6:17:23:28 |
| 17 | Lobster | G. Horgan | 1.126 | 5:23:31:31 | 6:17:36:34 |
| 18 | Crazy Horse | Nigel Rollo | 1.075 | 6:07:19:40 | 6:18:40:38 |
| 19 | People Group | M. Boyd | 1.147 | 5:22:35:00 | 6:19:32:35 |
| 20 | Moonduster | D. Doyle | 1.145 | 5:23:07:15 | 6:19:52:24 |
| 21 | Fenix | R. Balding | 1.268 | 5:12:41:10 | 7:00:14:46 |
| 22 | State O'Chassis | M. O'Connell | 0.995 | 7:01:49:45 | 7:00:58:48 |
| 23 | RNLI Wild Goose | N. Condon | 0.96 | 7:12:50:15 | 7:05:36:14 |
| 24 | Clarion of Wight | B & Y Turner | 0.968 | 7:12:40:19 | 7:06:53:26 |
| 25 | Tokio | M.O'Brien & CO. | 1.452 | 5:13:46:00 | 8:02:13:45 |
| 26 | Damp Store | M. Davis | 0.949 | 9:05:57:05 | 8:18:37:55 |
| | Rebellion | J. Hughes | 1.072 | Retired | |
| | Trident | A. Mills | 0.995 | Retired | |

## Sport Ireland Round Ireland 2002 - Overall Results

| Place | Yacht | Entrant | TCF | Elapsed | Corrected |
|---|---|---|---|---|---|
| 1 | Cavatina | Eric Lisson | 0.926 | 4:15:24:11 | 4:07:09:33 |
| 2 | Imp | George Radley | 1.026 | 4:06:59:46 | 4:09:40:26 |
| 3 | Hippocampus | Michael Greville | 0.933 | 4:17:53:00 | 4:10:15:11 |
| 4 | Changeling | Kieran Jameson | 0.991 | 4:13:23:54 | 4:12:24:49 |
| 5 | Tiger | Oliver Sheehy | 1.078 | 4:05:35:35 | 4:13:31:02 |
| 6 | Sapphire | Frank Clarke | 1.069 | 4:06:31:55 | 4:13:36:24 |
| 7 | Joker | John Maybury | 0.997 | 4:14:12:49 | 4:13:52:59 |
| 8 | Team Tonic | Nick Hewson | 1.315 | 3:11:34:50 | 4:13:54:30 |
| 9 | Cracklin Rosie | Roy Dickson | 1.109 | 4:03:25:26 | 4:14:15:40 |
| 10 | Errislannan | Paul Kirwan | 0.997 | 4:15:52:09 | 4:15:32:01 |
| 11 | Xerxes | M. Liddy | 1.068 | 4:09:10:57 | 4:16:20:06 |
| 12 | White Rooster | Dermot Cronin | 0.966 | 4:20:20:45 | 4:16:23:24 |
| 13 | Aquelina | James Tyrrell | 1.074 | 4:08:45:41 | 4:16:30:49 |
| 14 | Azure | Bob & Barbie Stewart | 1.154 | 4:01:44:51 | 4:16:48:02 |
| 15 | Little Princess | Fiona Naisbitt | 1.127 | 4:04:31:16 | 4:17:17:14 |
| 16 | Trinculo of Howth | M. Fleming | 1.058 | 4:11:24:52 | 4:17:38:40 |
| 17 | Fenix | Richard Balding | 1.258 | 3:18:42:20 | 4:18:06:27 |
| 18 | Something Fishy | Johnny Morgan | 0.983 | 4:20:10:35 | 4:18:12:05 |
| 19 | Lobster | Gary A. Horgan | 1.128 | 4:05:18:54 | 4:18:17:00 |
| 20 | Lancastrian | Neil Eatough | 1.072 | 4:11:12:20 | 4:18:55:28 |
| 21 | Endeavour | Conor Phelan | 0.966 | 4:23:09:30 | 4:19:06:25 |
| 22 | Thalia | Lemass, Tennyson, et al | 1.061 | 4:13:14:11 | 4:19:53:59 |
| 23 | Maiden | Terry Nielson | 1.177 | 4:03:25:41 | 4:21:01:37 |
| 24 | Irisha | Adrian F. Lee | 1.139 | 4:07:41:20 | 4:22:06:06 |
| DNS | Pichenette | Samuel Caillault | 0.927 | DNS | DNS |
| retired | Jabberwokky | Tim Costello | 1.075 | retired | retired |
| retired | Fusion | Micheal O'Carroll | 1.046 | retired | retired |
| retired | State O' Chassis | Kevin Buckley | 0.997 | retired | retired |
| retired | Fandango | Terence Fair | 0.934 | retired | retired |

| Place | Yacht | Entrant | TCF | Elapsed | Corrected |
|-------|-------|---------|-----|---------|-----------|
| | **BMW Round Ireland 2004 - Overall Results** | | | | |
| 1 | Calyx Voice & Data | Eamonn Crosbie | 1.046 | 4:05:38:33 | 4:10:19:05 |
| 2 | Jazz | Chris Bull | 1.197 | 3:17:27:35 | 4:11:05:00 |
| 3 | Cavatina | Eric Lisson | 0.928 | 4:20:25:00 | 4:12:02:05 |
| 4 | Chieftain | Ger O'Rourke | 1.075 | 4:06:04:47 | 4:13:44:09 |
| 5 | Blondie | Eamonn Rohan | 1.035 | 4:11:47:36 | 4:15:33:58 |
| 6 | Freya | Conor Doyle | 1.106 | 4:05:09:05 | 4:15:52:24 |
| 7 | Inis Mor | Bernard & Laurent Gouy | 1.019 | 4:13:59:43 | 4:16:05:07 |
| 8 | Do Dingle.com - (2) | Fitzgerald & Lemonnier | 1.096 | 4:06:30:00 | 4:16:20:24 |
| 9 | City Jet Solune | Jean P. Chomett | 1.429 | 3:07:25:41 | 4:17:30:10 |
| 10 | Endeavour | Conor Phelan | 1.025 | 4:14:48:26 | 4:17:34:39 |
| 11 | Tonnerre de Breskens | Piet Vroon | 1.288 | 3:16:26:35 | 4:17:54:53 |
| 12 | Second Love | Gerard Cok | 1.257 | 3:18:59:34 | 4:18:22:41 |
| 13 | White Rooster | Dermott Cronin | 0.96 | 4:23:20:31 | 4:18:34:06 |
| 14 | Minnie the Moocher | Anthony Richards & Ian Travers | 1.158 | 4:03:05:20 | 4:18:44:42 |
| 15 | Galileo | Kelleher, Lemass & Tennnyson | 1.096 | 4:08:45:50 | 4:18:49:16 |
| 16 | Cecille | George Radley | 0.921 | 5:04:43:21 | 4:18:52:10 |
| 17 | Changeling | Kieran Jameson | 0.988 | 4:20:17:30 | 4:18:53:46 |
| 18 | 02 Team Spirit | David Nixon | 1.496 | 3:04:48:39 | 4:18:54:32 |
| 19 | Zwerver | Frans Van Schalk | 1.037 | 4:14:52:19 | 4:18:58:27 |
| 20 | White Tiger | Oliver Sheehy | 1.112 | 4:08:00:46 | 4:19:39:44 |
| 21 | Aquelina | James Tyrrell | 1.031 | 4:16:14:50 | 4:19:43:37 |
| 22 | Thunder 2 - (2) | Robert Boulter | 1.112 | 4:08:41:20 | 4:20:24:51 |
| 23 | Lobster | Gary Horgan | 1.124 | 4:08:39:35 | 4:21:38:15 |
| 24 | Trinculo of Howth | Michael Fleming | 1.056 | 4:15:47:13 | 4:22:02:49 |
| 25 | Nunatak - (2) | Mike Jaques | 1.087 | 4:12:47:17 | 4:22:15:09 |
| 26 | Isobar | Tom Roche | 1.08 | 4:14:10:02 | 4:22:58:50 |
| 27 | Hark | Roy Conway | 1.099 | 4:12:31:30 | 4:23:16:08 |
| 28 | Xerxes | Laurence O'Neill | 1.066 | 4:16:29:25 | 4:23:54:53 |
| 29 | Genevieve | Diarmuid Good | 0.976 | 5:04:21:01 | 5:01:21:57 |
| 30 | Moontiger - (2) | Alan Bell | 1.015 | 4:23:53:41 | 5:01:41:35 |
| 31 | State of Chassis | Kevin Buckley | 0.995 | 5:06:28:15 | 5:05:50:19 |
| 32 | Confusion | Ruth Scanlon & Lucy Walters | 1.028 | 5:03:52:53 | 5:07:21:00 |
| 33 | Lancastrian | Neil Eatough | 1.083 | 5:00:26:26 | 5:10:26:14 |
| 34 | Nike | Des Rogers | 1.012 | 5:14:31:04 | 5:16:07:55 |
| 35 | Enshallah | John Sweeney | 0.907 | 6:18:16:16 | 6:03:10:48 |
| 36 | Celtic Spirit | Michael Holland | 1.02 | 6:00:59:03 | 6:03:53:02 |
| 37 | Felix | Andrew Guerin | 0.988 | 6:13:03:35 | 6:11:10:30 |
| | Clarionet | Paul March | 0.917 | | |
| | Errislannin | Paul Kirwan | 0.995 | | |
| | Fidessa Fastwave | Chris Browne | 1.209 | | |
| | Groupe Partouche | Christophe Coatnoan | 1.102 | | |
| | Irisha | Adrian Lee | 1.138 | | |
| | Joker | John Maybury | 0.995 | | |
| | Megalopolis | Matt Davies & Andrew Corrie | 1.017 | | |
| | Oz Privateer | Don & Heather Kennedy | 1.086 | | |
| | Saber - (2) | James Eyre | 0.902 | | |
| | Broadsword | Ken & Anna Hudson | 1.062 | | |

| Place | Yacht | Entrant | TCF | Elapsed | Corrected |
|---|---|---|---|---|---|
| | **BMW Round Ireland 2006 - Results** | | | | |
| 1 | Cavatina | Eric Lisson | 0.927 | 153:20:20 | 142:08:43 |
| 2 | Teng Tools | E. Crosbie | 1.047 | 137:14:36 | 143:41:38 |
| 3 | Pepperbox | C & M Farrelly | 0.937 | 153:40:48 | 143:59:53 |
| 4 | Ireland's West | A. Fitzgerald | 1.061 | 136:15:20 | 144:34:02 |
| 5 | Imp | G. Radley | 1.018 | 142:28:40 | 145:02:33 |
| 6 | Inis Mor | B & L Gouy | 1.025 | 141:32:35 | 145:04:54 |
| 7 | Aquelina | J. Tyrrell | 1.03 | 142:15:02 | 146:31:05 |
| 8 | Jeronimo | N. Dowling | 1.13 | 129:40:53 | 146:32:24 |
| 9 | Blondie | Jenny Winter | 1.035 | 142:07:18 | 147:05:45 |
| 10 | Whitetiger | T.O. Sheehy | 1.115 | 133:29:30 | 148:50:36 |
| 11 | Isobar | T. Roche | 1.07 | 141:35:50 | 151:30:33 |
| 12 | Lascar | J & B Berry, C. O'Mahony | 0.923 | 164:12:17 | 151:33:39 |
| 13 | Panda Nova II | D. Matthews | 0.989 | 153:18:00 | 151:36:49 |
| 14 | Independent Bear | M. Davis & A. Cormori | 1.144 | 132:34:13 | 151:39:37 |
| 15 | Nadie | S. McCarthy | 1.157 | 131:29:09 | 152:07:45 |
| 16 | Roxy 9 | R. Davis & A. Creighton | 1.223 | 124:59:48 | 152:52:15 |
| 17 | Minnie The Moocher | Anthony Richards | 1.155 | 132:23:42 | 152:54:58 |
| 18 | Alice 11 | Mike Henning | 1.237 | 123:59:07 | 153:22:11 |
| 19 | Altana Chieftain | G. O'Rourke | 1.319 | 117:07:08 | 154:28:47 |
| 20 | Freya | Conor Doyle | 1.106 | 139:58:08 | 154:48:20 |
| 21 | Moontiger | A. Bell | 1.014 | 152:45:40 | 154:53:59 |
| 22 | Creative Play | A. Greenwood | 1.184 | 131:00:49 | 155:07:12 |
| 23 | Legally Blonde | Paul Egan | 0.963 | 162:00:00 | 156:00:22 |
| 24 | Albatross | Jim Ryan | 1.04 | 151:00:31 | 157:02:56 |
| 25 | Blackjack | Peter Coad | 0.947 | 166:07:39 | 157:19:22 |
| 26 | Ulula | N. Ogden | 1.04 | 153:08:15 | 159:15:47 |
| 27 | State o Chassis | J. Collins | 0.989 | 166:10:15 | 164:20:35 |
| 28 | Spirit of Kilrush | T. Whelan & Co. | 1.423 | 116:04:57 | 165:11:07 |
| 29 | Konica Minolta Zana | S. Thwaites | 1.643 | 100:57:30 | 165:52:28 |
| 30 | Whisper | M. Cotter | 1.438 | 116:14:32 | 167:09:23 |
| 31 | Galileo | Kelleher, Lemass & Tennyson | 1.094 | 152:57:55 | 167:20:38 |
| 32 | Fizz | C. Geoghegan & C.Chavasse | 1.042 | 161:10:25 | 167:56:34 |
| 33 | Lyons Solicitors | B. Lyons &T. Lenehan | 1.438 | 117:24:02 | 168:49:19 |
| 34 | Lancastrian | N. Eatough | 1.074 | 158:44:44 | 170:29:34 |
| 35 | Solune | JP. Chomette | 1.507 | 116:01:18 | 174:50:41 |
| 36 | Quite Correct | J. Roberts | 1.095 | 165:26:39 | 181:09:41 |
| | Nunatak | Mike Jaques | 1.082 | Retired | Retired |
| | Sarnia | M. Creedon | 0.904 | Retired | Retired |
| | Southbound.ie | Y. Lemonnier & M. Greely | 1.093 | Retired | Retired |

**BMW Round Ireland 2008 - Overall Results**

| Place | Yacht | Entrant | TCF | Elapsed | Corrected |
|---|---|---|---|---|---|
| 1 | Ireland West | Ireland West & Aodhan Fitzgerald | 1.06 | 96:01:57 | 101:47:40 |
| 2 | Dinamite-Tee | Glyn Shefield | 1.075 | 95:50:16 | 103:01:32 |
| 3 | McCarthyMotors.ie | George Radley | 1.012 | 102:01:19 | 103:14:46 |
| 4 | Galileo | Kelliher/Lemass/Tennyson & Sean D Lemass | 1.093 | 94:36:53 | 103:24:50 |
| 5 | Cavatina | Eric Lisson & Ian Hickey | 0.927 | 112:52:22 | 104:37:59 |
| 6 | Mumbo.ie (2H) | Patrick Cronin | 0.993 | 105:23:20 | 104:39:04 |
| 7 | Bjaysus | Alan Hannon | 1.104 | 94:56:33 | 104:48:59 |
| 8 | Team Kingspan | Matt Davis | 1.127 | 93:09:58 | 104:59:54 |
| 9 | Slingshot (2H) | Michael Boyd & Niall Dowling | 1.015 | 103:58:04 | 105:31:38 |
| 10 | Ocean Spirit of Carlingford | Peter Finegan | 1.006 | 105:06:25 | 105:44:15 |
| 11 | Jalfrezi (2H) | Gareth Thomas & Brian Millea | 1.068 | 99:01:55 | 105:45:58 |
| 12 | Nadie | Ciam McCarthy | 1.159 | 91:15:45 | 105:46:24 |
| 13 | Aquelina | James Tyrell | 1.033 | 102:48:35 | 106:12:09 |
| 14 | Blackjack (2) | Darren & Clifford Nicholson | 0.938 | 115:32:46 | 108:22:56 |
| 15 | Lee Overlay | Adrian Lee | 1.336 | 81:09:35 | 108:25:46 |
| 16 | Another Nods (2H) | Richard & Helen Booth | 1.078 | 100:58:40 | 108:51:15 |
| 17 | White Tiger | Anthony J. O'Brien | 1.114 | 98:49:51 | 110:05:51 |
| 18 | Cheetah Cub (2H) | Yacht Action Sailing & Robin Wooton & James Walker | 1.052 | 106:00:00 | 111:30:43 |
| 19 | Formidable 3 | Piet Vroom | 1.38 | 81:38:52 | 112:40:26 |
| 20 | FMB-Noyeks | Tom Fitzpatrick & Des Glennon | 1.023 | 111:17:57 | 113:51:33 |
| 21 | Cracker (2H) | Anthony & Alice Kingston | 0.999 | 114:17:59 | 114:11:08 |
| 22 | Alburn | Robbie Milhench & Kenny McCullough | 1.414 | 81:28:36 | 115:12:29 |
| 23 | Chancer | Carroll Bros. | 1.038 | 111:25:39 | 115:39:42 |
| 24 | Quite Correct | John Roberts | 1.094 | 107:30:00 | 117:36:18 |
| 25 | Persistance | Jerry Collins | 0.986 | 120:06:04 | 118:25:11 |
| 26 | Gusilliam | Mark Wynne Smith | 1.283 | 92:20:13 | 118:28:06 |
| 27 | Earendil | Pierre & Samuel Caillault | 1.025 | 115:48:02 | 118:41:44 |
| 28 | Lancastrian | Neil Etough | 1.07 | 113:16:57 | 121:12:44 |
| 29 | ICAP Leopard 3 | ICAP Leopard & Mike Slade | 1.888 | 65:48:47 | 124:15:18 |
| 30 | Cassiopeia | John Clarke & William Maher | 0.998 | 124:31:14 | 124:16:17 |
| | Alegre | Andres Soriano | 1.533 | Retired | Retired |
| | First of September | Jerry Whiston | 1.018 | Retired | Retired |
| | Inis Mor | Laurent & Bernard Gouy | 1.132 | Retired | Retired |
| | IRL 107L (2H) | Glen Ward & Marie Hercelin | 1.128 | Retired | Retired |
| | Jacana | David Munro & John Syms | 1.109 | Retired | Retired |
| | Joker | David Gibbons & Mike Broderick | 0.986 | Retired | Retired |
| | Lascar | Brian Berry | 0.923 | Retired | Retired |
| | Legally Brunette | Cathal Drohan & Paul Egan | 1.122 | Retired | Retired |
| | McConnells Chieftain | McConnells Chieftain & Ger O'Rourke | 1.68 | DNS | DNS |
| | Mighty Max 2 | Neil Thomas | 1.081 | Retired | Retired |
| | Ruffian (2H) | Peter McIntyre & Emma Nutt | 0.938 | Retired | Retired |
| | Sarnia | Michael Creedon | 0.893 | Retired | Retired |
| | Star Dancer (2H) | Rob Packham & Tim Wright | 0.938 | Retired | Retired |
| | Ulula (2H) | Nick Ogden | 1.09 | Retired | Retired |
| | Voador (2H) | Simon Curwin & Paul Peggs | 1.105 | Retired | Retired |
| | WSI | Cormac & Mandy Farrelly | 0.936 | Retired | Retired |